*Aging in America*

SOCIOLOGY IN THE TWENTY-FIRST CENTURY

*Edited by John Iceland, Pennsylvania State University*

This series introduces students to a range of sociological issues of broad interest in the United States today and addresses topics such as race, immigration, gender, the family, education, and social inequality. Each work has a similar structure and approach as follows:

- introduction to the topic's importance in contemporary society
- overview of conceptual issues
- review of empirical research including demographic data
- cross-national comparisons
- discussion of policy debates

These course books highlight findings from current, rigorous research and include personal narratives to illustrate major themes in an accessible manner. The similarity in approach across the series allows instructors to assign them as a featured or supplementary book in various courses.

1. *A Portrait of America: The Demographic Perspective*, by John Iceland

2. *Race and Ethnicity in America*, by John Iceland

3. *Education in America*, by Kimberly A. Goyette

4. *Families in America*, by Susan L. Brown

5. *Population Health in America*, by Robert A. Hummer and Erin R. Hamilton

6. *Religion in America*, by Lisa D. Pearce and Claire Chipman Gilliland

7. *Diversity and the Transition to Adulthood in America*, by Phoebe Ho, Hyunjoon Park, and Grace Kao

8. *Aging in America*, by Deborah Carr

# Aging in America

Deborah Carr

UNIVERSITY OF CALIFORNIA PRESS

University of California Press
Oakland, California

© 2023 by Deborah Carr

Library of Congress Cataloging-in-Publication Data

Names: Carr, Deborah (Deborah S.), author.
Title: Aging in America / Deborah Carr.
Other titles: Sociology in the 21st century (University of California
    Press) ; 8.
Description: Oakland, California : University of California Press,
    [2023] | Series: Sociology in the twenty-first century ; 8 | Includes
    bibliographical references and index.
Identifiers: LCCN 2022025069 (print) | LCCN 2022025070 (ebook) |
    ISBN 9780520301283 (cloth) | ISBN 9780520301290 (paperback) |
    ISBN 9780520972162 (ebook)
Subjects: LCSH: Aging—Social aspects—United States. | Aging—
    Economic aspects—United States. | Older people—United States—
    Social conditions. | Older people—Care—United States.
Classification: LCC HQ1064.U5 C355 2023 (print) | LCC HQ1064.U5 (ebook)
    | DDC 305.260973--dc23/eng/20220628
LC record available at https://lccn.loc.gov/2022025069
LC ebook record available at https://lccn.loc.gov/2022025070

32  31  30  29  28  27  26  25  24  23
10  9  8  7  6  5  4  3  2  1

To my family, past and present

# Contents

# Illustrations

# Acknowledgments

When John Iceland, editor of the *Sociology in the Twenty-First Century* series, invited me to write a book about aging for this series, I enthusiastically agreed. The aging of the US and global populations is one of the most profound and consequential shifts in contemporary society, and I'm honored to have the opportunity share my passion for this topic with readers. My thanks to John for including me in this important series, and to Naomi Schneider, executive editor at University of California Press, for her guidance, encouragement, patience, and support as I completed this manuscript. The anonymous reviewers provided thoughtful and constructive feedback; their wise words have improved the manuscript. My gratitude also goes to Sara Bubenik for her assistance with the reference list, and Samyuktaa Jayakrishnan for ably preparing the book's figures.

This book would not be possible without the pathbreaking research of the many scholars whose insights informed my understanding and appreciation of population aging. There are far too many to name, but I am grateful to the many authors who published in *Journal of Gerontology: Social Science* during my editorship. Their work is woven throughout the book. I am also grateful to my many brilliant collaborators through the years, including Kathrin Boerner, Jennifer Cornman, Shinae Choi,

Ken Ferraro, Vicki Freedman, Jung-Hwa Ha, James House, Ellen Idler, Chioun Lee, Elizabeth Luth, Sara Moorman, Eun Ha Namkung, Tetyana Pudrovska, Carol Ryff, Pam Smock, Kristen Springer, Rebecca Utz, and many others.

My deepest gratitude goes to "my boys," Sam and Brisket (the beagle). Writing a book while chairing an academic department during a global pandemic is a challenge, to say the least. Sam's continual good humor, support, and baking skills sustained me through the writing process, and filled even the darkest days with light and laughter.

# Introduction

AGING IN AMERICA

Close your eyes and think about what your life might be like when you're seventy-five years old. What will you look like? Where will you be living? Who will you live with? Will you be healthy and active, filling your days with the hobbies and interests that you enjoyed in your younger years? Or do you expect that health problems and diminishing sight, hearing, or memory might limit what you do each day? Will you live extravagantly, enjoying the best of everything, or frugally on a fixed income?

Some readers may have no idea what their future might look like. Others might find this mental exercise to be difficult and even frightening, presuming that "old age" is synonymous with illness, loneliness, and imminent death. Some believe they will resemble their grandparents or great-grandparents, presuming the apple doesn't fall far from the tree. Others think they'll be nothing like their grandparents, whom they see as belonging to a generation that is less nimble with a smartphone, more traditional in their views toward things like politics and sexuality, and more likely to eat meat and potatoes for dinner rather than healthier vegan fare.

The imaginary crystal ball we are peering into reveals some important truths about aging. None of us (even those with a penchant for cosmetic surgery) will look the same at age seventy-five as we did at age twenty.

Biological changes are an inevitable part of growing old. The dewy skin tone, lustrous hair color, clear vision, sharp hearing, firm muscle tone, mental quickness, and strong heart and lungs that many young people have will change with passing years. Yet other characteristics that we might associate with old age, like conservative political views or a preference for jazz music, aren't necessarily linked to one's biological age. Rather, age also reflects the year in which we were born, making us members of a particular generation or *birth cohort*. Cohorts born in the 1930s who were children during World War II have different life experiences than those born in the 1950s and 1960s who grew up during the Vietnam War era. Those two cohorts, in turn, differ from persons born in later decades. Sweeping economic, technological, and cultural changes throughout the twentieth and twenty-first centuries mean that older adults in 2050 will have led very different lives than those who are retirement-age today, transforming what "old age" looks and feels like—an important process that social scientists call *cohort replacement* (Mannheim 1952).

Cohorts are an important yet contested concept in sociology. Some scholars argue that snappy monikers like "Baby Boomer" are meaningless and perpetuate baseless stereotypes, such as "Gen Xers are slackers," "Millennials are addicted to technology," and members of "Generation Z live their lives on TikTok." Another critique is that any single cohort, like the Baby Boomers born between 1946 and 1964, is so large and diverse that its members can't be universally characterized (Cohen 2021; Duffy 2021). Despite these concerns about cohort labels, experts agree that the historical period someone grows up in can shape key aspects of their lives, including when and if they marry and buy a home, the kind of jobs they hold, and how they grow old. Throughout the book, I will use these (contested) labels as shorthand only to identify persons born in the following years: Silent Generation (born 1928–1945), Baby Boomers (born 1946–1964), Generation X (born 1965–1980), Millennials (born 1981–1996), and Generation Z (born 1997–2012).

Although members of a single cohort are born at roughly the same time, cohort members are highly diverse. They differ from one another on the basis of characteristics like their sex, sexual orientation, race, ethnicity, education, social class, and more. Our social characteristics—and the structural opportunities and obstacles associated with those characteristics—shape our lives at every age and set the stage for how we grow old. For example, let's meet the two oldest living Americans as of January 1, 2021: Hester Ford, who celebrated her 115th birthday in August 2020, and Iris Westman, who is just two weeks younger.[1] Hester was born in South Carolina in 1905. As a child, she and her parents labored on a farm picking cotton, plowing, and cutting wood. Hester married at age fifteen, and went on to have 12 children, 53 grandchildren, 120 great-grandchildren, and a remarkable 126 great-grandchildren. She worked as a nanny and volunteered at her church in North Carolina, where she and her family moved in the 1950s (*QCity Metro* 2019). Hester shares her extreme longevity with Iris, yet their lives have few other similarities. Iris was born in North Dakota, and her parents were farmers. From a young age, Iris knew she would attend college. She earned her degree from the University of North Dakota in 1928 and was an English teacher before becoming a school librarian (Wallevand 2020). Like Hester, Iris was active in her church and sang in the choir. But their family lives couldn't be more different; Iris never married or had children, whereas Hester had dozens of offspring.

These divergent life paths, of two women born just two weeks apart, reveal the power of social, legal, and historical forces in shaping the life course, a theme that weaves throughout this book (Elder 1994). Hester, an African American woman, had limited opportunities for schooling as a child in the Jim Crow South; at that time, segregation laws codified a system of racial oppression. By law, Hester's home state of South Carolina had separate but vastly unequal schools for Black and white children. In the 1910s, annual school expenditures in South Carolina averaged about $15 for each white child, but just $2 for each Black child. In rural areas like Hester's hometown of Lancaster, schools for Black children ran just 70 days a year, compared to 140 days for white children (Bartels 1994). Children from poor families and Black families often dropped out of school and worked to support their parents and siblings. In stark contrast, Iris Westman had the good fortune to graduate high school and college and to work for decades in a professional career. She never married, which was a relatively common pattern among college-educated women in the early twentieth century. Women at that time often had to choose between a career and a family—a choice that may seem unimaginable to college women in the twenty-first century who are raised to believe they can "have it all" (Solomon 1985). The lives of Hester and Iris provide clues into why individual experiences in old age vary so widely; their birth cohort, geographic location, race, gender, and socioeconomic status shape their life paths.

Social factors like education also matter at the *population* level. Whether a society is young or old, rich or poor, or highly educated or poorly educated, has important consequences for all members of that society and for the social policies intended to protect them. For instance, in 1950, just 20 percent of US adults ages sixty-five and older had graduated high school, whereas 80 percent of older adults in 2020 have earned their diploma. This historical shift means that older adults today, on average, have greater health, financial, and legal literacy than the generations that came before them. Societal-level increases in education are a key reason why the US population is aging so rapidly: more education is associated with longer lives. Education is linked with healthy behaviors like not smoking, a major factor in reducing deaths from smoking-related causes like lung cancer throughout the late twentieth and early twenty-first centuries (Meara, Richards, and Cutler 2008). Populations with higher levels of education also tend to marry at older ages, waiting until after they've finished their schooling to wed and have children. As a result, couples are having fewer children today than they did in the mid-twentieth century, a social pattern that affects the overall age structure of a society (Rindfuss and Sweet 2013).

The ways that individuals and populations age is a fascinating and timely topic. The United States population is older than ever before; in 2020, adults ages sixty-five and over accounted for 17 percent of the total population, as shown in figure 1. One in five Americans will be age sixty-five or over by 2030, and a remarkable one in four will have reached old age by 2060. The "graying" of America will affect nearly every aspect of life. Population aging creates demands for doctors and caregivers to tend to older patients' health needs, advertising executives keen to sell prescription medications and anti-wrinkle creams to this large and profitable market, elder care lawyers who help their clients with legal matters like estate planning, biomedical engineers who create assistive devices like hearing aids and robotic helpers, and architects who design homes and

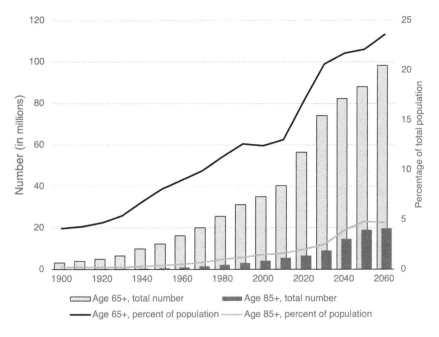

*Figure 1.* Growth of population ages sixty-five and over, 1900–2060. SOURCE: Federal Interagency Forum on Aging-Related Statistics (2020). Data for 2020 through 2060 are projections.

apartments with ramps and other features to meet the needs of older residents (Hannon 2011). Economists and policy makers caution that a population with many retirement-age persons who receive Social Security and Medicare benefits yet relatively few working-age persons paying federal income taxes could lead to a financial crisis. These challenges were intensified by the COVID-19 pandemic, which first threatened global health in 2020, with older adults particularly vulnerable to both the disease and the social isolation required to limit exposure to the virus. The burning question for citizens and policy makers alike is: how will our nation care and provide for the projected ninety-eight million older Americans in 2060?

This question is one of many at the core of the demography of aging. *Demography* is an academic field that focuses on the size, distribution, and composition of a population. *Size* refers to how large a population is, such as the number of persons ages sixty-five and older in the United States in 2020 (fifty-six million) versus 2060 (projected at ninety-eight million). *Distribution* tells us how a population is dispersed across space, such as whether they are densely clustered in cities or sparsely spread across rural towns. For example, rural areas make up 97 percent of the US land area but are home to just 19 percent of the overall population. That's because residents are concentrated in urban and suburban areas, leaving vast swaths of land unpopulated or very sparsely populated, primarily in the western and central United States (US Census Bureau 2016). *Composition* tells us about the characteristics of a population, such as their age, race, ethnicity, physical health, or national origin. For instance, a college town like Ann Arbor, Michigan, has a high proportion of residents who are ages eighteen to twenty-four, whereas a retirement community like The Villages in Florida is home almost exclusively to older adults. Building upon these three foundational concepts, this book will explore the reasons why the age sixty-five-plus population is growing so dramatically, how the demographic and socioeconomic characteristics of older adults shape their everyday lives, and the implications of population aging for the future of US and global society. Before delving more fully into the causes and consequences of population aging, it's important to first identify precisely what aging is, the measures demographers use to document aging, and the demographic processes that drive population aging.

## DEFINING OLD AGE AND AGING

What is "old age"? Folksy sayings tell us that "age is a state of mind," and "you're only as old as you feel." But demographers have a much more concrete definition. Older adults are defined as persons ages sixty-five and older. Recognizing that sixty-five-year-olds have little in common with those in their nineties, demographers further identify three subgroups: *young-old*, who are ages sixty-five to seventy-four; *middle-old*, who are ages seventy-five to eighty-four; and the *old-old* or *oldest old*, who are ages eighty-five and older. *Centenarians*, or persons ages one hundred and older, are distinguished as a special group. Although centenarians like Hester Ford account for only 0.2 percent of the US population, scientists extensively study these very aged individuals because they provide clues into the biological and social factors linked with extremely long lives (Santos-Lozano et al. 2016).

These fine-grained age distinctions are important because they help to challenge ageist, outdated, and overly coarse notions about older adults. For instance, we often hear myths like "all old people are senile," yet researchers know that these overgeneralizations aren't true (Cook 2017). In 2020, just 3 percent of adults ages sixty-five to seventy-four had Alzheimer's disease, a progressive brain disease that destroys memory and other important mental functions. Clearly, 3 percent does not constitute "all" or even "most" older people. This very low rate jumps to 17 percent among those ages seventy-five to eighty-four, and increases more than tenfold, to 32 percent among those ages eighty-five and over (Alzheimer's Association 2020). Even in the oldest-old group, however, the proportion with dementia is modest. These distinctions are important not only for squashing harmful myths about old age, but also for helping health care providers and policy makers target their work to those with the greatest needs.

## Four Dimensions of Individual Aging

Classifications like young-old or oldest-old refer to *chronological age* only, meaning the number of years a person has been alive. However, a single numerical value cannot adequately capture personal capabilities, nor does it reflect the fact that people age at different paces along four different clocks: biological, functional, social, and psychological. *Biological aging*, also called *senescence*, refers to physiological changes that occur with each passing year. For instance, immune systems gradually weaken with age, leaving older adults vulnerable to infection and illness, as the COVID-19 pandemic painfully revealed (Centers for Disease Control and Prevention [CDC] 2021a). *Functional aging*, by contrast, refers to changes in how a person functions or manages their everyday activities. Our daily functioning is affected by factors like eyesight, hearing, mobility, balance, strength, cardiopulmonary function, concentration, and memory. When these changes happen, older adults may need to adapt their routines, for example, by giving up a strenuous hobby, such as cycling, or relying on supports, like a walker, hearing aid, or daily reminder list.

It's not just our bodies that change as time passes; we also experience social and psychological aging. *Social aging* encompasses the changing social roles that occur as we age, such as transitions from student to worker, worker to retiree, married person to widow(er), and parent to grandparent. *Psychological aging* refers to changes in our thinking and feeling processes over time. Despite negative stereotypes that old age is a time of sadness and senility, researchers have documented that psychological aging is not uniformly a process of decline. Although memory, reasoning, and the speed at which we process new information may decline, other processes like abstract reasoning, wisdom, and the capacity to control one's emotions can improve or increase with age (Harada, Love, and Triebel 2013).

The pace at which one ages along these four different dimensions varies based on one's social characteristics. In general, people who have faced greater adversity, stress, and economic disadvantage tend to age more quickly than their counterparts who have had more privileged lives. To take an extreme case, homeless adults in their late fifties and early sixties have more health problems and greater difficulty carrying out daily activities like bathing and eating, compared to eighty-year-olds who have safe and secure housing (Brown et al. 2017). The daily wear and tear of living on the streets or in shelters speeds up functional and biological aging processes. Social aging also is stratified; for instance, youth who do not complete high school tend to form romantic partnerships, have their first child, and become a grandparent at younger ages than their peers who delayed marriage and childbearing until after they have finished college or graduate school (Pew Research 2015). People with fewer years of schooling also start to experience memory problems at younger ages and the pace of decline is faster, relative to those with more schooling (Clouston et al. 2019). These four dimensions of aging—biological, functional, social, and psychological—are important because they help us to understand why some people enjoy happy, healthy long lives, whereas others do not, and to identify potential interventions to slow processes of decline.

## Population Aging: Concepts and Measures

Just as individuals grow old, populations also age. *Population aging* refers to the process whereby the *mean* (average) or *median* age of a population

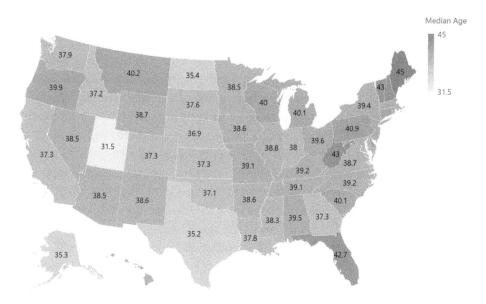

*Figure 2.* Median age of US states, 2020. SOURCE: US Census Bureau (2021). © GeoNames, Microsoft, TomTom

grows older, or the age composition of a society shifts so that older adults account for an increasingly large share of the overall population. The concept of population aging is complex, and can be measured with several different indicators, each of which tells us something different about a population. The most straightforward measure is the *median* age of a population. That is the age that divides a population into two equally sized groups, such that half are older and half are younger. The median age in the United States was thirty-eight in 2020, although this statistic varies across the fifty states, as shown in figure 2. Utah has the youngest median age at just 31.5 years, whereas West Virginia, Florida, and the northern New England states of Maine, Vermont, and New Hampshire are the oldest, with median ages above 42 years. On a global scale, these differences are even more extreme. Niger has the world's youngest median age of 15, whereas Japan has one of the oldest at around age 50 (Central Intelligence Agency 2020).

Another indicator of population aging is the *proportion of persons who are age sixty-five or older.* Two US states are tied for the rank of "oldest" according to this metric: in both Maine and Florida, persons aged sixty-five and older account for about 20 percent of their overall populations. Utah is the youngest, with 10 percent of state residents over sixty-five (Kaiser Family Foundation 2019). On a global scale, the proportion of people over sixty-five in a population ranges from a low of 2 percent among nations in Sub-Saharan Africa to a high of 28 percent in Japan (United Nations 2019). This is a helpful statistic for policy makers, as it tells us how many people will rely on age-based social programs like Social Security and Medicare in the United States, or who might use publicly-funded support services like ride vans or assistance for victims of elder abuse. However, the proportion of people over sixty-five is a static measure and cannot help policy makers predict future needs for age-based supports and services. Nor does it tell us much about the population under age sixty-five. Is the under-sixty-five population made up mainly of children or working-age adults? For these reasons, demographers also rely on population pyramids to help understand population aging.

A *population pyramid* is a simple tool that provides a wealth of information on the population of a particular geographic area, such as a nation, state, or city. Figures 3a and 3b show population pyramids for Florida, one of the oldest US states, and Utah, the youngest state, with data plotted for 2019. A population pyramid is made up of stacked bars indicating the proportion of a population in every age group, typically in five- or ten-year bands, starting from the bottom up with ages under five, five to nine, and so on. The left-hand side of the pyramid shows bars for men, and the right-hand side shows bars for women.

The shape of the pyramid tells us how old or young a population is. A pyramid with a heavy base and a narrow top is a relatively young population, one with a heavy middle and top is an older population, and one that bulges out in the middle (sometimes referred to as "the pig in the python" shape) depicts a largely middle-aged population. For example, Utah's pyramid has a very heavy base, where boys and girls under age five each make up about 4 percent of the population, yet men and women ages eighty-five and older each make up less than 1 percent of the population. Florida's shape is very different, with far fewer young children and many more middle-aged and older adults. The oldest-old make up roughly 3 percent of Florida's population, a proportion several times greater than the oldest-old population of Utah. The pyramid shapes are even more extreme in the oldest nation in the world, Japan (figure 3c), and the youngest, Niger (figure 3d). Japan's shape has very small base and very large top, whereas Niger's shape resembles a pyramid with a very narrow spire, showing relatively few old people live in that nation.

The pyramid's tilt, or how lopsided it is, tells us about sex differences in the age of a nation's population.[2] Most pyramids lean more heavily toward the right, especially in the top tiers, because men are more likely than women to die at all ages, especially at advanced ages. As such, the share of a population that is male decreases as we progress through the age groups, and the pyramid becomes more asymmetrical with more women than men. The relative sizes of the population of women and men help us to calculate another important indicator: a sex ratio. A *sex ratio* refers to the number of men relative to women in a population. Among babies and young children, the ratio is relatively balanced. However, by age eighty-five there are only fifty-six men for every one hundred women, and by age one hundred, just thirty men per one hundred women in the United States (Mather and Kilduff 2020). It may come as no surprise that of the ten oldest living Americans today, all ten are women. You might have observed a similar pattern when visiting a grandparent in an assisted-living facility, noting that the women residents far outnumber the men. Sex ratios have important implications for older adults' family lives, and experiences of giving and receiving care, as we will see later in the book.

The tiers of the population pyramid help us to understand another important ratio: a *dependency ratio*. This statistic is intended to show what demographers call the "burden" of a dependent population, where dependents are defined as those too young and too old to work for pay. A *total dependency ratio* refers to the number of people under age eighteen plus those ages sixty-five and older, divided by the number of persons ages eighteen to sixty-four. Those ages eighteen to sixty-four are presumed to be employed and paying income taxes, whereas younger and older adults are not. A high dependency ratio suggests that the working-age population and government programs may be "burdened" by those deemed financially dependent. However, it doesn't tell us which age group, specifically, is imposing the burden. That's why demographers also calculate a *youth dependency ratio* (population under age eighteen divided by those

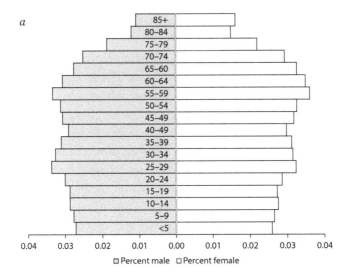

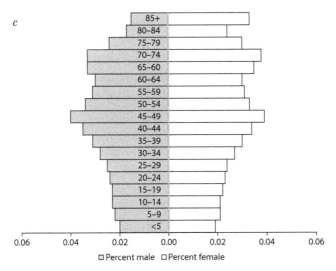

*Figure 3a–d.* Population pyramids of Florida (a), Utah (b), Japan (c), and Niger (d), 2019. SOURCE: US Census Bureau (2020b); United Nations (2019).

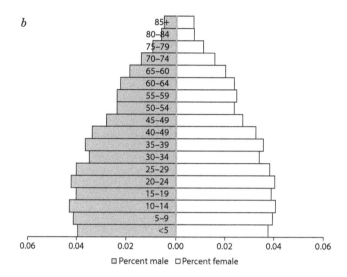

*b*

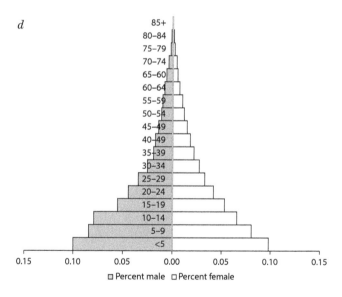

*d*

ages eighteen to sixty-four), and an *old-age dependency ratio* (population age sixty-five and over divided by those ages eighteen to sixty-four). Each of these ratios provides different pieces of information that may be useful to policy makers and planners. For instance, a very high old-age dependency ratio suggests that there may not be enough working-age people to provide care to the older adults who need it, whereas a very high youth dependency ratio suggests a heightened need for day care, schools, summer camps, and investments in school lunch programs. For instance, in Japan there are now 48 older adults per every 100 working-age adults, whereas in Niger, there are just 5.4. However, the youthful population poses a dependency burden in Niger, where there are 104 youth for every 100 working-age adults (United Nations 2019). These dramatically different population distributions necessitate different social policies.

Population pyramids help us to understand the past and project the future. When we look at the population pyramid for Florida, we see that the bars are widest for the fifty-five-to-fifty-nine and sixty-to-sixty-four age groups. These bars are wide, in part, because today's adults ages fifty-five to sixty-four were born in the late Baby Boom years of the 1950s and 1960s. The many babies born during those "boom" years are now reaching old age in record numbers, and they are an important reason why the older population is projected to skyrocket over the next three decades. The pyramids for both Utah and Florida, however, show us another large and important birth cohort: the twenty- and thirty-somethings of the Millennial cohort born in the late 1980s and 1990s. This large cohort is projected to surpass the Boomers as the largest living birth cohort by 2060 (Fry 2020a).

## HOW DO POPULATIONS AGE?

By any measure, it's clear that the US population has aged at a rapid pace over the past century and will continue to do so in the coming decades. In 1900, just 3.1 million Americans (or 4 percent of the US population) had celebrated a sixty-fifth birthday. By 2020, more than 55 million had passed this milestone, accounting for more than 17 percent of all Americans. But how did this happen? How do populations age? At first blush, this seems like a very simple question. Populations, we might reason, grow older every year just as individuals grow older with each passing birthday. The actual story of how a population ages is much more complex and requires us to understand three key demographic processes: fertility, mortality, and migration. *Fertility* refers to the number and timing of babies born in a particular time period, like the high birth rates in the post–World War II years of 1946 to 1964 when 75 million Baby Boomers were born. That's part of the reason why the US population is aging so rapidly in the twenty-first century; the large cohort of Boomer "babies" is now in or nearing their retirement years.

High fertility in a particular time or place contributes to the overall age structure of a population, as the population pyramids reveal. One reason why Utah is the youngest state in the United States and Niger is one of the youngest nations in the world is that their birth rates are very high. In Utah's case, their high birth rate is due partly to the state's religious makeup. More than 60 percent of Utah residents are Mormons, or members of the Church of Latter-Day Saints (compared to 2 percent of the United States overall). Members of this faith tend to marry younger and have more babies, on average, than other Americans (Lipka 2015). High birth rates contribute to population growth in an additional way; two to three decades later, many of those babies will begin having babies of their own. In stark contrast, states or nations with large numbers of persons in their fifties and older, like Florida and Japan, will not keep birth rates as high, because women's biological capacity to give birth diminishes dramatically after age forty-five.

Fertility patterns do not fully explain population aging, however. We also need to consider *mortality*, or the rates and ages at which people in a population die. In order for a cohort of babies, like the large Baby Boom generation, to contribute to the graying of society they must survive until old age in large numbers. For this reason, declining mortality rates throughout the twentieth century are the driving force behind the aging of the US population. If babies die in infancy, childhood, or young adulthood, they will not live long enough to contribute to the aging of a population.

Consider the fact that in 1900, one hundred out of every one thousand babies born would die before their first birthday. By the year 2020, this rate plummeted to six deaths per one thousand babies (Centers for Disease

Control and Prevention 2019). The precipitous drop in infant mortality is due to improvements in nutrition and hygiene including simple practices like regular handwashing, and major technological advances like water chlorination and milk pasteurization. Low rates of infant and child deaths contributed to the steep rise in life expectancy over the past century; *life expectancy* is an estimate of the average number of years that members of a particular birth cohort will live. A baby boy born in 1900 could expect to live to age forty-six on average, while a baby girl could expect to live until age forty-eight. In 2020, newborn girls and boys are projected to live until ages seventy-six and eighty-one, respectively. Rising life expectancies in the early twentieth century were due primarily to successes in fighting infectious diseases like pneumonia and tuberculosis, whereas medical advances—especially those that reduce cardiovascular deaths—contributed to longer life spans from the 1950s forward (Cutler and Meara 2004).

Fertility and mortality are powerful forces that have contributed to the aging of America. A third demographic process, *migration*, or the movement of people into or out of a nation or region, cannot account for the rising number of older adults overall in the United States because it is a rare person who moves into the United States from another nation after their sixty-fifth birthday. However, migration explains why some states, like Florida, are so old. Florida, known as the Sunshine State, has long been one of America's most popular retirement destinations. Older adults are drawn to the state's warm climate, sunny skies, low taxes and cost of living, amenities like golf courses and beaches, health care facilities tailored to older adults' needs, and large retirement communities like The Villages, home to more than fifty thousand older adults. Some older adults live in Florida year-round, while others are "snowbirds" who winter in Florida but return to their homes in the Northeast and Midwest during the summer.

Migration *into* a state like Florida affects its age structure, but migration *out* of a state also can shape a state's age distribution. You might have been surprised to read that states like Maine and West Virginia are among the oldest in the nation. It's not because older adults are flocking there for retirement; rather, younger people are leaving to find more lucrative or appealing opportunities elsewhere. As young people depart, older adults account for a disproportionately larger share of the overall population staying behind. That's why states with dying coal industries like West

Virginia, or rural states with few bustling cities like Maine, are losing their young residents to other states. Young adults may leave the state for college, the military, or careers elsewhere, and never return. The loss of young people can have serious economic impacts, with large numbers of retirees relying on the services provided by relatively few (or even insufficient numbers of) working-age persons. That's why the state of Maine started a series of programs a decade ago, like tax credits for recent college graduates and media campaigns to recruit young workers to the state, all in an effort to help fill the many empty job openings (Sugarman 2018).

The aging of America will reshape how we live, transforming the workforce, politics, the economy, health care, families, urban design, popular culture, the social safety net (including the solvency of Social Security and Medicare), and more. Growing populations of older adults also may help to squash ageism, or the pernicious yet deeply entrenched biases that people hold about old age. The future impacts of population aging depend on the composition of who older adults are in the future; if many get by on a limited income, they'll spend little in our consumer-driven economy. However, older adults who are healthy and engaged have the potential to contribute to our society in myriad ways, as volunteers, mentors, workers, caregivers, and keepers of family memories and traditions.

## PLAN FOR THE BOOK

The goal of this book is to provide a lively, nuanced, and timely portrait of aging in the United States, showcasing the diversity of the older adult population. A key message is that the US population of older adults is larger and more diverse than ever before, challenging myths and outdated notions about old age. My methodological approach is demographic, using national population-level data to document the personal characteristics, family lives, health and well-being, and economic security of older adults. The life course paradigm provides a theoretical foundation for the book, emphasizing that differences between older adults who are healthy versus unhealthy, rich versus poor, socially integrated versus isolated—do not emerge suddenly on one's sixty-fifth birthday. Rather, disparities in health, wealth, and happiness unfold gradually over time—a product of the advantages and disadvantages that we experience throughout childhood, adulthood, and ultimately, old age. Understanding the reasons why old age can be the best of times or worst of times is the key to developing social policies and community programs to meet the needs of an aging society.

The book begins by introducing readers to the history of aging in the United States, and the ways that theoretical approaches to understanding aging have evolved alongside this history. Chapter 1 begins with a concise history of old age in the United States, highlighting how major social, economic, and technological changes have affected older adults' lives. I show how the creation and expansion of Social Security and Medicare have boosted the financial security and health of older adults and shifted how Americans think about old age. I then summarize classic and contemporary theories used to understand aging and old age and highlight how these frameworks can either perpetuate or challenge ageist notions about older adults' competencies and capacity to contribute to society.

Chapter 2 provides a statistical portrait of older adults in the contemporary United States, detailing their demographic characteristics like race, sex, and immigrant status; their socioeconomic resources like education, income, and wealth; whether they are working or retired; and their living arrangements, including where and with whom they reside. A recurring theme is that older adults today are very different from what future generations of older adults will look like. Demographic forces like declining birth rates, and ebbs and flows of international migration, as well as shifting cultural, political, economic, and technological forces are creating a context in which Generation X, Millennial, and Generation Z cohorts will experience old age differently from their Baby Boomer grandparents and Greatest Generation great-grandparents.

Chapter 3 examines older adults' families and social relationships. The transformation of US families has been one of the most dramatic demographic changes in the twentieth and twenty-first centuries and carries important implications for how, where, and with whom Americans grow old. Declines and plateaus in fertility mean older adults today have fewer biological children to care for them, relative to prior generations. Divorce and remarriage have created a context in which older adults may have several romantic partners over a lifetime, and may have to navigate complex decisions regarding caregiving, end-of-life decision-making, and inheritance with current and former spouses or cohabiting partners, and biological and stepchildren. Rising numbers of older adults are custodial grandparents to their grandchildren, due in part to social problems that have undermined their children's capacity to parent—including mass incarceration, the ravages of HIV and COVID-19, addiction, premature illness and death, unemployment, and other adversities that have their roots in economic and racial oppression. Yet rising numbers of older adults also are aging alone, without a romantic partner, children, or parents. Some find support from siblings and friends, whereas others suffer from social isolation and loneliness—problems that were intensified by social distancing practices during the COVID-19 pandemic (Brooke and Jackson 2020).

Chapter 4 delves into the health and well-being of older adults, underscoring social disparities in who gets sick. I show how sociodemographic factors like race, gender, and economic resources affect three dimensions of health: physical, mental, and cognitive. An important theme is that health disparities don't emerge suddenly in old age, but rather are the end result of disadvantages and advantages that accumulate over the life course. The COVID-19 crisis provides a dramatic example, revealing how social inequalities in where we live, the jobs we hold, and our access to health care set the stage for how we age.

Chapter 5 shows how public policies affect the well-being of older adults and their families. I begin by providing a global snapshot of population aging, to place the United States in an international context. I then focus on three main types of public policies: *economic policies* like public pensions, *health care policies* like publicly funded health insurance, and *family and caregiver policies*, such as programs to support family givers and expand the paid care workforce. I point out shortcomings in US policies and provide examples from other nations to illustrate the creative ways that governments and community initiatives like volunteer programs can enhance the well-being of all older adults. The chapter concludes by highlighting the contributions that older adults make to society, and the importance of providing opportunities so that older adults can use their skills and knowledge, to the extent that their health and preferences allow.

The conclusion looks into the future and proposes ways that future cohorts of older adults may experience old age. Much of what we know about later life is based on research focused on members of the Greatest

Generation, born in the 1920s and 1930s, and the oldest members of the Baby Boom cohort born in the 1940s. But what will old age look like for the small Generation X and large Millennial and Generation Z cohorts that follow? I describe contemporary social and economic patterns that may shape the experience of old age for future cohorts and conclude by showing how today's younger generations can help make the United States a more just, equitable, and safe place to grow old.

# 1 Historical and Contemporary Perspectives on Aging

Over the hill to the poorhouse I'm trudgin' my weary way,
I a woman of 70 and only a trifle gray,
I, who am smart an' chipper, for all the years I've told,
As many another woman that's only half as old . . .
What is the use of heapin' on me a pauper's shame?
Am I lazy or crazy? Am I blind or lame?
True, I am not so supple, nor yet so awful stout:
But charity ain't no favor, if one can live without.

(Carleton, 1872)

"Over the Hill to the Poor House" was one of the most popular songs in the United States in 1872. It was so popular that it inspired a 1920 movie musical of the same name (see figure 4). The lyrics capture the dread that older adults felt about going to the "poor house," the dreary and downtrodden public facilities that housed impoverished older adults, orphaned children, widows, persons with mental illness, unwed mothers, jobless men, criminals, and other people considered to be needy, dependent, or a drain on society (Wagner 2005). Poor houses were common in the United States from the mid-nineteenth through early twentieth centuries and were the home of last resort for many older adults. At that time, older people had few if any savings, their bodies were often too frail to work in farming or factories, and a national old-age pension program would not exist until the passage of the Social Security Act in 1935 (Fischer 1978). Those without families or whose families were unwilling or unable to take them in had no choice but to live in these "wretched quarters" (Fleming, Evans, and Chuka 2003a:916).

*Figure 4.* Poster for 1920 film *Over the
Hill to the Poor House.* SOURCE: Fox
Film Corporation.

Fast-forward roughly one century to 1988, when the *New Republic*
magazine published a controversial cover story on "greedy geezers." Jour-
nalist Henry Fairlie's (1988) article described "selfish" older adults who
were living lavishly, grabbing Social Security and Medicare benefits from
the federal government, and robbing younger generations of their future.
In the decades that followed, media headlines implored us to "Meet the
Greedy Grandparents: Why America's Elderly Are So Spoiled" (Chapman
2003) and told us "Here's Another Way Boomers are Screwing Us" (Kripke
2017). Political cartoons showed unflattering images like smug older
adults sitting in golf carts, urging debt-strapped, under-employed Millennials to hurry up and find good jobs to "keep funding our Social Security
and Medicare." As Chapman (2003) told readers, "America's elderly have
never had it so good. They enjoy better health than any previous generation of old people, [and] high incomes and ample assets. . . . Still they are
not content. From gratefully accepting a basic level of assistance back in
the early decades of Social Security, America's elderly have come to expect
everything their durable little hearts desire."

While Carleton's and Fairlie's sensationalist writings may sell movie
tickets and magazines, they offer misleading, simplistic, and potentially
dangerous depictions of old age in the United States. These extreme

images—abandoned and impoverished on one end of the continuum and on the other end, ungrateful and avaricious—belie the more nuanced realities of older adults' lives. It is true, at the population level, that the *average* level of health, wealth, and longevity of older adults has improved dramatically over the past two centuries (a COVID-related dip in longevity not withstanding). However, a simple statistical snapshot conceals the important fact that not all older adults have benefitted equally from these gains, with minoritized populations, women, and persons who grew up with social and economic disadvantages often left behind. The words of Carleton and Fairlie vividly demonstrate that public perceptions and stereotypes about old age, and the respect (or contempt) bestowed on older adults have changed dramatically throughout US history. These cultural transformations have little to do with the character or morals of older adults, and instead are tied to economic trends, changing families and household structures, social policies, and medical and technological advances that influence the quality of older adults' lives. This chapter provides a historical overview of the older population in the United States, and traces changes in their economic security and health over the past three centuries. Scholarly views of old age have changed alongside popular views, so the chapter also shows how the theoretical frameworks used to understand aging both perpetuate and challenge ageist notions about older adults' competencies and capacity to contribute to society.

## A BRIEF HISTORY OF OLD AGE IN THE UNITED STATES

### Social and Cultural Perspectives

Older adults were a rare and exalted population in the earliest days of the United States. From 1650 to 1850, adults ages sixty-five and older accounted for less than 2 percent of the nation's population. Even as late as 1870, they made up just 3 percent of the US population, and persons ages eighty and older accounted for less than 0.5 percent (Chudacoff 1989). The reasons for older adults' sparse numbers at that time reflect the demographic processes of fertility, mortality, and migration. Many babies were born during this time period; in 1800, the average woman gave birth to seven infants in her lifetime (Haines 2008). Yet infant and child mortality rates also were very high, so few infants survived until young adulthood, never mind old age. At the same time, European settlers were moving to North America in large numbers. A trans-Atlantic passage was treacherous before the advent of modern steamships, so most of these travelers needed to be young and healthy enough to survive the journey in crammed wooden ships (Guillet 1963). As the youthful ranks increased, older people accounted for a diminishing share of the total population (Posner 1995).

Because relatively few Americans survived until old age in colonial America, they were revered as special, wise, and knowledgeable. Older adults were respected and venerated, holding prestigious religious and political positions and other distinctions of high status—such as seats at the front of their church congregations. Puritan religious texts and sermons taught young people to behave benevolently and even deferentially toward older members of their communities. Consistent with this ethos of "respect for elders," most older persons lived with family members, typically their children—with unmarried children most likely to take in their parents (Fischer 1978). Even as late as 1850, nearly 70 percent of older adults lived with an adult child (Ruggles 2007). Caring for one's older relatives was seen as an honor rather than a burden.[1]

Popular fashions of the day were designed to make young people appear older and more dignified, a trend at odds with our modern youth-inspired culture. Young men would don white powdered wigs and wear clothing that appeared to make their backs look slightly hunched over, to mimic the appearance of their elders. Historical analyses of Census data from the early 1800s showed a slight tendency toward people *over*-reporting their actual age. This desire to be and appear older is a jarring contrast from the contemporary trend whereby middle-aged job applicants, Hollywood celebrities, and dating app users strategically shave a few years off their lives, whether due to vanity or fears of ageism. Yet this reverence for older persons was not due solely to the ethos of "respect for elders." The high status of older adults also reflected another reality: older men controlled the family wealth. Those who survived until advanced ages typically were from more privileged backgrounds; like today, the strains of poverty such as poor nutrition, unsafe housing, and physically onerous work conditions shortened life spans. Wealthy landowners had great economic power over their children (Fischer 1978). The patriarch owned and controlled their family's farmland and properties, and their sons (and daughters, after inheritance laws changed by 1800) would inherit these assets only when their father died—so the young had self-interested reasons for deferring to their elders. Or more accurately, deferring to white male landowning elders. Blacks, women, and immigrants who could not own land were not granted the same privilege and status as their white male counterparts (Carr 2019).

In the years that followed, the cultural and political tides turned, and youthful energy replaced sage wisdom as a status symbol. In the decades during and after the American Revolution, a new "youth culture" emerged. In the nineteenth century, older people no longer laid claim to the prestigious front-row pews at churches and meetinghouses. Powdered wigs gave way to more contemporary-looking toupees, and clothing styles no longer mimicked the frame and posture of older persons. Trends like age over-reporting on the Census started to wane. Retirement started to become mandatory at age sixty or seventy for some public office holders, reflecting the emerging desire to overthrow the "tyranny of age" (Fischer 1978). Even language changed; the emergence of ageist language, including new terms like "old fogey" or "old coot" were first recorded (Fleming et al. 2003a). The first documented use of the term "codger," meaning an "old miserly man," was in the late eighteenth century. Lexicologists suspect the word evolved from the antiquated verb "cadge," meaning to beg or sponge off others (Kyff 2012). These new slang terms equating old age with economic dependence mirrored dramatic changes in the financial status of older adults that would occur in the coming decades.

The waning status and honor bestowed on older adults plummeted even further throughout the late nineteenth and early twentieth centuries. Industrialization and urbanization afforded ambitious young people appealing job opportunities in cities and factories, far away from their parents' farmland (Burgess 1960). While 75 percent of US workers held agricultural jobs in 1800, this proportion fell to just over 30 percent by the early twentieth century (Ruggles 2007). Factory work in the late nineteenth and early twentieth centuries required youthful, strong bodies. Technical jobs that emerged in the mid-twentieth century, following the 1946 debut of the first modern computer, were believed to require nimble fingers and quick minds that could easily master the latest technical innovation. Early twentieth-century advances in sanitation, hygiene, and medicine meant that more people were surviving until old age, so older adults were no longer considered a rare or special population (Achenbaum 2020). For much of the early and mid-twentieth century, older adults were seen as physically and financially dependent, incapable of making productive contributions to society, and in desperate need of public support. Old age was described as a "roleless role," as older adults had few if any opportunities for productive activity (Burgess 1960). These dual forces of pity and paternalism helped impel two of the most important and successful policy reforms of the twentieth century: the establishment of Social Security in the 1930s, and the expansion of Social Security and birth of Medicare in the 1960s.

Since the late twentieth century, attitudes toward older adults have shifted once again. The current cultural narrative about old age is more bifurcated than in the past. On one hand, some older adults are still viewed as dependent, weak, and out of touch. National surveys find that more than 80 percent of older adults say they have been the target of ageism—like being the butt of insensitive jokes, being treated as if incompetent, and being passed over for a workplace promotion in favor of a younger or less experienced coworker (Palmore 2001; Roscigno et al. 2007). Laboratory experiments using Implicit Attitude Tests (IAT) consistently show that people associate negative words like *weak* with older adults, and more positive words like *strong* with younger adults (Levy and Banaji 2004).[2] Many experts believe that negative attitudes toward and discriminatory treatment of older adults have intensified during the COVID-19 pandemic. Some reports suggest that younger people may blame older adults for pandemic-related business shutdowns and strict masking and social distancing rules. Employers may be reluctant to hire or retain older workers in the future, presuming that they will be especially vulnerable to illness or in need of costly workplace adjustments (Brooke and Jackson 2020). Cruel memes referring to COVID-19 as the "BoomerRemover" illustrate the pervasiveness of beliefs associating old age with death, disease, and despair (Meisner 2020).

On the other end of the continuum is the narrative that older adults are doing just "fine" (Samuelson 2019). In fact, they're doing better than "fine"; current generations of retirees are characterized as healthier, wealthier, and more politically powerful than ever (Samuelson 2019). They're portrayed as unfairly gobbling up jobs and Social Security benefits—resources that should be reserved for the struggling younger generations behind them (Chapman 2003; Fairlie 1988; Kripke 2017). In his 2019 book *The Theft of a Decade: How the Baby Boomers Stole the Millennials' Economic Future*, the *Wall Street Journal* writer Joseph Sternberg reported that Baby Boomers are almost twice as likely as Millennials to expect Social Security to provide a major source of the retirement income. Sternberg cites data showing that Baby Boomers were more likely to own homes and less likely to carry crushing educational debt in their younger years, compared to the beleaguered Millennial generation.[3]

The "older adults are doing fine" narrative also refers to non-economic indicators like health, happiness, and longevity. Feel-good news stories on TV and the internet inspire us with images of super-human older adults like centenarian senior master swimmer Maurine Kornfeld. Nicknamed "Mighty Mo," Kornfeld has earned fourteen world championship gold medals, set twenty-eight world records, and was inducted into the International Swimming Hall of Fame at age ninety-seven. The most inspiring part of the story? She only started competitive swimming at age sixty-five (Yuccas 2020). Similarly, in 2020, ninety-year-old billionaire and Berkshire Hathaway chief executive Warren Buffett announced that he was planning to stay on the job, joking that he plans to run the company from his grave (Warner 2020). Five years earlier, at age eighty-five, Buffett famously told *Fortune* magazine that it would be "crazy" for him to stop working. Retirement, he said, "is not my idea of living" (LaRoche 2015). In January 2021, Joe Biden became the forty-sixth president of the United States at age seventy-eight, making him the oldest president in our nation's history. These late-life achievements would have been unimaginable at the turn of the twentieth century.

What accounts for these discrepant portrayals of older adults today—on one end of the spectrum a target of ageism and disrespect and on the other end an inspirational model of strength, competence, and leadership? The answer lies partly in the demography of aging. The over-sixty-five population is larger and more diverse than ever, so it is difficult if not impossible to generate a single narrative that aptly characterizes fifty million people (US Census Bureau 2020). Older adults' experiences vary dramatically, such that some enjoy good health, stimulating hobbies, comfortable homes, ample income and savings, and loving supportive relationships, whereas others suffer from poor health, unsafe housing, poverty, and so-cial isolation (Carr 2019). Recognizing these differences is critical to en-suring that the needs of all older adults are met through well-designed social policies.

## The Shifting Economic Fortunes of Older Adults

Cultural portrayals of older adults, like the 1920 film *Over the Hill to the Poor House* and a 2011 political cartoon of entitled Boomers sneering at debt-strapped Millennials partly mirror economic realities. This section provides a historical overview of the economic status of older adults and shows how their fortunes are shaped by policies like military pensions in the nineteenth century, the establishment of Social Security in the 1930s and its dramatic expansion in the 1970s. Yet social programs are not a per-fect solution for improving a population's well-being because they often are designed in such a way that they do not close the gap between the rich and poor, men and women, married and single, or Blacks and whites. That's why dramatic disparities in older adults' health and well-being per-sist in the twenty-first century, as we will see in the following chapters (Carr 2019).

During the first two centuries of the United States' history, old age was a time of poverty and dependency, other than for a small elite of wealthy elders (Haber and Gratton 1993). Historians estimate that in the early to mid-1800s, older adults needed roughly $230 per year to live, a stan-dard that only 20 percent attained. The financial plight of women, espe-cially widows, as well as immigrants and Black older adults (especially those who had been enslaved) was even more dismal (Fischer 1978). Older adults had two main options for financial security: work until they were too frail to do so or live with their adult children (Ruggles 2007). Thomas Paine, the political activist and revolutionary best known for his pamphlet *Common Sense* (1775–1776), was remarkably prescient and called for a third option: the establishment of a national old-age pension program. In his pamphlet *Agrarian Justice* (1795), Paine wrote that such a program would enable older adults to "live without wretchedness . . . and go de-cently out of the World." However, it would take nearly 150 more years for Paine's vision to become a reality.

In the absence of a national pension program, local townships developed their own charitable programs to provide for older adults who could neither work nor rely on kin. Following the model of English poor laws established in the seventeenth century, local governments and churches provided assistance with food and housing and established almshouses. Almshouses, a more genteel euphemism for "poor houses," provided housing for needy members of their local communities (Katz 1996). Widows, childless older adults, and those too frail to work were considered "worthy poor," meaning that they were poor due to no fault of their own and lacked the capacity to care for themselves. In stark contrast, those who were viewed as healthy enough to work were considered "undeserving poor" and thus unworthy of charity (Gans 1995). Not all older adults were welcomed to almshouses, however; an older adult with living family members would be denied charitable relief.

The accommodations provided by almshouses were barebones and have been described as "wretched" and "filthy" (Fleming et al. 2003a:916). The expenditures per resident were barely enough to provide for their basic nutrition and comfort. One 1897 examination of a poor farm in West Virginia estimated that only twelve cents per day was spent on each resident (Brammer 1994). An 1823 study of poor houses in New York State similarly found annual expenditures of thirty-five dollars per resident (less than ten cents per day), or about 15 percent of average annual wages at that time (Hannon 1984). Residents were expected to work around the house unless they were too frail to do so. They were referred to as "inmates," underscoring the stigmatized and demeaning existence of those who lived in these facilities. Older residents carried an additional stigma: the recognition that they did not have family willing or able to take them in (Katz 1996). Squalor and shame were part of everyday life: as the seventy-year-old narrator sang in *Over the Hill to the Poor House*, "charity ain't no favor, if one can live without." (Carleton 1872).

The nineteenth century ushered in pension programs for workers and military personnel. Pensions provided income for workers or military personnel upon their retirement; often this income would continue to flow after the worker's death, to his widow or other dependents. In 1861, Congress instituted a military pension system shortly after the start of the Civil War. The program was designed to recruit soldiers, bolster national pride, and provide a financial cushion for soldiers who were injured in combat and the widows of those who died (Blanck 2001). In the decades that followed, several trade unions for industrial workers established homes for their older members and experimented with pension programs to provide a regular income stream for their retired workers. Other employers, including the railroads, large public utilities, metal and mining trades, and corporations, also began to set up private pension plans. In 1911, Massachusetts became the first state to establish a retirement plan for state employees. Major cities also offered retirement and disability benefits to civil servants like firefighters and police officers; by 1917, more than 85 percent of US cities with populations of more than 100,000 had pensions for police officers (Clark et al. 2003).[4] By 1930, all federal workers received pension benefits, and twenty-one states had retirement plans for their teachers (Bortz 2012).

This progress toward older adults' economic security started to unravel in the 1930s, in the wake of the 1929 stock market crash and Great Depression. In 1910, about 25 percent of older adults lived in poverty. However, inflation and stock market tumbles in the Depression years led to a steady climb in old-age poverty rates, from 30 percent in 1930, to 50 percent in 1935, to an astonishing 65 percent by 1940 (Haber and Gratton 1993). Widespread unemployment meant that working-age adults could no longer afford to support their aged kin. Formerly middle- and upper-class older adults lost their savings and investments, contributions to charities plummeted, and ballooning numbers of impoverished older adults overwhelmed the state and local resources available to help them (Schieber and Shoven 1999). Against this backdrop of financial devastation, President Franklin D. Roosevelt enacted the Social Security Act of 1935 as part of the New Deal. Upon signing the legislation, Roosevelt proclaimed, "We have tried to frame a law which will give some measure of protection to the average citizen and to his family against the loss of a job and against poverty-ridden old age" (Martin and Weaver 2005).

Social Security was a history-changing program; the 1935 Act created a social insurance program that paid retired workers aged sixty-five or older (and their dependents) a continuing income after retirement. However, the original program was not sufficient to eradicate late-life poverty. During its first three decades, Social Security benefits barely provided

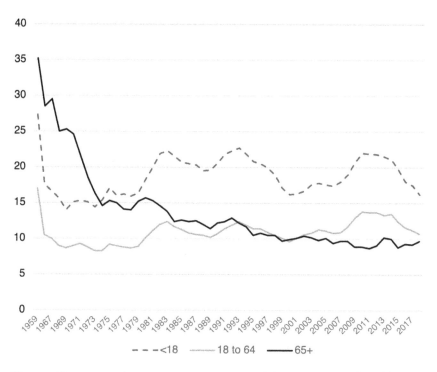

*Figure 5.* Poverty rates by age, 1959–2018. SOURCE: US Census Bureau (2019b).

a minimum standard of living because monthly payments were not adjusted annually to offset inflation. The first-ever beneficiary of Social Security, retired legal secretary Ida May Fuller, received a benefit of $22.54
in January 1940, and her monthly checks stayed at that amount for more
than a decade. In 1950, benefits increased for the first time, and were
expanded dramatically in 1972. That was the historical tipping point at
which older adults went from living in poverty in large numbers, to being
the age group with the lowest risk of poverty (Martin and Weaver 2005).

   Figure 5 shows the proportion of persons in the United States living
beneath the federal poverty line from 1959 through 2018, by age group.
Through the mid-1960s, more than one in three adults ages sixty-five
and older lived in poverty. In a now legendary broadcast in the 1960s,
newscaster Walter Cronkite described the plight of impoverished older
adults who had no choice but to eat dog food because they couldn't afford

groceries (Nyce and Scheiber 2015). Shortly thereafter, President Lyndon B. Johnson passed the Social Security Act Amendments as part of his Great Society program. The Act also created Medicare and Medicaid, the national public health insurance programs for older adults and low-income persons, respectfully; the Act helped protect older adults from potentially devastating medical bills. In 1972, the Social Security program was expanded again with a 10 percent across-the-board increase in benefits and automatic annual Cost of Living Adjustments (COLAs) to keep pace with inflation (Martin and Weaver 2005).[5]

The proportion of older adults living in poverty dropped to just 15 percent by 1974, and it continued to decline to about 10 percent in the 1990s and 2000s. In stark contrast, poverty rates among children under age eighteen increased and now fluctuate between 15 and 25 percent—rates considerably higher than those documented for older adults. Since 2010, late-life poverty rates also have dipped beneath the rates for working-age persons ages eighteen to sixty-four. This turn-around, whereby childhood and adult poverty rates are substantially higher than old-age poverty rates, has sparked intense debates about the appropriateness of continued investments in social programs that benefit older adults relative to younger adults (Preston 1984). However, this debate regarding "which generation has it worse" is misguided and counterproductive. First, the current *overall* old-age poverty rate of 10 percent conceals the fact that older women, especially older Black and Latinx women, have poverty rates nearly three times the national average. Second, the federal poverty line is not an ideal indicator for measuring late-life poverty, because it does not adjust for the very high medical expenditures of older adults, which can deplete their limited incomes.[6] Third, social programs that benefit one generation necessarily benefit the generations older and younger, given the importance of family members in providing financial and social support to one another (Carr 2019). Consequently, it is incorrect to conclude that older adults are "doing just fine" and that investments in one generation hurt the generations that follow.

### The Improving Health and Longevity of Older Adults

The bifurcated stereotypes of older adults we see today portray some as healthy, strong, and vigorous, and others as frail and weak. On one end of the continuum, we see awe-inspiring athletes like centenarian competitive swimmer mighty Mo Kaufman, octogenarian CrossFit Games competitor Jacinto Bonilla, and centenarian yoga master Tao Porchon-Lynch, who taught weekly classes up until her death at age 101 in 2020 (Blanton 2020; Weekman 2020). These aged athletes epitomize Chapman's (2003) claim that older adults today "enjoy better health than any previous generation of old people." Yet at the other end of the continuum, we see tragic media images of frail older COVID patients slumped over in their wheelchairs in overcrowded hospital hallways and dying nursing home residents waving to their grandchildren outside their windows. Statistical data also convey the vulnerability of older adults to COVID-19. While adults ages sixty-five and over account for 17 percent of the US population, they account for one-third of all COVID-19 cases, half of related hospitalizations and ICU admissions, and a staggering 80 percent of deaths associated with the virus (Carr, Boerner, and Moorman 2020).

How do we make sense of these two health extremes, of vigor versus vulnerability? The answer requires a brief look at historical trends in health and an understanding of the epidemiologic transition (Omran 1971). *Epidemiologic transition* refers to the historical process whereby infectious diseases were replaced by chronic illnesses as the leading causes of death in the United States. As a result of this transition, *overall* life expectancy increased dramatically, yet gender, race, and socioeconomic disparities emerged—fueling the disparate images of old age we see today (Olshansky and Ault 1986). In the eighteenth through the early twentieth centuries, most US deaths were due to infectious diseases like influenza, pneumonia, and tuberculosis (Kunitz 1984). These diseases struck quickly and unexpectedly, and they were relatively egalitarian in that people from all backgrounds were at risk. The spread of infection could not be easily controlled, and death could not be prevented even if a person had social advantages like a good income. As historians observed, "bacteria did not respect social or economic conditions. . . . A person's health was dependent on that of others" (Preston and Haines 1991: 20).

By the mid-twentieth century, infectious diseases were largely eradicated in the United States due to improved sanitation and personal hygiene, less crowded housing, better understanding of infectious disease transmission, and new technologies like milk pasteurization, vaccinations, and penicillin. As infectious diseases disappeared, infant and childhood mortality rates declined, and people were surviving to middle and old age in unprecedented numbers. Infectious diseases were replaced by chronic diseases that strike later in life, such as cancer, heart diseases, and diabetes (Omran 1971). Yet while infectious diseases would strike anyone, chronic diseases are closely tied to social and behavioral factors. That's why health and mortality have become so stratified by socioeconomic status and race over the past century. Those with greater advantages are more likely to eschew smoking and drinking, maintain a healthy diet and body weight, and have access to quality housing, safe neighborhoods, good jobs, medications, a regular health care provider, and other health-enhancing benefits (Olshansky and Ault 1986).

Medical breakthroughs over the past century also disproportionately enhance the health of those with greater social and economic advantages. Innovations like effective cancer screenings and surgical techniques like angioplasty for heart patients benefit those with access to doctors at top-notch hospitals using cutting-edge technologies. Public health campaigns against risky behaviors like smoking are most likely to benefit those who are literate and who have the means and support to kick unhealthy habits and adopt healthy new behaviors. That's part of the reason why Blacks are more likely than whites, and high school dropouts more likely than high school graduates to become ill and die prematurely of nearly all causes, including COVID-19 (Cunningham et al. 2017; Raifman and Raifman 2020). The concept of disparities or unequal outcomes, a core theme of this book, helps to explain an important paradox. The aging of the US population is largely a good news story in the *aggregate*, where average life spans, income levels, housing quality, health, and functioning have improved dramatically over the past three centuries. Yet, when we dig more deeply, we see a "best of times, worst of times" scenario, where some older adults are thriving while others are suffering (Carr 2019).

## THEORETICAL PERSPECTIVES ON AGING

A historical lens helps us to describe how and why older adults' lives have changed over time. Sociological theories help us to move beyond description, and provide a framework for understanding, explaining, and interpreting social realities. Theories are a product of their time and are shaped by the historical and cultural contexts in which they developed. This section provides a brief introduction to the most influential theoretical frameworks that social scientists use to understand aging processes.[7]

## Early and Mid-Twentieth-Century Perspectives

Sociological theories about aging are relatively new, with the first wave emerging in the mid-twentieth century. Given the high rates of poverty and limited opportunities for social and intellectual engagement among older adults in the 1950s and early 1960s, it's not surprising that one of the most influential theories of that era—disengagement theory—focused on explaining and rationalizing older adults' position on the sidelines of society. Subsequent theories, most notably activity and continuity theory, countered that older adults should engage rather than withdraw in order to enhance their health and well-being (Bengtson and Settersten 2016).

### DISENGAGEMENT THEORY

Disengagement theory proposed that it is best for older adults to reduce and ultimately withdraw or "disengage" from their social roles (Cumming and Henry 1961). Consistent with paternalistic views at the time, this perspective suggested it is best for aging minds and bodies to pull back from the demands of everyday life, and to focus on their inner needs to prepare psychologically and spiritually for death. This withdrawal also would benefit the larger society as it would open up opportunities for younger generations; retirements of older people would create job openings for younger persons.

Disengagement theory is now seen as out of step with contemporary views of old age, which encourage social engagement (Friend 2017) and recognize the meaningful ways that older adults can contribute to their families, communities, and society (Rowe and Kahn 2015). It also presumes that chronological age is an accurate marker of one's physical and cognitive capacities, failing to recognize that people age socially, psychologically, and biologically at different paces based on their social and economic positions. Blue-collar workers may stop working as young as their forties or fifties, if injuries or early health problems prevent them from carrying out tasks requiring physical strength and stamina. Warren Buffett has had privileges that enable him to lead Berkshire Hathaway even as he enters his nineties. Older adults working in professional jobs with health benefits, comfortable working conditions, and flexible schedules may have the capacity to remain active, engaged, and vital even into extreme old age.

## ACTIVITY AND CONTINUITY THEORIES

In the 1960s and 1970s, scholars started to challenge the notion that it was best for older adults to withdraw, countering that keeping busy was the path to health and happiness. Activity theory proposed that staying involved and engaged is essential to well-being (Havighurst 1963). People lose important social roles when they get older, such as worker (when they retire) and spouse (when they become widowed), yet proponents of activity theory argue that these voids can be filled with meaningful substitutions. The main theme of activity theory is strongly supported by research: social activities— whether volunteering; visiting friends and family; attending religious services; working for pay; and participating in activities like travel, sports, and the arts—are linked with older adults' well-being. Activity theory also was a driving force behind the development of social programs like senior volunteer corps and lifelong education programs such as Elderhostel (since renamed Road Scholar), which began in 1975.

However, a limitation of the theory is that almost any activity is considered beneficial regardless of whether it's something an older adult enjoys. For a shy bookish retiree, the thought of playing bingo at a senior center or taking a bus trip to Atlantic City may be seen as punishment rather than pleasurable. They may be much happier reading a novel or watching a PBS documentary in their home alone. This critique was an impetus behind the development of continuity theory, which argues that merely staying busy is not sufficient for enhancing older adults' well-being. Rather, older adults should hold roles and perform activities similar to those carried out during their younger years (Atchley 1989). A retired schoolteacher might volunteer to tutor children at an afterschool program, or a former bricklayer may help build homes for Habitat for Humanity. Yet this emphasis on continuity neglects the fact that some older adults might not have chosen or enjoyed the daily activities, relationships, and locales that filled their younger years. This may especially be the case for those who faced blocked opportunities on the basis of their race, gender, sexual orientation, or social background.

## Contemporary Life Course Perspectives on Aging

Contemporary perspectives extend classic frameworks in two major ways. First, they recognize that older adults' experiences are a product of the many roles, relationships, opportunities, and constraints that they have encountered, dating back to childhood and even in-utero. Second, these perspectives emphasize the importance of social structures, or the systems of stratification on the basis of race, class, and gender, that influence our lives. Two of the most prominent frameworks for studying the sociology of aging today are the life course paradigm (Elder 1985) and cumulative inequality perspectives (O'Rand 1996).

### LIFE COURSE PARADIGM

Life course sociologists are motivated by the recognition that "aging starts at birth." Our experiences in old age reflect a lifetime of influences including the comfort (both material and emotional) we enjoyed or lacked in childhood, how far we went in school, the jobs we held, the nature of our family relationship, the neighborhoods we lived in, our exposure to racism or sexism, and much more. The life course paradigm rests on four foundational assumptions. First, lives are shaped by historical contexts. Social and historical changes including cultural shifts in attitudes toward old age, public policies related to pension and health benefits, and biomedical and technological advances powerfully influence the lives of older adults. This theme helps us to understand why old age may look very different for those born in 1930 versus 1960 versus 1990; each cohort grew up under very different sociohistorical circumstances.

Second, timing matters in that the long-term impact of a personal experience or historical event is contingent on one's age when it occurred. Exiting the paid workforce at age fifty (rather than the "usual" retirement age of sixty-five) due to disability or caregiving demands means fewer savings, lower pensions, and less accumulated wealth in the longer-term. In general, making a transition earlier than one's peers (or "off-time") poses challenges and deprives one of the supports that could help them adapt to the transition (George 1993). Being widowed at thirty-five makes one an anomaly, whereas being widowed at age seventy-five means that one can draw support and advice from empathetic peers going through a similar experience.

Third, human lives are embedded in networks of social relationships—with parents, children, siblings, friends, coworkers, in-laws, romantic partners, and others. This theme helps us understand how and why childhood and adolescent conditions can affect one's physical, emotional, social, and financial well-being even five or six decades later. It also shows how daily experiences in old age are shaped by social ties. A sixty-five-year-old who is providing care to their spouse, eighty-five-year-old parent, and teenage grandchild will experience old age very differently than their peer with no caregiving responsibilities. As chapter 3 will show, social relationships affect nearly every aspect of older adults' health, longevity, emotions, and economic well-being.

The final theme guiding life course research is that individuals direct their own lives through their choices and actions—yet within the constraints of social circumstances. Sociologists' heavy emphasis on historical, economic, and intergenerational influences might seem deterministic, allowing little room for innovation or resilience in how people respond to the opportunities and obstacles before them. Yet life course approaches explicitly consider the role of personal choices, goals, and other factors that help to explain why two people facing the same constraints may have very different outcomes. In his classic book *American Lives*, John Clausen (1993) followed a cohort of school-age youth for more than sixty years and found that children who showed "planful competence" were more likely to have successful careers, stable and rewarding interpersonal relationships, and good health in old age. Planful competence encompasses traits like self-confidence, intellectual investment, and dependability. These attributes help people from all social backgrounds to achieve in school, develop thoughtful plans for the future, and pursue their goals effectively. This theme helps us to understand how social structures influence but do not wholly determine how one experiences old age.

## CUMULATIVE INEQUALITY PERSPECTIVES

Cumulative inequality perspectives build on life course principles by showing how inequalities in health, wealth, and well-being widen over the life course. The core assumption is that advantages give rise to further advantages, and disadvantages give rise to further disadvantages, such that small differences early in life widen over time (Dannefer 1987; O'Rand 1996).

It's easy to understand how disparities between the advantaged and disadvantaged could increase over time. Imagine that two elementary school classmates, James and John, differ in one way: one is born into a family that struggles financially, and the other is born into a family with financial comfort. James, the child born into poverty, might drop out of high school to help support his family, taking whatever low-paying or even physically dangerous job is available to a young person who lacks a high school diploma. His strenuous work might give him minor aches and pains in the short-term. Over time, James's muscle aches intensify, and he might sooth the pain with a few beers each night. After showing up for work with a hangover, he loses his job and health insurance and can't afford to get the health care he needs, worsening his health problems.

This scenario, whereby one adversity begets another, may create an increasingly vast divide between James and John, his classmate who had the good fortune to graduate high school, earn a college degree, find a good job, buy a home, and have few financial worries. While the differences between these two childhood friends might have been barely noticeable when they were young, over time these differences widened such that James struggled to make ends meet during his retirement years, whereas John enjoyed comfort and good health.[8] Cumulative inequality perspectives are useful for explaining disparities in later-life health, and help us to understand the two competing images of contemporary old age mentioned earlier in this chapter—with frail and lonely COVID-19 patients on one hand, and the hale and hearty Mo Kornfeld on the other (Crystal and Shea 1990; Ferraro and Shippee 2009). Old age is powerfully shaped by long-term, persistent, and accumulating inequalities over the life course.

## 2 Who Are Older Adults Today?

A CONTEMPORARY SNAPSHOT

What do music legends Bruce Springsteen and Carlos Santana, Massachusetts senator Elizabeth Warren, action film star Samuel L. Jackson, *Star Trek* actor and Twitter celebrity George Takei, business mogul turned space-travel entrepreneur Richard Branson, and talk show host and philanthropist Oprah Winfrey have in common? All are rich and famous and have been trailblazers in their professions. These icons share another similarity: all are older adults who are years past their sixty-fifth birthdays. While they may defy stereotypes of old age, they do reveal the great diversity of older adults today. The age sixty-five-and-over population in the United States is diverse with respect to race, ethnicity, national origin, education, family lives, sexual orientation, and more. Richard Branson, the British billionaire founder of multinational corporations, dropped out of high school at age sixteen, whereas Elizabeth Warren graduated college and law school. Carlos Santana was born in Mexico and migrated to California as a teenager, while Bruce Springsteen was famously born and bred in New Jersey. Hollywood star Samuel L. Jackson has been married to his wife LaTanya for more than forty years and has an adult daughter, George Takei has been married to his husband Brad for two decades and has no children, and Oprah Winfrey has not legally married her partner of four decades, Stedman Graham.

These luminaries are not representative of all older adults, due to their wealth and prominence, but they do help us to think about the diversity of that population. This chapter provides a statistical portrait of older adults in the contemporary United States, detailing demographic characteristics like sex, sexual orientation, race, immigration status, and marital status; socioeconomic characteristics such as level of education, employment status, and economic resources; and residential characteristics, like whether they live in a private home or long-term-care facility. All of these factors bear on older adults' social relationships (chapter 3), health and longevity (Chapter 4), and use of social programs and supports (Chapter 5). Another theme is that today's older adults differ from future generations of older adults. Demographic forces like declining birth rates, rising rates of late-life divorce, and waxing and waning levels of international migration, as well as shifting cultural, political, and economic forces are creating a context in which Generation X, Millennials, and Generation Z will experience old age differently from the Boomer and Greatest Generation cohorts before them.

## DEMOGRAPHIC CHARACTERISTICS

Demographic characteristics like age, sex, sexual orientation, race, ethnicity, nativity status, and marital status are key components of a population's composition. These characteristics also are linked with important outcomes like health and well-being because population subgroups may be vulnerable to particular obstacles or may enjoy important structural opportunities.

### Sex and Sexual Orientation

#### SEX

A casual visit to an older adults' residential community reveals an obvious demographic reality: the population is overwhelmingly female.[1] In 2020, the population of those aged sixty-five and older in the United States comprised more than thirty million women but just over twenty-four million men, meaning that older women outnumbered their male peers by five to four (Administration for Community Living 2020). The feminization of the US population increases with age; among those ages eighty-five and older women outnumber men two to one, and among centenarians this ratio is three to one (Mather and Kilduff 2020). The imbalanced sex ratio reflects the fact that men are more likely than women to die at every age, and thus have an overall life expectancy that is five to six years younger (seventy-six versus eighty-one years old). The gender gap in mortality is a consequence of biological and social factors. Baby boys are more likely than girls to die during their first year of life due to biological factors like boys' weaker cardiopulmonary systems, a greater genetic susceptibility to illness, and a higher risk of birth injury due to their larger heads (Mathews and MacDorman 2013). As children, teens, and young adults, boys are more likely to die from violent causes like automobile accidents, homicide, suicide, and drug- or alcohol-related conditions (Read and Gorman 2010). These gender gaps largely reflect differences in behavior rather than biology, in that boys are socialized to take physical risks and act in aggressive ways that are considered "brave" and "manly" even if they lead to injury and death. Some experts also attribute boys' riskier behavior to biological factors, including the slower development of the male brain's frontal lobe, which controls judgment and reason (Johnson, Blum, and Giedd 2009).

In adulthood, women are protected by the biological benefits of estrogen, also known as the female sex hormone. Estrogen protects against heart disease by lowering levels of harmful cholesterol. Women also tend to have stronger immune systems because testosterone, the male sex hormone, is linked to immunosuppression (Read and Gorman 2010). That's part of the reason why men are more likely than women to die of COVID-19 (Scully et al. 2020). Social and behavioral factors also contribute to men's health problems and shortened life spans in adulthood and old age. Men are more likely to smoke, drink alcohol, and work in physically dangerous occupations like construction worker, fisher, and logger (Bureau of Labor Statistics 2019). Men also may ignore troubling health symptoms, neglect routine health screens, and skip regular doctor's visits. These behavioral patterns are another reason why men died of COVID-19 at roughly twice the rate of women; they were more likely to refuse vaccinations and face masks, even though both are effective steps against infection (Griffith et al. 2020). These multifaceted biological and social factors contribute to men's greater mortality risk and lower chances of surviving until old age (Springer and Mouzon 2011).

SEXUAL ORIENTATION

Social scientists have only recently begun to document the number and characteristics of older adults who identify as lesbian, gay, bisexual, transgender, or queer (LGBTQ). Large population-based studies have not asked older adults about their sexual orientation until fairly recently, and national surveys vary in their measures and estimates. The Gallup Poll suggests that about 5 percent of US women identify as lesbian, 4 percent of men identify as gay, and less than 1 percent say they are transgender (Newport 2018). In stark contrast, federal data from the National Health Interview Survey (NHIS) reports that 1.6 percent of US adults identify as gay or lesbian, 0.7 percent as bisexual, and 1.1 percent identify as "something else," or refuse to answer the survey question (Ward et al., 2014). These discrepancies reflect a reluctance to report a behavior or identity that may be stigmatized in one's community. Some people who are attracted to same-sex partners or who have had only occasional same-sex relations also may be hesitant to label themselves as gay or lesbian (Wolff et al. 2017).

Despite these discrepancies in the exact proportion of US adults who identify as LGBTQ, research consistently shows that current cohorts of older adults are less likely than younger cohorts to identify as gay. As figure 6 shows, a 2018 Gallup Poll found that 1.4 percent of the Greatest Generation cohort, 2.4 percent of Baby Boomers, and 3.5 percent of Gen Xers identified as LGBTQ, compared to more than 8 percent of Millennials. These patterns reflect the fact that discrimination and prejudice against, and the legal rights afforded to LGBTQ persons have improved over the past several decades. The data suggest that future cohorts of older adults will include considerably larger shares of LGBTQ persons than we see today (Newport 2018).

The nearly three million older LGBTQ adults in the United States have faced multiple sources of institutional and interpersonal mistreatment. However, in 2015 the US Supreme Court ruled that same-sex marriage is legal in all fifty states. Given the recency of this ruling, older LGBTQ persons are less likely than their straight peers to be married or partnered, to live with a significant other, or to have children. They also are especially

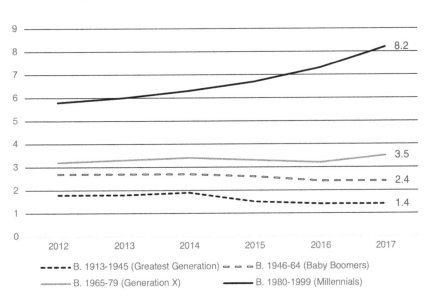

*Figure 6.* Percentage of population identifying as LGBTQ by birth cohort, 2012–17. SOURCE: Newport (2018).

vulnerable to economic adversity and poorer physical and mental health due to a lifetime of exposure to what epidemiologist Ilan Meyer (2003) calls "minority stress." Social isolation also is a concern, although LGBTQ older adults enrich their social lives with friends and "families of choice" who meet their socioemotional and caregiving needs (Goldsen 2018).

## Race and Ethnicity

Most US older adults today are white, yet each successive birth cohort is more racially and ethnically diverse than the one before it. Demographers predict that by the end of the twenty-first century, the population of US older adults will become "majority minority," meaning that groups histori-cally known as racial or ethnic minorities will make up more than half of the population. In 2018, 77 percent of adults ages sixty-five and older but less than half of all children under age eighteen were white (Frey 2021). Among the 23 percent of older adults (or 12.3 million persons) identifying as a racial or ethnic minority in 2018, 9 percent were African Americans, 4 percent Asian, less than 1 percent American Indian, Alaska Native, or

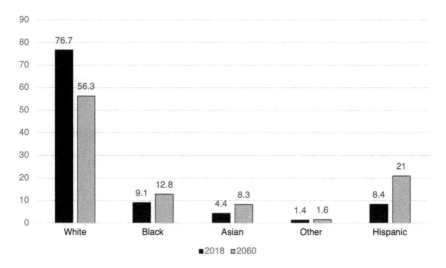

*Figure 7.* Racial and ethnic composition of population ages sixty-five and over, 2018 and 2060 (projected). NOTE: White, Black, Asian, and Other refer to non-Hispanics. SOURCE: William H. Frey analysis of US Census population estimates released June 20, 2019.

Native Hawaiian/Pacific Islander, and 1 percent multiracial (see figure 7). Persons of Hispanic ethnicity, such as those with Mexican, Dominican, Cuban, or Puerto Rican ancestry, represented 8 percent of the older population in 2018.

By the year 2060, racial and ethnic minority populations ages sixty-five and over are projected to jump from 12.3 to 27.7 million, accounting for more than one-third of all older adults. Whites account for more than three-quarters of older adults today, yet that share will drop to just over half (56 percent) by 2060. In sharp contrast, Hispanics are the most rapidly growing ethnic group, accounting for just over 8 percent of all older adults today, but a projected 21 percent by 2060 (US Census Bureau 2020). The proportion identifying as Black and Asian also will increase, with the share of older Asian adults nearly doubling from 4.4 percent in 2018 to a projected 8.3 percent in 2060, while the proportion of older Black adults will increase from 9.1 percent to 12.8 percent.

The reasons behind these dramatic shifts in the racial and ethnic composition of the older population reflect the three demographic processes of mortality, fertility, and migration. First, a major reason why current cohorts of older adults are disproportionately white, relative to the overall US population, is differential mortality. Put simply, Black Americans die younger than white Americans at every stage of life. Despite large declines in infant mortality rates in the United States over the past century, Black newborns are more than twice as likely to die as white newborns (Kaiser Family Foundation 2019). In adolescence and adulthood, Blacks (especially men) have a much greater risk of dying than whites, and thus are less likely to survive until midlife and old age. Black-white disparities in deaths due to homicide, HIV/AIDS, cancer, diabetes, heart disease, and, most recently, COVID-19 are a devastating consequence of long-standing systemic racism in the United States (Hooper et al. 2020; Kawachi, Daniels, and Robinson 2005).

Second, race and ethnic differences in fertility, or the number of babies a woman gives birth to in her lifetime, contribute to rising diversity among future cohorts of older adults. White women today are having fewer children on average than Latinas and, to a lesser extent, Black women. In 2017, the average total fertility rate (TFR) in the United States was 1.77, meaning that the average woman gives birth to just under two babies in her life. The TFR ranged from a low of 1.67 among white women to a high of 2.01 among Latinas, with Blacks in the middle at 1.82 (Mathews and Hamilton 2019). Due to these differences in childbearing, recent birth cohorts are rapidly becoming majority-minority. In 2015 for the first time ever, white newborns were outnumbered by infants of color, albeit by a slight margin (49.8 versus 50.2 percent).

Demographers project that the number of white births will continue to decrease, while the total number of births to Black, Latinx, and Asian women will increase for a further reason: the different age structures of each ethnic group. The white population today is much older than the populations of other racial/ethnic groups, so a smaller fraction of white women have the biological capacity to become parents. Most women today give birth in their twenties and thirties, with far fewer in their forties and virtually none in their fifties becoming biological mothers, due to diminishing reproductive capacity with age (Rowe 2006). In 2018, the median age of whites was forty-four, and the modal (or most common) age was fifty-eight; as such, large numbers of white women are past the age at which they are biologically capable of giving birth. In stark contrast, the median ages of the Black, Asian, and Latinx populations were thirty-four, thirty-seven, and thirty, respectively. Even more extreme, the modal age for these three groups in 2018 was twenty-seven, twenty-nine, and eleven, respectively (Schaeffer 2019). These data show that there are many young Latinx, and to a lesser extent, Black and Asian women who are likely to become mothers, and they tend to give birth to a slightly greater number of babies on average than white women. These babies, in six to seven decades, will account for the rapidly growing share of older adults who are of Latinx descent.

Third, migration patterns affect the ethnic and racial composition of the older population. In recent decades, immigrants to the United States have come primarily from Latin America, Asia, and, to a lesser extent, Africa, whereas in the first five decades of the twentieth century, immigration from Europe and Canada was more common. These patterns affect the racial and ethnic composition of the US population across different birth cohorts (Abdul-Malak and Wang 2016). In 2018, just five countries accounted for nearly half of all new immigrants to the United States: Mexico, China, India, the Philippines, and El Salvador. As these cohorts of new Americans grow old in the coming decades, the racial composition of the sixty-five-and-over population will look very different than it does today (Budiman et al. 2020).

*Nativity Status*

Older adults today are slightly less likely than younger persons to have been born outside the United States, and those who did migrate to the United States are slightly more likely to hail from Europe or Canada, relative to the generations that followed them. In 2018, a record forty-five million immigrants were living in the United States, accounting for 14 percent of the overall population. This fraction varied slightly across cohorts, ranging from just 14–15 percent of Baby Boomers and members of the Greatest Generation, yet more than 20 percent of Generation X. As figure 8 shows, the national origin of US immigrants varies across the generations, such that Europe, Canada, East and Southeast Asia, and the Caribbean account for a somewhat larger share among cohorts now in their seventies and older, whereas Mexico, South Asia, and Central America are more common origins for midlife and younger adults, with Sub-Saharan

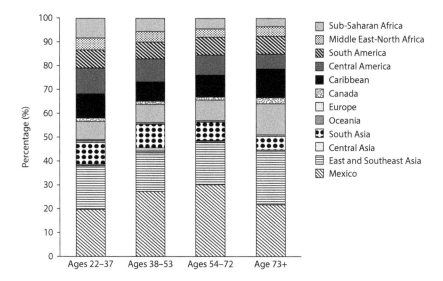

*Figure 8.* Country of origin among immigrants living in the United States by age group, 2018. SOURCE: Budiman et al. (2020).

Africa also accounting for a considerable share of the youngest cohorts of Millennials (Budiman et al. 2020).

Older Americans born outside the United States are a heterogeneous group, so it is difficult to offer a simple snapshot of who they are. One key source of difference is whether one moved to the United States as an older adult, or whether one migrated early in life and grew old in the United States. For most of the twentieth century, it was a rare older adult who would migrate to the United States, given the social disruption that immigration entails. Most migrants were working-age adults seeking economic opportunities for themselves and their children. Even as recently as 2000, just 2 percent of new immigrants were ages sixty-five and older, although this proportion crept up to 6 percent by 2017. Part of this increase reflects rising numbers of older immigrants who are coming to the United States on "parent" green cards, sponsored by their adult children who had previously moved to the United States and became citizens (Camerota and Zeigler 2019). These green cards enable older parents to live close to their adult children and grandchildren. Most older adults born outside the United States migrated at much younger ages, however, typically in their twenties or thirties either to work or to be reunited with family members who had arrived earlier. Data from the 2010 US Census show that more than 90 percent of all immigrants ages sixty-five and older have been in the United States for more than ten years and 60 percent for more than 40 years (Wilmoth 2012).

Older immigrants' experiences in the United States vary based on when they arrived in their new country. Those who came as children or young adults, like celebrated guitarist Carlos Santana, resemble their native-born counterparts, whereas those who arrived in later life are more likely to experience social and linguistic isolation, meaning they may struggle with little or no proficiency in the English language, limited work experience in the United States, and weak ties to the local communities in which they have settled (Wilmoth 2012). These disadvantages are further compounded by the fact that those who migrate in later life are more likely to be women, to have limited education, to be widowed, and to have health problems—the reasons their children may have insisted on bringing their aged parents to the United States in the first place (Wilmoth 2012).

New immigrants to the United States cannot receive benefits from social welfare programs like Medicare and Social Security unless they become naturalized citizens. Of the 14 percent of older adults who were born outside the United States, about 10 percent are naturalized citizens and 4 percent are not citizens (Roberts et al. 2018). Naturalization is the legal process through which an immigrant gains US citizenship, after meeting the strict requirements established by Congress in the Immigration and Nationality Act (INA). One condition is to "be proficient in basic spoken and written English and demonstrate knowledge of US history and government," a standard that may be difficult for older immigrants with limited English literacy.[2] Nearly three-quarters of recent older immigrants cannot speak English fluently or have limited proficiency, compared with just one-third of older immigrants who arrived in the United States decades earlier (Wilmoth 2012). The most common language spoken by older immigrants is Spanish, followed by European and Asian languages (Roberts et al. 2018).

## Family Statuses

Family relationships, including romantic partnership and parental statuses, are critical to older adults' health, happiness, financial security, and capacity to live safely and comfortably in their own homes. Marital status refers to whether one is married, divorced, separated, widowed, cohabiting with a romantic partner, or never married. For current cohorts of older adults, marriage is a nearly universal experience. Just 5 percent have been single for life, with this share inching upward in each successive generation, as shown in figure 9. Older men are more likely than older women to be married, and this gender gap widens with age. Among adults ages sixty-five to seventy-four, 73 percent of men yet just 58 percent of women are currently married. By age eighty-five and older, 54 percent of men are still married, compared to just 17 percent of women (US Census Bureau 2020). Women are more likely to be widowed, a gap that widens with age. By age eighty-five, women are twice as likely as men to be widowed (72 versus 36 percent). The widowhood gap is due to the fact that wives tend to outlive their husbands, a reality exacerbated by men's tendency to marry women two to three years younger than themselves. Black women are especially likely to become widowed due to Black men's mortality disadvantage.

A further reason for the gender gap in marriage is that older men are more likely than women to remarry after becoming widowed or divorced. The category of "married" includes people in long-term marriages as well as those who have lost a spouse to death or divorce and have since remarried. One-half of older adults whose marriages ended eventually remarry, although men are more likely than women to remarry (66 versus 40 percent). This gender gap reflects both demographic constraints and personal preferences (Livingston 2014). Lopsided sex ratios, where women outnumber men, mean that older women seeking a same-age male partner will find few eligible candidates. This is especially the case for Black women. Yet research and anecdotal evidence show it's not simply that women can't remarry; rather, some don't want to. Interviews with older women reveal that some don't want to remarry because they don't want to provide round-the-clock care to an older husband once he becomes ill (Bennett, Hughes, and Smith 2003). Some women don't want to remarry because their social and emotional needs are met by their friends, children, and siblings (Carr 2004a).

Divorce is relatively uncommon among current cohorts of older adults, yet each successive cohort is more likely to end their marriages through

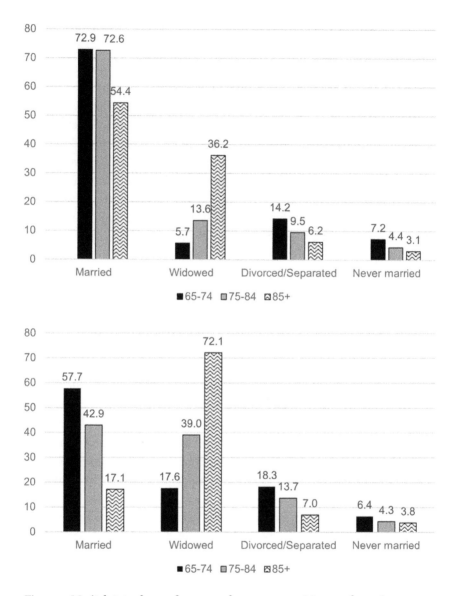

*Figure 9.* Marital status by age for men and women, 2019. Men are shown in top panel, women are shown in bottom panel. SOURCE: US Census Bureau (2020a).

divorce rather than spousal death. As figure 9 shows, 14 percent of men and 18 percent of women Baby Boomers (ages sixty-five to seventy-four) are currently divorced, although these proportions are just 6 and 7 percent among members of the Greatest Generation (ages eighty-five and older). For the cohorts of late Baby Boomers and Generation X that follow, the proportion who divorce will be even higher (Raley, Sweeney, and Wundra 2015). There are two ways to become an older divorced person. Some people in the "divorced" category ended their marriages when they were young and never remarried, whereas others had long marriages and then divorced later in life. The latter pathway, dubbed "gray divorce" or divorce among people in their fifties and older, has become much more common in recent decades. Since 2010, divorce rates have increased at a particularly steep pace for those ages sixty-five and over (Brown and Lin 2022). Midlife and older adults recognize they have many healthy and active years ahead and may decide they don't want to grow old with their current partner (Brown and Lin 2012).

Divorced, widowed, and never married older adults are not necessarily "single," however. Rising numbers of unmarried midlife and older adults are in cohabiting unions, meaning that they live with a steady romantic partner, although they are not legally married. The proportion cohabiting increases across successive cohorts; just 2 percent of unmarried persons ages seventy and older live with a romantic partner, compared to 7 percent among those in their sixties, and nearly 10 percent in their fifties (Brown, Lee, and Bulanda 2006). These generational differences reflect cultural shifts in attitudes toward sexual relations outside of legal marriage.

Marital status is closely linked to living arrangements; not surprisingly, married and cohabiting individuals typically live with another person and have the support of a coresidential partner. Older women are more likely than men to live alone, because they are less likely to be partnered. More than 95 percent of older adults live in their own homes, with only a small fraction living in institutions like nursing homes. Of those who live in their own homes, women and especially Black women are more likely than whites and men to live alone. As figures 10a (men) and 10b (women) show, Black women are more than twice as likely as white men (43 versus 20 percent) to live alone. Conversely, white and Asian men are three

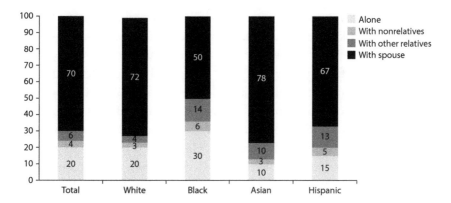

*Figure 10a.* Older men's living arrangements by race/ethnicity, 2016.

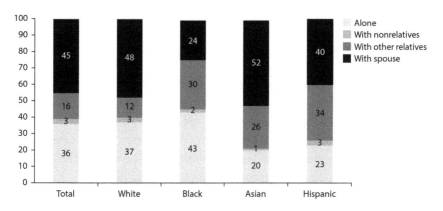

*Figure 10b.* Older women's living arrangements by race/ethnicity, 2016. NOTE: White, Black, and Asian refer to non-Hispanics. SOURCE: Federal Interagency Forum on Aging-Related Statistics (2016).

times as likely as Black women to live with a spouse (72 versus 24 percent). These gaps are troubling, because living alone can be an isolating and even dangerous experience for older adults who want to "age in place" or remain in their own homes rather than move to an assisted living facility. Older adults who live alone lack a coresidential companion who can assist with preparing meals, getting dressed, bathing, going shopping, or taking medications. Some people who live alone have the financial means to pay for assistance like home health services, yet these options often are out of reach to women, and especially Black women and Latinas, who are at particular risk of financial insecurity in old age (Carr 2019).

Spouses and romantic partners are an important source of socioemotional and practical support, yet most older adults also receive support from (or give support to) children and grandchildren. About 85 percent of older adults today are parents, and 70 percent have at least one grandchild (American Association of Retired Persons 2002). Blacks and women report more supportive and close-knit relationships with their children than do whites and men (Sarkisian and Gerstel 2008). Black, Latinx, and Asian older adults are more likely than whites to live with their children or grandchildren in multigenerational households and to be involved in their grandchildren's day-to-day activities.

## SOCIOECONOMIC CHARACTERISTICS

Socioeconomic characteristics indicate the social standing or social class of an individual or group. It encompasses a range of resources, including education, income, occupation, wealth, and poverty risk. These resources have a powerful influence on the quality of older adults' lives, as they provide a means to purchase the goods and services or generate the helpful social connections that are critical to health and well-being.

### Educational Attainment

Richard Branson, the space travel entrepreneur and billionaire founder of multinational conglomerate Virgin Group famously dropped out of high school at sixteen, following his struggles with dyslexia. The septuagenarian's remarkable financial success is atypical, however. Educational attainment, or the years of formal schooling one has completed, is one of the most powerful predictors of later-life well-being. Education is linked to the kind of job one holds and how much money one earns and saves. It is a flexible resource that is linked with healthier behaviors and effective coping skills that can enhance one's quality of life. Throughout the twentieth century, educational attainment in the United States increased dramatically for women and men, Blacks and whites, and poor and rich. However,

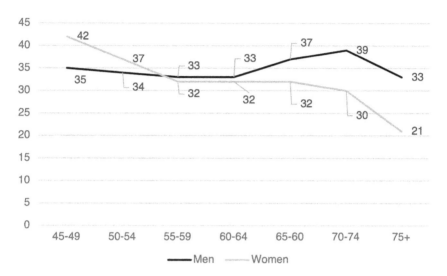

*Figure 11.* Percentage of adults with college degree, by age and sex, 2019. SOURCE: US Census Bureau (2020b).

significant gaps in high school and college graduation rates persist, and these gaps are driving disparities in physical and mental health, financial security, and other aspects of late-life well-being.

In 1950, less than 20 percent of adults ages sixty-five and over had earned a high school diploma; by 2019, 88 percent had reached this milestone. College graduation rates also increased, quintupling from less than 5 percent of persons in this age group in 1950 to more than 31 percent in 2019 (US Census Bureau 2020c). Among current cohorts of older adults, men are more likely than women to have graduated college, although this gender gap has narrowed among Baby Boomers and has closed and even reversed slightly among Generation X and the cohorts that follow (US Census Bureau 2019b). As figure 11 shows, the proportion of midlife and older men with a college degree has held steady around one-third across recent cohorts, although each successive cohort of women is more likely than their predecessors to have graduated college. The proportion of Generation X women now in their forties and fifties with a college degree is twice that of women now in their seventies (42 versus 21 percent), and slightly higher than their male peers.

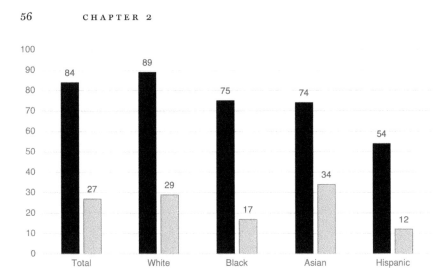

*Figure 12.* Educational attainment of persons ages sixty-five and over by race/ethnicity, 2015. NOTE: White, Black, and Asian refer to non-Hispanics. SOURCE: Federal Interagency Forum on Aging-Related Statistics (2016).

Although all racial and ethnic groups have seen educational gains, disparities persist, as shown in figure 12. In 2015, nearly 90 percent of older white adults had a high school diploma, compared to 75 percent of Black and Asian older adults, and just 54 percent of Latinos. While one in three white and Asian older adults today has a college degree, these proportions are considerably lower for Black and Latinx older adults (17 and 12 percent, respectively). The GI Bill is a factor underlying these disparities. The Servicemen's Readjustment Act of 1944, popularly referred to as the GI Bill, provided stipends for tuition and living expenses for military veterans attending college or trade schools. These education benefits continued until 1956, while the Veterans Administration (VA) offered insured loans until 1962. The Readjustment Benefits Act of 1966 extended these benefits to all veterans of the armed forces, including those who had served during peacetime. However, women were less likely than men to serve in the military in the mid-twentieth century, because social conventions at that time encouraged women to put their marriages and children ahead of education and careers (Goldin 2006). Black military veterans could not take full advantage of the GI Bill tuition benefits, due to racial discrimination on the part of college and university admissions officers and banks providing loans (see Rothstein 2017 for extensive discussion).

Older adults with limited schooling face challenges such as lower levels of financial and health literacy. College graduates are more likely than high school graduates to have proficient levels of health literacy, meaning a capacity to read and understand things like instructions on their prescription medical vials (Kutner et al. 2006). College graduates also are more facile with technology, an increasingly important and even necessary component of everyday life. The importance of being tech-savvy was apparent during the peak of the COVID-19 pandemic, when videoconferencing replaced face-to-face encounters as the primary means of social interaction for older adults. Internet access also was essential for signing up for vaccines and COVID tests. While two-thirds of Americans ages sixty-five and older used the internet and 42 percent owned smartphones in 2016, these proportions vary by level of schooling, as shown in figure 13 (Pew Research Center 2017). Just half of older adults with a high school diploma or less schooling used the internet in 2016, compared to more than 90 percent of college graduates. College graduates are more than twice as likely as high school graduates or dropouts to use smartphones (65 versus 27 percent) and social media (56 versus 20 percent). Internet use is an important pathway to information and social connectedness, and it contributes to widening disparities between those with more or fewer socioeconomic resources.

*Employment*

A common stereotype is that older adults don't work for pay, with rare exceptions like the erudite museum docent or college professor. Yet that stereotype does not align with reality. The proportion of older adults who are working for pay has climbed steadily over the past three decades, and will likely continue, especially as the US economy bounces back from the COVID-19 pandemic. In 2019, more than ten million adults sixty-five and older worked for pay, a record high number that included about 20 percent of all older adults. Labor force participation rates decline with age, as age-related health concerns or a desire to retire take older adults out of the

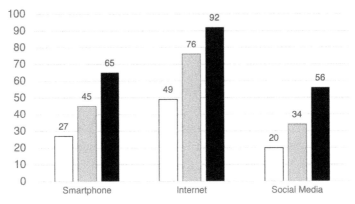

*Figure 13.* Internet use of persons ages sixty-five and over by educational level, 2016. SOURCE: Vogels et al. (2020).

work force. One in three adults ages sixty-five to sixty-nine, 20 percent of those seventy to seventy-four, and just 9 percent of those seventy-five and older were working for pay in 2019 (Federal Interagency Forum on Aging-Related Statistics 2020). About 15 percent of older workers have retired and then reentered the labor force, while 40 percent work part-time, clocking fewer than 35 hours per week (Cahill, Giandrea, and Quinn 2015).

Older adults' labor force participation rates have ebbed and flowed throughout the twentieth and twenty-first centuries. In 1950, nearly half of older men and 10 percent of women ages sixty-five and older worked for pay. At that time, many adults needed to work because public pensions were meager. As Social Security benefits increased throughout the 1970s, more older adults could afford to retire. Older men's employment rates dropped to just 16 percent in 1985. Since that time, this rate has risen to about 25 percent in the 2010s, as shown in figure 14. Women's labor force participation rates are consistently lower than men's but started to creep up in the 1970s, due in part to expanding occupational opportunities in the wake of the women's movement. Rising divorce rates sent newly single women back into the workforce so that they could earn enough to support themselves and their children. In 2019, older men's and women's employment rates reached 25 and 16 percent, respectively. These rates vary

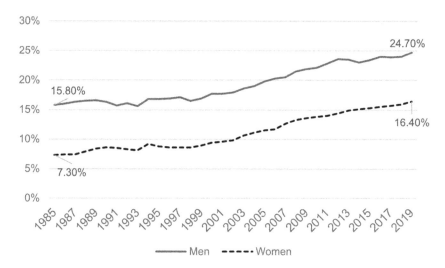

*Figure 14.* Labor force participation of persons ages sixty-five and over by sex, 1985–2019. SOURCE: Bureau of Labor Statistics (2020).

somewhat by race and ethnicity, ranging from a low of 19.5 among Black men to 25.7 percent among Asian men, and from 14.3 among Latinas to 17.7 among Asian women.

Older adults' employment throughout the late twentieth and early twenty-first centuries reflects both "pull" and "push" factors. Healthy older adults want to work because it provides a sense of identity, purpose, and social integration, as well as a paycheck. Financial need forces some people to work, even if they would prefer to retire. Policy shifts also have affected older adults' employment. Mandatory retirement ages have been largely abolished, dating back to 1967 when Congress enacted the Age Discrimination in Employment Act (ADEA). Another major policy shift will keep future cohorts of older adults working longer: the age at which workers are eligible to receive full Social Security benefits has increased. Workers born before 1942 are eligible for full benefits at age sixty-five, yet this age of eligibility increases to sixty-six for those born between 1942 and 1960, and sixty-seven for those born after 1960 (Social Security Administration 2022).

The COVID-19 pandemic and its aftermath may reshape older adults' labor force participation. On one hand, it might create new and unexpected opportunities for older workers. A "great resignation" occurred in 2021 and 2022, when millions of workers quit their jobs, weary from the pandemic. These new openings provided unexpected opportunities for some older adults to start new careers or reenter the workforce. A workplace shortage meant that employers were offering hiring bonuses and higher starting salaries, an option that was appealing to healthy older adults looking to remain engaged in the labor force (Moran 2022).

On the other hand, the immediate economic downturn of the pandemic was felt especially hard by older workers. In times of economic downturns, older workers tend to be particularly vulnerable. During the 2008 recession, adults sixty-two and older were the age group least likely to find a new job after being laid off, and they were most likely to quit a job search within nine months. With an abundance of job applicants, employers may unwittingly discriminate against older applicants (Morrow-Howell et al. 2020). The 2020 economic downturn also disproportionately affected older workers. As of July 2020, roughly four months into the pandemic, 13 percent of workers ages sixty-five and older (topping one million people) had lost their jobs, with rates of job loss even higher for older workers of Asian or Latinx ethnicity (19 percent). Older workers in the leisure and hospitality industry, like restaurant staff, were the hardest hit, with nearly one-third losing their jobs. Some who were lucky enough to keep their jobs chose to retire early, rather than face the health risks of close contact with coworkers and customers (Fry 2020b). Some small business owners retired earlier than expected or closed up shop as a result of the dip in business during the recession and the high costs of reconfiguring their workplace to accommodate social distancing rules (Jacobson, Feder, and Radley 2020).

Older adults hold many different types of jobs, despite stereotypes like the genial Walmart greeter or prim museum tour guide. The five most common jobs held by men ages sixty-two and older in 2017 were truck driver, janitor, farmer, college professor, and lawyer, while the top five for women were teacher, secretary, personal care aide, registered nurse, and childcare worker (Johnson and Wang 2017). These patterns largely reflect historical factors. Women growing up in the early and mid-twentieth century were channeled into traditionally "female" jobs like secretary and teacher, rather than engineer or lawyer (Goldin 2006). When Senator

Elizabeth Warren entered law school in the 1970s, only 4 percent of law-yers were women, although this proportion reached 12 percent by 1980 and is just over 50 percent today (Bowman 2009). Older men entered the labor market during a time when agricultural jobs were common. Farmers often work until very old age because they do not have younger relatives who want to take over the family farm (US Department of Agriculture 2020). Blue-collar jobs like truck driver were heavily unionized and pro-vided workers a good income and benefits through the mid-twentieth century; however, policy changes like the deregulation of the trucking in-dustry in 1980 meant that wages and benefits plummeted, driving away younger cohorts from the profession.

*Income and Poverty*

Older workers rely on their earnings to pay their bills. But how do the forty-six million older retirees support themselves? Retirement income, or the money that older adults have to live on after they leave the work force is described as a "three-legged stool," where the three legs are Social Security income, private pensions, and personal savings and investments (along with the interest those investments generate). For some older adults, the stool also has a fourth leg: earnings from wages, salary, or self-employment income.[3] Although earnings historically were considered a less important leg of the stool, given that most older adults exited the labor force, more and more older adults are working for pay today, for reasons presented earlier in this chapter. The types of income that older adults rely on are critical to their financial security. Older adults who depend primarily on their monthly Social Security benefits are the most threat-ened by cuts to public programs, whereas older adults with other income sources have a financial cushion. Figure 15 shows the breakdown of older adults' annual income by source, based on one's per capita family income.

Social Security is the most important source of income for older adults, especially those with meager savings and no private pension from their for-mer employer. On average, Social Security accounts for about half of older adults' per capita income, although women, ethnic and racial minorities, and those with lower incomes rely on it most heavily. Older immigrants who are not naturalized do not qualify for such benefits, however, forcing many

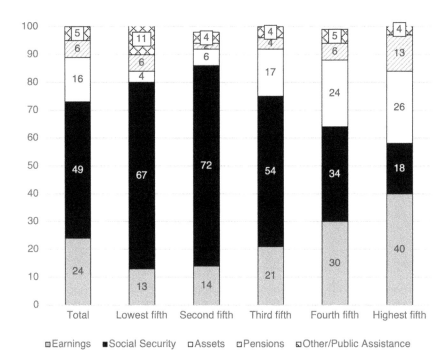

*Figure 15.* Sources of per capita family income for persons ages sixty-five and over, by income quintile, 2015. NOTE: The "other/public assistance" category includes unemployment compensation, workers' compensation, veterans' payments, and personal contributions. The quintile limits are $12,492, $19,245, $29,027, and $47,129. The data refer to the civilian noninstitutionalized population in 2014. SOURCE: Federal Interagency Forum on Aging-Related Statistics (2016).

to work into their later years. The Social Security system is progressive, meaning that those who had lower earnings during their working years receive a higher percentage benefit. In 2020, the average monthly payment was about $1,800 for a retired worker, and about $2,500 for a couple in which both spouses were receiving benefits. Without Social Security, 40 percent of older adults rather than the current 10 percent would be poor (Romig and Sherman 2016).

Social Security benefits account for more than two-thirds of the monthly incomes of lower-income households, but just 34 and 18 percent for those with per capita incomes in the top fourth or fifth of the income distribution, respectively. Black and Latinx families and women are particularly dependent on Social Security as their main or only source of income. One in five Black and Latinx older households gets by on their monthly Social Security checks alone, compared to 13 percent of white households. Women are more likely than men to rely on Social Security as their main or only income source.

Employer-provided pensions are the second most important source of retirement income, although only half of private sector employees now receive private pensions. Workers for larger firms, typically around one hundred or more employees, and higher income workers are most likely to receive these benefits. Because Blacks, Latinos, and women are less likely to work for large firms or in higher-wage jobs, they are less likely to have their own employer-provided pension plan. Married women may receive a pension through their spouse's work; this is another factor that puts private pensions out of reach for Black women, who are less likely to marry and stay married (Raley et al. 2015). Private pensions also are changing in such a way that they are a less dependable source of retirement income, especially for lower-income workers. Up until the mid-twentieth century, most private pensions were defined-benefit (DB) plans; retirees would receive lifetime retirement pay from their employer, based on how long they were with their employer and their final salary. Yet since the 1970s, DBs have been gradually replaced by defined contribution (DC) plans, where retirement income is much more uncertain. Workers now contribute to their pension plan, if they can afford to, and also must make choices about how those investments are managed. Workers who cannot afford to contribute to their plan, or who lack the financial savvy to invest wisely may find their private pension income to be inadequate once they retire (Dushi, Iams, and Tamborini 2011).

Personal savings and interest from one's savings, assets, and investments are the third major source of retirement income. Whites and families with higher incomes are more likely than Blacks and lower-income families to have accumulated wealth in the form of home ownership, other real estate, savings, and investments, and to have their monthly incomes boosted by interest income (US Census Bureau 2016). Wealth—whether a healthy savings account or a home that one could sell if need be—provides a financial buffer when a crisis strikes, such as job loss, retirement, death of a spouse, or illness. Race and ethnic gaps in wealth (and consequently, interest income) are vast, reflecting long-standing patterns of race-based discrimination in the labor market, institutional discrimination like bank lending practices, and public policies that disadvantage Blacks, like the GI Bill (Traub et al. 2017). Black and Latinx persons also are more likely to have educational, medical, and housing debt; high monthly interest payments make it difficult to save money at the end of the month (Oliver and Shapiro 2013). The financial downturns and volatility resulting from the pandemic further eroded some older adults' retirement savings and investments (Makaroun et al. 2020; Morrow-Howell et al. 2020).

Wages and salary from one's job are not technically a "leg" in the traditional three-legged stool of retirement, yet they are an important income source for the rising number of older adults who are working for pay. As figure 15 shows, the proportion of monthly income coming from earnings is 40 percent among the highest income households, yet just 13 percent among the lowest income households. This reflects the fact that poorer adults experience health problems at younger ages, which can shorten their work careers. Workers who are on their feet all day, like waitresses and grocery store cashiers, or who do heavy lifting and bending, like stockroom or construction workers, may retire early when their aches and pains make work impossible. Higher-income older adults tend to hold comfortable desk jobs like accountant or lawyer that allow them to work and earn income until a ripe old age.

The median income for older adults in 2019 was about $27,000, with this number ranging from $15,000 for Latinas to $41,000 for white men. Figure 16 shows median annual incomes in 2019 for older men, women, and households (i.e., the total income of persons who share a home headed by a person aged sixty-five or older) on the basis of race and ethnicity. Men consistently had higher incomes than women regardless of their race or ethnicity. Black and Latinx older adults have consistently lower incomes than Asians, who have less than whites. The one exception is that median household incomes are higher among Asians than whites ($55,000 vs. $50,000) in part because they are more likely to live in intergenerational households, with multiple generations of earners (US Census Bureau 2020a).

About 10 percent of older adults live beneath the federal poverty line, which in 2019 was an annual income of about $13,000 for those who live alone and $17,000 for those who live with another person, typically a

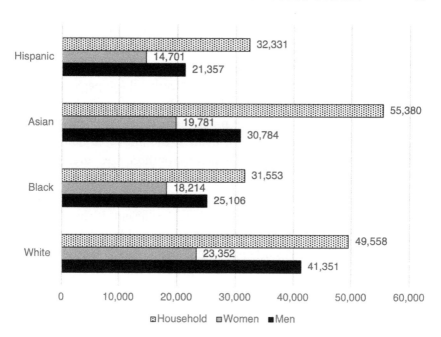

*Figure 16.* Median income for men, women, and households ages sixty-five and over by race/ethnicity, 2019. SOURCE: US Census Bureau (2019b).

spouse. The 10 percent poverty statistic would suggest that most older adults enjoy financial security, yet a more in-depth look reveals a less rosy picture. One-third of older adults say they have no money left at the end of the month and many dip into their meager savings accounts to pay their monthly bills (National Council on Aging 2017). Black and Latinx older adults are twice as likely as whites to live in poverty, with one in five living below the poverty line. Across all racial and ethnic groups, women on their own are 1.5 to 3 times as likely as men to be impoverished, reflecting multiple factors including labor market exits to care for their families, working in lower-paying jobs, and less access to pensions.

## HOUSING

A common stereotype is that older adults are "dumped" in nursing homes because their adult children are too selfish to care for them. That stereotype could not be further from the truth. The overwhelming majority of older adults live in their own homes or apartments up until very old ages, when they require medical care or other supports that outstrip what their family members and caregivers can manage. Nearly all (98 percent) adults ages sixty-five to seventy-four live independently in a private home or apartment in the community. That proportion declines with age, yet even among the oldest-old, independent living is the most common housing arrangement. As figure 17 shows, 93 percent of those ages seventy-five to eighty-four, and 77 percent of those ages eighty-five and older live on their own. Living "on one's own" doesn't necessarily mean that one is alone, nor does it mean that a person is completely self-sufficient. It simply means that they live in a home in the community; some reside with their spouse or an adult child, whereas others live alone and receive assistance from family, paid caregivers, or community services like Meals on Wheels (Federal Interagency Forum on Aging-Related Statistics 2016).

Most older adults have a strong desire to stay in their own homes. The dread of going to a long-term care facility was vividly portrayed in the classic HBO drama *The Sopranos*, when crime boss Tony Soprano moved his mother Livia from her own home into the Green Grove facility. Livia was so enraged that she enlisted two hitmen to kill her son. That reaction may be extreme, but the underlying fear is common. US surveys show that around 90 percent of older adults want to "age in place" or remain in the homes where they raised their families and in the neighborhoods where they have regular routines like grocery store visits and morning walks with friends. However, "aging in place" is not appropriate for everyone, especially people living in homes that are not well suited for older bodies. A majestic home with slippery polished hardwood floors, loose antique rugs, a grand curved staircase, and an ornate clawfoot bathtub is unsafe for older adults with mobility problems. A run-down apartment with cracked bathroom tiles, dim lighting, or a broken handrail on the front stoop can be dangerous for residents with an unsteady gait. Remaining in one's longtime home is best when one's home and community provide the physical supports that enable one to live safely

The COVID-19 pandemic has cast a global spotlight on the problems of congregate care facilities like nursing homes, yet older adults who dread the thought of living in such a facility seldom have that fear realized.

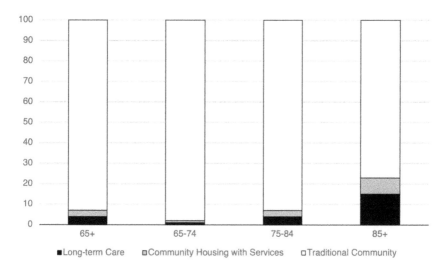

*Figure 17.* Distribution of community and institutional residence, by age group, 2013. NOTE: Community housing with services refers to persons living in retirement communities or apartments, senior housing, CCRCs, assisted living, board and care facilities, and similar settings and who report that they had access to one or more services such as meal preparation, housekeeping services, or medication assistance. Long-term care facilities refer to residences that are certified by Medicare or Medicaid, or have three or more beds, are licensed as a nursing home, and provide at least one personal service or provide round-the-clock supervision by a non-family paid caregiver. SOURCE: Federal Interagency Forum on Aging-Related Statistics (2016).

Although half of older adults will spend at least some time in a skilled nursing facility, for most it is a temporary stay to recover from an illness or injury, or a place to live out one's final days, as roughly 20 percent of older adults die in a nursing facility. Even among the oldest-old, however, only one-quarter live in an institution for long time periods. Physical health matters more than age for these residential arrangements; older adults who have difficult carrying out daily tasks like bathing, dressing, or preparing their own meals are especially likely to live in a long-term care setting (Federal Interagency Forum on Aging-Related Statistics 2020).

The term *nursing home* is used casually (and imprecisely) to describe places where older adults live together, often with professional or medical services. However, institutional living is a broad category that includes different types of settings. About 3 percent of all older adults (although 8 percent of those ages eighty-five and older) live in residential communities that feel like a private home yet also offer amenities, like meals, laundry service, and assistance with medications. Another 4 percent of those age sixty-five and over (yet 15 percent of the oldest old) live in long-term care facilities, which include nursing homes. Nursing homes fall along a continuum, where some feel like an antiseptic hospital and others are designed to look and feel as much like home as possible. Long-term care facilities usually offer round-the-clock services for their residents with serious medical needs. Many have a special "memory care" corridor or wing, where patients with dementia live and are cared for. Women are more likely than men to reside in long-term care facilities because they tend to live to very advanced ages when continuous care may be needed. However, race and socioeconomic differences in living arrangements are modest; this reflects the fact that nursing home care is largely paid for by Medicaid, the public insurance program for low-income Americans.

This chapter has revealed the great diversity of older adults today. Popular media images of old age—from advertisements for life insurance to classic sit-coms—overwhelmingly portray this population as white, middle-class, and female like the best friends Rose, Dorothy, and Blanche of *Golden Girls*. However, the truth is much more complex. Now that we've provided a snapshot of older adults' demographic, socioeconomic, and residential characteristics, we will show how they navigate the joys and challenges of their family lives and personal relationships.

# 3  Family and Social Relationships

Two special birthday parties were held in the summer of 2020. On August 15, Hester Ford celebrated her 115th birthday at her Charlotte, North Carolina, home. Hester sat on her front steps, a nursing aide by her side, and waved as a fleet of cars drove by carrying some of her forty-eight grandchildren, and more than two hundred great- and great-great-grandchildren. Her family and friends waved from the motorcade and dropped off cards and gifts at the end of Hester's driveway. Party guests got out of their cars to sing a socially distanced rendition of "Happy Birthday" to America's oldest living person, mindful of the threat of COVID-19 (Raymond 2020). Just two weeks later, Iris Westman followed in Hester's footsteps by celebrating her own 115th birthday on the front lawn of her nursing home residence in Northwood, North Dakota, just twenty-five miles from the farm where she grew up. Iris never married or had children, but she had plenty of celebrants in her birthday procession, including her ninety-year-old niece, great-great grandnieces and nephews, firefighters sounding their sirens, cyclists, and neighbors in the small town that Iris called home (Wallevand 2020).

For people of any age, social relationships can be one of the greatest sources of joy, providing a sense of meaning, support, companionship, and community. As the COVID-19 pandemic painfully revealed, social isolation and loneliness can be devastating for old and young people alike (Saltzman, Hansel, and Bordnick 2020). Yet precisely who our social ties are varies considerably throughout the population. Some people, like super-centenarian Hester Ford have grown old with a spouse or partner, children, grandchildren, great-grandchildren, and even great-great-grandchildren. Others, like Iris Westman, find love and support from siblings, nieces, nephews, and life-long friends who are often considered "families of choice" (Himes and Reidy 2000). Some people have complex families, including current and former spouses, and biological and stepchildren or grandchildren. The number, types, and quality of older adults' social ties are critical to their well-being. Supportive relationships provide practical assistance as well as emotional and physical health benefits, whereas conflictual or strained relationships can undermine health and happiness. Satisfying sexual relationships can bolster one's mental and physical health. The deaths of loved ones can be heartbreaking, yet many older adults discover inner strengths and establish new relationships or interests that help them cope with the losses that occur in later life (Carr and Mooney 2021).

The transformation of families in the United States and worldwide has been one of the most profound demographic changes in the twentieth and twenty-first centuries, and it has shaped how and with whom we grow old (Smock and Schwartz 2020). Declining birth rates mean older adults today have fewer biological children to care for them, relative to the generations before them. Widespread divorce and re-partnering mean that older adults may have had several spouses and both biological and stepchildren from these unions, complicating decisions about caregiving and inheritance. Grandparenthood brings joy to many older adults, but for some that joy is tempered by the daily challenges of raising their grandchildren, especially when one's children face obstacles that prevent them from parenting effectively (Hayslip, Fruhauf, and Dolbin-MacNab 2019). Rising numbers of older adults worldwide are aging alone, without a romantic partner, children, or siblings (Carr 2019). Some of these "elder orphans" or "solo agers" relish their solitude and independence, whereas others rely on their friends and neighbors, and others still suffer from social isolation and loneliness—problems that were intensified by social distancing practices, quarantines, and stay-at-home orders during the COVID-19 crisis (Brooke and Jackson 2020). Despite the many benefits of our social connections, these ties also can have an ominous side. Some older adults are mistreated physically or emotionally, preyed on financially, or neglected by the very people who should be caring for them. They also may be overwhelmed by intensive caregiving duties or demoralized by encounters with ageism.

This chapter delves into older adults' social relationships (or the lack thereof), including marriage and romantic partnerships like dating or cohabitation, intergenerational relationships with children and grandchildren, and other social ties such as siblings and friends. Social relationships have been reinvented over the past two decades, as face-to-face visits, phone calls, and letters have been replaced by (or supplemented with) email, text messaging, and videoconferencing, helping older adults to have meaningful visits with their loved ones miles or oceans away (Cotten 2021). The chapter then considers the painful side of social relationships, shedding light on five common challenges among older adults: loss and bereavement, loneliness and social isolation, elder mistreatment and abuse, intensive caregiving, and ageism. Older adults from all backgrounds are susceptible to these struggles, yet socially and economically disadvantaged older adults are especially vulnerable, contributing to ever-widening gaps in well-being over the life course (Carr 2019).


## LATE-LIFE FAMILY AND SOCIAL RELATIONSHIPS

Demographic shifts have created a context in which older adults' family lives in the twenty-first century differ from earlier generations. Decreasing numbers of adults are growing old with their first and only spouse, with rising numbers divorcing, remarrying, or cohabiting with a new partner, forming nonmarital romantic unions, or living single by choice (Brown and Wright 2017; Waite and Xu 2015). Economic trends, including rising debt and constricting career opportunities for young people, have transformed intergenerational ties, with some grandparents acting as provider rather than recipient of support (Doley et al. 2015). These trends have restructured the exchange of care and support within and across older adults' legal, biological, romantic, and kin-like relationships.

*Marriage, Cohabitation, and Romantic Partnerships*

Marriage is the most common romantic partnership among US adults ages sixty-five and older, with higher percentages among men, whites, and persons ages sixty-five to seventy-four, relative to women, Blacks, and adults ages eighty-five and older. In 2018, 70 percent of men but just 46 percent of women ages sixty-five and older were currently married. The proportion of older adults who are married declines with age, as rates of widowhood increase. Among those ages eighty-five and older, 60 percent of men but just 17 percent of women are married (Federal Interagency Forum on Aging-Related Statistics 2020). Roughly half of all married older adults are in a second or higher-order marriage (Livingston 2014). Rising rates of divorce in the 1970s and 1980s mean that many older adults today remarried decades ago, after their first marriages ended. For those who had more recent "gray divorces" in their fifties, sixties, or older, these second (or third) marriages have been entered into much more recently. Data from the national Health and Retirement Study (HRS) show that about 20 percent of women and 25 percent of men re-partner following gray divorce, with women more likely to remarry and men more likely to live with their romantic partner without formally remarrying (Brown et al. 2019). Spouses in remarriages report marital quality and happiness that is every bit as good as their peers in long-term first marriages (Cooney, Proulx, and Snyder-Rivas, 2016).

Yet rising numbers of older adults are opting out of marriage (or remarriage) and are entering other types of romantic partnerships that better meet their social, emotional, and even financial needs. One of the most significant changes has been the dramatic increase in cohabitation, or living with an unmarried romantic partner. In 1996, just 2 percent of adults ages sixty-five and over were cohabiting; this figure nearly tripled to 6 percent by 2017 and is projected to rise even higher (Gurrentz 2019). After a "gray divorce," the newly single are now more likely to cohabit rather than marry (Brown et al. 2019). Most older cohabitors are as committed to and happy with their relationship as married people are, with these unions lasting more than ten years on average and ending due to a death rather than a break-up (Brown, Bulanda, and Lee 2012). Unlike remarriage, cohabitation generally allows a widow(er) to continue receiving their late spouse's pension benefits. Some divorced older adults, especially women, may prefer cohabitation to marriage, as it carries less rigid gendered expectations regarding household roles such as spousal caregiver (Noël-Miller 2011). As many older women say, they don't want to be a "nurse or a purse" to a new spouse.

Some older adults have a long-term exclusive relationship with a romantic partner, but choose to live separately in their own homes, an arrangement called "living apart together" (LAT). About 7 percent of older adults in the United States are in LAT relationships; nearly all are relationships that formed after one's long-time marriage ended following a death or divorce. The LAT arrangement gives partners the freedom of living in their own homes, and the flexibility to choose when to spend time together (Connidis, Borrell, and Karlsson 2017). LAT relationships also spare older adults from the stress of relocating and combining households, the legal complexities regarding co-owning a home with their partner, and complications for their offspring's inheritance. Older adults who live with their grown children or grandchildren are especially likely to prefer LAT arrangements, so as not to disrupt their offspring's lives (de Jong Gierveld and Merz 2013). Some researchers have found that women are more likely than men to prefer LATs, observing that "men want someone to come home to, and women want someone to go out with." LATs offer companionship without taking away their freedom (Davidson and Fennell 2017).

Some older adults prefer an even more casual form of romantic partnership. About 15 percent of unmarried older adults are currently dating, with rates considerably higher among men than women (27 versus 7 percent) (Brown and Shinohara 2013). Older men and women are equally likely to want to date, yet women have fewer opportunities due to an imbalanced sex ratio and men's desire to date younger women (Brown and Wright 2017). Not all men are successful in their dating goals, however. More educated, healthy, wealthy, and socially connected men are considered better "catches" and are more likely to date (Brown and Shinohara 2013). Some older adults are following the lead of younger people and are now using dating websites and apps to meet new partners. As of 2018, 13 percent of single adults ages sixty-five and over had gone online to find a partner, compared to half of adults ages eighteen to twenty-nine (Vadnal 2020). The loneliness and isolation wrought by the pandemic has drawn even more to try online dating (American Association of Retired Persons [AARP] 2020). Yet many single older adults are perfectly happy on their own. Three-quarters of single people ages sixty-five and older say they're not looking to date—nearly twice the rate of young adults eighteen to twenty-nine who are opting out of the dating market (Brown 2020).

While romantic partnerships are an important source of emotional and practical support for many older adults, they also bring a further benefit: sexual intimacy. Despite outdated stereotypes that older adults are uninterested in sex, research consistently shows that a healthy and loving sexual relationship is an important part of older adults' lives. One recent study found that three-quarters of men and half of women in their sixties, seventies, and older said that sex was an important part of their life (Waite et al. 2021). Age-related biological changes like drops in estrogen and testosterone mean that some older couples must adapt their sexual activities, with foreplay, oral sex, or cuddling often replacing intercourse (Liu, Shen, and Hsieh 2019; Waite et al. 2009). Still, one in four partnered adults ages seventy-five to eighty-five reports having sexual relations at least once a week (Waite et al. 2009). Couples with the happiest and most supportive unions tend to report the greatest sexual satisfaction, although a common problem is a discrepancy in partners' sexual interest, especially if one has serious health declines. But most long-married couples say sexual and physical intimacy is a source of comfort and fulfillment. As octogenarian couple David and Anne told the *New York Times*, their sex life is now better than when they first married six decades ago. Their awareness that time may be running out makes their intimacy feel more special. Now, after sex, they say to one another "Thank you, God, for one more time" (Jones 2022).

*Parenthood*

Parenthood, like romantic partnerships, comes in many forms today. Most older adults have at least one biological child, although some have lost a child through death, while others no longer have contact with their adult child(ren) due to family tensions or estrangement (Coleman 2021). Some researchers estimate that as many as 25 percent of older adults today do not have a child they can turn to for emotional or practical support, with

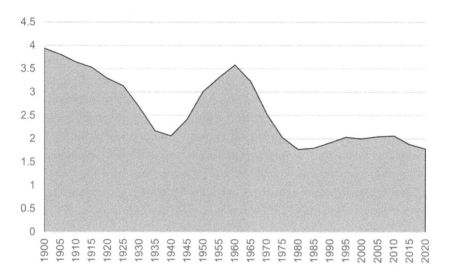

*Figure 18.* Total fertility rate in the United States, 1900–2020. SOURCE: Osterman et al. (2021).

this proportion projected to increase among aging Baby Boomers and the Generation X cohort that follows, due to rising rates of childlessness in recent decades (Carney et al. 2016). The average number of biological children also has inched downward in recent decades, with future cohorts of older adults having fewer children than the generations before them. As figure 18 shows, the total fertility rate in the United States ranged between 3 and 3.5 in the 1950s and 1960s, the period in which current cohorts of older women gave birth to their children. The TFR declined in the 1960s and 1970s, reaching a low of 1.77 in 1980, and has fluctuated between 1.8 and 2.1 ever since (Osterman et al. 2022). Declining birth rates have raised the concern that future cohorts of older adults may not have sufficient numbers of children to care for them, a topic we revisit in chapter 5.

Although birth rates have declined, many older adults have expanded their families by remarrying and acquiring stepchildren. Stepfamilies are formed when one or both partners have children from previous relationships. For remarriages in which the wife is of childbearing age, the couple also may have biological children together, creating blended families with both biological and stepchildren. About 40 percent of middle-aged and older parents have stepchildren (Lin, Brown, and Cupka 2018), while 20 percent of grandparents have at least one step-grandchild, whether through their own, a spouse's, or an adult child's remarriage (Yahirun, Park, and Seltzer 2018). However, stepchildren do not provide the same level of care and support as biological children, especially when family ties are fraught (Sherman, Webster, and Antonucci 2013). Stepchildren tend to be more helpful if their biological parent remarried when the child was young and views their stepparent as "mom" or "dad"—like President Joe Biden who married his wife Jill when his sons Beau and Hunter (from his first marriage) were ages three and four. However, in stepfamilies that formed when the couple's children were adults—like former President Donald Trump who married third wife Melania when the children from his two prior marriages were adults—the two generations may feel like "strangers," especially if their contact has been limited (Berger 1998: 75).

## Grandparenthood

More than 80 percent of older adults have grandchildren, and two-thirds of grandparents have at least four grandchildren. For most, the experience is one of joy and pride. A national survey asked Americans ages 65 and older to name the best part of getting old, and the top two answers were "spending time with family," and "spending time with grandchildren" (Krogstad 2015). According to the AARP (2019), two-thirds of grandparents see a grandchild at least every two weeks, and more than 80 percent are in touch regularly through email, telephone, videoconferencing, or mail. Most grandparents view their role as a playmate, confidante, or mentor rather than disciplinarian. The activities that grandparents see as their main responsibility are spoiling the children, teaching them family history, and giving them treats or surprise gifts.

Older adults are spending more time in the grandparent role (and even great-grandparent role) than ever before, as increases in life expectancy have resulted in more families with three or more generations alive at the same time (Margolis and Wright 2017). As people delay marriage and have children at older ages, they are becoming grandparents at older ages. As a result, grandparents today are older, on average, than previous generations, yet they are playing a larger role in caring for grandchildren.

About one in five grandparents help with grandchild care regularly in a given year, while most others say they help or provide care "occasionally" or less (Krogstad 2015). These patterns vary somewhat by socioeconomic status and race. Economically well-off older adults tend to provide occasional help with babysitting, transportation, and recreational activities, whereas Blacks and those of lower socioeconomic status tend to take on more time- and labor-intensive roles, like serving as custodial caregiver when their own children are unable to care for their offspring (Meyer and Kandic 2017). The share of US children living in a grandparent's household has more than doubled over the past five decades, from 3 percent in 1970 to 8 percent in 2015 (Wu 2018). More than 6 million children live with a grandparent, and about 2.4 million live in a household headed by grandparents without a birth parent in the home (i.e., skip-generation), leaving the older adult fully responsible for the child.

The strains of being a grandchild's primary caregiver can be immense. Custodial grandparents often are distressed by the problems that rendered their children unable to care for their offspring, such as addiction, imprisonment, unemployment, premature death, and other adversities that have their roots in economic and racial oppression (Carr 2019). Because the custodial role frequently is entered into by those already facing physical or financial challenges, the added demands of raising a child can be overwhelming (Hayslip et al. 2019). Roughly 21 percent of custodial grandparents live beneath the poverty line, 25 percent have a disability, and 40 percent have provided this care for more than five years (Ellis and Simmons 2014). The challenges facing custodial grandparents intensified with the COVID-19 pandemic, as they homeschooled their grandchildren, helped them manage their own fears, and worried that their grandchildren might bring the virus home (Barahmpour and Schmidt 2020). Yet there is often a silver lining; grandparents feel a sense of pride in helping to nurture and support these children.

### Siblings, Friends, and Animal Companions

Siblings and friends are an important (if not the only) source of practical support for unmarried and childless older adults, and they are a cherished source of emotional support for nearly all older adults. Sibling relationships are often the longest and most enduring tie one has, dating back to birth for some (Robinson and Mahon 1997). A brother or sister is our first friend, confidante, playmate, and role model. Among adults ages sixty-five and older, more than three-quarters have at least one living sibling, and most describe these ties as close and mutually supportive (White 2001). Sibling relationships can wax and wane over the life course and may become strained when one sibling (typically a sister) feels that they are unfairly shouldering the burden of caring for aged parents (Rurka, Suitor, and Gilligan 2020). Statistics support this perception; about three-quarters of older adults receive help from one child only, with this care averaging about fifty hours a month. However, as parents grow older and more frail, they depend on more of their children, with the workload shared more equitably among the siblings (Lin and Wolf 2020).

Friends and confidantes outside the family are another important source of support to older adults. Friendships, unlike family ties, are entered into by choice rather than blood or law. Their primary purpose is companionship, so friendships may be abandoned when they are no longer emotionally or socially fulfilling (Allan 1998). Older adults tend to limit their social networks to include only their closest and most meaningful ties, so the friendships they maintain are deep bonds rather than fleeting attachments (Charles and Carstensen 2007). Friends protect against the despair that some older adults experience when they first retire (Kail and Carr 2020) and are an essential source of support for older adults who are "kinless," meaning they have no spouse or children (Mair 2019). Widows and widowers are especially likely to rely on friends; many find that friends fulfill their social and emotional needs so well that they no longer feel a need or desire to remarry (Carr 2004b; de Vries et al. 2014).

For older adults who are alone or isolated, non-human friends are a surprisingly important source of support. The adage that dogs are "man's best friend" takes on special resonance for older adults, roughly half of whom live with a pet. Dogs and cats provide a daily routine through feedings and walks, social connectedness to other pet owners in the neighborhood, and unconditional affection (Wood et al. 2015). Pets were a great comfort during the COVID-19 shutdowns, when families old and young welcomed "pandemic puppies" to their homes. Researchers have found that dogs were especially meaningful for older adults living alone during the shutdowns (Oliva and Johnston 2020). As one older adult confided, "at least there is someone to talk to and see during the days/nights. . . . Although they don't answer, it is a distraction from the nothingness."

## FAMILY CLOSENESS, CONTACT, AND COOPERATION

Just as demographic changes have transformed who makes up our families, migration patterns and technological advances have reinvented how families maintain contact. For much of the twentieth century, parents, children, and grandchildren kept in touch through face-to-face visits, especially during time periods when multiple generations of a family remained in the same neighborhood (Adams 1999). Having children and grandchildren nearby meant that most older adults could rely on their kin for help with things like household chores, transportation, shopping, doctor's visits, meals, and medications. Healthy older adults look after grandchildren (Rossi and Rossi 1990). However, as work opportunities have enticed adult children and grandchildren to far-off locations and as physically and financially well-off older adults have moved to retirement communities in warm locales like Florida and Arizona, families (especially white middle-class families) often are separated by the miles.

Despite these migratory trends, most older adults still have at least one adult child or grandchild who lives close by. Just 7 percent live more than five hundred miles away from their nearest child (Choi et al. 2020). Likewise, about two-thirds of older adults live within fifty miles of their closest grandchild (AARP 2019). From the adult child's perspective, 20 percent live within a few hours' drive of a parent or parent-in-law (Bui and Cain Miller 2018). Consequently, many older adults rely on nearby family for personal care, while those whose loved ones live far away may rely on them for financial assistance or emotional support.

Despite ageist stereotypes portraying older adults as "dependent" on the younger generation, many older adults provide assistance and financial support to their children and grandchildren up until very advanced ages. Wealthy and successful comedian Jerry Seinfeld famously joked about receiving a birthday card with a $10 check every year from his Nana. Seinfeld is among many adults who still receive financial gifts from their less well-off aged relatives. These processes of exchange, both up and down the rungs of the intergenerational ladder, are a common source of support for older and younger family members alike (Wiemers and Park 2021).

### Exchanges across the Generations

We usually think of "family" as synonymous with "love." But social scientists have found that families also provide benefits that are less warm and fuzzy, most notably exchanges or "transfers" of time and money. *Time transfers* refer to the time that family members give to one another, in the form of practical assistance like childcare or errands. *Financial transfers* refer to the money that family members give to one another, whether a gift, help with a down payment on one's home, or paying off one's college debt. Time transfers commonly go up the generational ladder from adult children to aged parents, and slightly less often go downward from aged parents to adult children. Financial transfers (like Nana's $10 annual birthday check to Jerry) usually flow downward from the older to the younger generation, revealing the endurance of the cultural norm that parents should provide for their children, no matter their age. Data from the Panel Study of Income Dynamics (PSID), a more than fifty-year-long study of intergenerational relations in the United States, show that roughly half of US households report giving time to a parent, whereas only one-third receive time from a parent.

The most common type of assistance that older adults receive from their children is personal care. The number of hours that parents receive from their children increases as the parent grows older, because each passing year typically brings more physical and cognitive limitations (Wiemers and Park 2021). Daughters dedicate more hours to parent care than do sons, consistent with gendered notions of caregiving. Sons with sisters are less likely than sons with brothers only to give care to their parents, reflecting long-standing beliefs that care is women's work (Grigoryeva 2017). Biological children dedicate more time to parent care than do stepchildren (Wiemers and Park 2021). Adult children with lower levels of income and education also are more likely to provide care, whereas children with professional jobs and higher incomes are more likely to move far away or can afford to pay for their parents' care.

Black and Hispanic adult children are more likely than whites to give time to their parents, reflecting their greater tendency to live close to or with parents, cultural norms that encourage giving back to parents, and fewer financial resources to help pay for home health aides, ride services and other sources of paid help (Sarkisian, Gerena, and Gerstel 2007). Interpersonal factors also shape caregiving; older adults often prefer that they receive care from the child with whom they are emotionally closest and share similar values (Pillemer and Suitor 2014).

While time flows for children to parents, money typically flows from parents to children. Aged parents are more likely to give money to adult children and to give a greater amount on average than the reverse. Analyses of PSID data from the 2010s show that adult children report giving about $247 on average to their parents compared to receiving over $800 in the typical year. Their parents, in stark contrast, report giving more than $2,500 to all of their adult children combined, yet they receive an average of only $138. These generational gaps in giving and receiving money do not narrow even as the parent reaches a very advanced age (Wiemers and Park 2021). Despite the cultural expectation that parents should treat their children all the same, researchers have found that parents give some children more than others. Studies using a "within-family difference" approach have found that within a single family, parents tend to give more financial support to those children who need it most and, surprisingly, those who need it the least, albeit for different reasons (Fingerman et al. 2009). Adult children who have more financial or health problems may require more help from their parents. Conversely, parents help their most successful children because they anticipate that these children will reciprocate the support when the parent is very old and in need of financial or practical help.

In general, Black and Latinx adult children are more likely than their white peers to make upward financial transfers to their aged parents, similar to the patterns documented for time transfers. Black and Latinx older adults are less likely to have private pensions and accumulated wealth, rendering them particularly dependent on their children for retirement income (Carr 2019). Their children also may feel a great sense of gratitude and obligation to the parents who sacrificed and provided for them during their younger years (Dilworth-Anderson et al. 2005).

*Maintaining Virtual Connections across the Miles*

Some of the most heartwarming images of the COVID-19 pandemic showed older adults waving and chatting at their computer screens, delighted and a bit awestruck at seeing their children and grandchildren in Hollywood Squares-style boxes. Information and communications technologies (ICTs) including video-chatting platforms like Zoom and Face-Time became essential lifelines when the pandemic kept older adults confined to their homes. Virtual connections were especially important for the nearly one-third of older adults who live alone and had no face-to-face interactions, sometimes for weeks on end. Yet not all older adults had this lifeline, either because they lacked internet access or because they were reluctant or nervous about learning new technologies. Older adults lag behind younger people in their rates of using iPhones, videoconferencing, texting, email, and other "high-tech" ways of maintaining social ties across the miles. In 2021, 61 percent of older adults used smartphones, and three-quarters had internet access, compared to near-universal use among younger persons (Faverio 2022).

The pandemic motivated family members and community volunteers to help older adults sharpen their tech skills. Programs like the online community Senior Planet and local "Villages" programs, which are volunteer-run grassroots organizations that provide supports to older adults living in their own homes, launched computer training programs. The training focused on many topics, offering instructions on how to participate in family calls or religious services through Zoom, access podcasts, take online fitness classes, watch concerts or films on YouTube, sign up for a vaccine or COVID test, and order groceries online (Poon and Holder 2021). One small silver lining of the pandemic may be that older adults are now better positioned to use online connections that are critical to their social engagement. Yet these benefits have not been afforded to all older adults; a "digital divide" persists, such that lower-income older adults, ethnic minorities, and those living in rural areas may lack connectivity, compounding their feelings of isolation and despair (Morrow-Howell et al. 2020). And virtual interactions, even for older adults with the latest model computer or smartphone, cannot capture the hugs and physical connections that boost physical and emotional health (Thomas and Kim 2020). Nearly two-thirds of older adults surveyed during the pandemic agreed that the internet was not a satisfactory replacement for face-to-face conversations (Vogels et al. 2020).

## THE BLEAK SIDE OF SOCIAL RELATIONSHIPS

For most people, social relationships are an essential source of meaning, happiness, and emotional security. Classic songs remind us "all you need is love" and "people who need people are the luckiest people in the world." International surveys consistently find that "family" tops the list when people are asked about the things that give their life meaning, while "friends" lag only slightly behind (Silver et al. 2021). Volumes of research dating back to pioneering sociologist Emile Durkheim's (1897) *Suicide* study show that social ties—whether with a romantic partner, children, friends, or members of one's religious community—protect and uplift us.

Yet for millions of Americans, older adults included, personal relationships can be fraught, frayed, or outright harmful. In his classic novel *Anna Karenina*, Tolstoy writes that "all happy families are alike; each unhappy family is unhappy in its own way," but researchers have found that unhappy social relationships follow some clear patterns. Five aspects of older adults' social ties (or lack thereof) can threaten their health and happiness: loss and bereavement; social isolation and loneliness; abuse and mistreatment; difficult caregiving demands; and ageism—that is, discriminatory and demeaning encounters based on one's age.

### Loss and Bereavement

The deaths of loved ones are among the most devastating events a person can experience. In their pioneering study of stress, Holmes and Rahe (1956) named "death of a spouse" as the most distressing of forty-three possible life events, while the deaths of a close family member and friend ranked fifth and seventeenth, respectively. Deaths of family and friends can be emotionally crushing because a close personal attachment is severed and cannot be replaced (Bowlby 1980). *Grief,* or the feelings of deep sadness, yearning, and emptiness experienced after the loss of a loved one has been poignantly described as "the price we pay for love, the cost of commitment" (Parkes and Prigerson 2013).

Bereavement is especially common in later life. Roughly three million Americans die each year, with about three-quarters of annual deaths befalling persons ages sixty-five and older (Kochanek et al. 2019). Consequently, older adults must adjust to the deaths of their age peers including spouse, siblings, and friends, as well as the deaths of generations above (parents) and, less frequently, generations below (children and grandchildren). Black older adults are especially vulnerable to experiencing multiple losses. Because of race gaps in mortality at every age, Blacks are more likely than whites to have experienced the death of a mother, father, or sibling during the first five decades of life, and the death of a child and spouse in later life (Umberson et al. 2017).

Heart disease, cancer, stroke, liver disease, and dementia consistently rank among the leading causes of death among older adults, with COVID-19 breaking into the top three in 2020 (Kramarow and Tejada-Vera 2019; Woolf, Chapman, and Lee 2020). Because the former five conditions are chronic or long-term illnesses, most older adults become bereaved after an extended period of giving care to a terminally ill loved one, or watching them suffer from physical discomfort, difficult breathing, and confusion or disorientation (Carr and Luth 2019). Although COVID-19 deaths often happen very quickly after a loved one becomes sick, these deaths are particularly distressing because family members often are separated from the dying patient, robbing them of final moments together and the opportunity for proper goodbyes. Many older adults, especially those living in congregate care settings, have lost several friends to the pandemic, intensifying their sorrow. Survivors of COVID deaths often cannot honor their loved one's life at an in-person funeral, due to social distancing rules. Although Zoom funerals offer some solace, they could not provide the hugs, face-to-face mourning rituals, and sense of community that can soothe grief-stricken loved ones during "normal" times (Carr et al. 2020).

## SPOUSAL AND PARTNER LOSS

Every death brings heartache, yet widowhood is the most consequential loss for older adults because it affects nearly every aspect of daily life. Widowhood, which refers to the death of one's spouse or romantic partner, is one of the most common and life-altering losses experienced by older adults, especially women. One-third of women and 11 percent of men ages sixty-five and older are currently widowed, with these proportions rising to 35 and 70 percent among those ages eighty-five and older, respectively (Federal Interagency Forum on Aging-Related Statistics 2020). When a spouse or cohabiting partner dies, their survivor often experiences emotional symptoms like sadness, loneliness, and a yearning for their beloved. They also face mundane challenges like managing the housework or financial tasks previously carried out by their late partner, as well as establishing new relationships and hobbies that provide a renewed sense of routine and purpose (Stroebe and Schut 2010). Despite the heartbreak of losing a spouse or partner, most older adults have short-lived symptoms of profound sadness, and find renewed happiness in the months and years following the death. Most researchers find that 20 to 40 percent of older widow(er)s report symptoms of depression, anxiety, or grief during the first six months of their loss, before returning to good mental health. About half are classified as "resilient," meaning that they experience few if any symptoms of prolonged depression and despair (Bonanno et al. 2002).

Some widows and widowers have more extreme emotional and physical reactions. About 15 percent experience a condition called "complicated" or "chronic" grief, which encompasses symptoms like extreme longing, intense emotional pain, anger, and withdrawal from activities or relationships for at least one year after the loss (Shear et al. 2011). Severe physical reactions including death, while rare, also are possible. We occasionally hear tragic stories on the evening news, where two spouses die within days or weeks of each other, with the widowed person dying of a "broken heart." Among the most famous was the death of country music legend Johnny Cash who died shortly after losing his wife and musical partner of nearly four decades, singer June Carter Cash. While romantic lore suggests that grief-stricken widow(er)s may "die of a broken heart," research offers a more scientific and less romanticized explanation.

The strain of caring for one's spouse in the months prior to their death, exacerbated by the actual shock of the death, can cause physiological harm—especially for cardiovascular health (Elwert and Christakis 2008). The loss of one's main helpmate, caretaker, and social secretary is especially harmful to husbands. Wives tend to monitor their husbands' diets, remind them to take daily medications, wear their seatbelts, get a good night's sleep, and give up bad habits like smoking, drinking, and second helpings of desserts (August and Sorkin 2010). That's why widowers are more likely than their married counterparts to die of accidents, alcohol-related deaths, lung cancer, and heart diseases, but are not more likely to die from causes less closely linked to health behaviors (Martikainen and Valkonen 1996). Wives also tend to be husbands' social lifeline; women are referred to as "kin keepers" because they maintain the couple's social calendar, and keep up their friendships, social activities, and visits with children and grandchildren—social ties that are critical to sustaining one's health and happiness (Hagestad 1986). For older women, especially those whose careers (and personal earnings) took a backseat to their husband's during their working years, the death of a spouse means a dip in one's economic resources, whether through the loss of a working husband's income or a retired husband's public or private pension (Angel, Jimenez, and Angel 2007). This new financial insecurity, along with the high costs of end-of-life medical care and funerals, may exacerbate the emotional stress of the loss (Carr 2019).

Older LGBTQ adults who have lost a spouse or partner face distinctive challenges yet possess distinctive strengths. On June 26, 2015, the US Supreme Court legalized same-sex marriage in all fifty states. This decision came relatively late in life for many LGBTQ older adults, who might have formed civil unions or long-term unmarried partnerships prior to the landmark 2015 ruling. As a result, older same-sex couples typically did not enjoy the same legal rights extended to different-sex married couples, including the opportunity to make health care and end-of-life decisions for dying partners. Some received inadequate emotional support upon their loss because their relationship was not acknowledged or legally recognized in the wider community. Especially for LGBTQ older adults who had concealed their relationship, some experienced conflicts with their deceased partner's family, particularly with respect to the dispersion of personal possessions (Green and Grant 2008).

Yet researchers also find that older gay men and lesbians have personal resources that help them cope with partner loss, most notably their close and emotionally supportive ties with friends and "families of choice" (Donnelly, Reczek, and Umberson 2018). They also may be better prepared than their straight peers to take on their late partner's tasks and chores after the death. Because they are less likely to adhere to gender-typed "his" and "hers" family roles, they may be better prepared to manage daily challenges and responsibilities related to housekeeping, home repairs, health, and finances (Almack, Seymour, and Bellamy 2010). Same-sex couples also have a more balanced approach to caregiving, in which partners are equally likely to provide personal care to one another—in sharp contrast to different-sex couples in which wives often bear the brunt for caring for their husbands. Consequently, same-sex partners experience less caregiving strain, and are less emotionally and physically drained when they make the transition from caregiver to bereaved partner (Umberson et al. 2016).

OTHER LOSSES

Older adults' daily lives change the most profoundly upon the loss of a spouse or partner, but the deaths of children, parents, siblings, and friends also are life-altering milestones. The death of an adult child can be emotionally devastating, especially for older women who shouldered most childrearing responsibilities when their children were young and maintained close ties even as their children became adults (Bratt, Stenstrom, and Rennemark 2018). The death of a child, no matter how old, shatters one's expectations that children should outlive their parents and that parents should protect their children from harm (Wheeler 2001). Child death affects a sizeable minority of older US adults. Data from the large Health and Retirement Study (HRS) show that 12 percent of adults over age fifty have lost a child (Umberson et al. 2017).

Losing a child can trigger mental health symptoms including anxiety, depression, grief, and suicidal thoughts, and physical health problems including cardiovascular disease. The trauma of child death also can threaten the quality and stability of one's marriage (Rogers et al. 2008). The death of one's only child or a child who lived close by deprives older adults of a caregiver and source of help with rides, shopping, and finances. If the deceased child leaves behind young children, the older adult may need to step in and serve as custodial grandparent, a rewarding yet taxing role. The loss is particularly difficult when an adult child dies from a stigmatized condition such as addiction, overdose, homicide, or suicide (Floyd et al. 2013), which may elicit insensitive rather than supportive responses from family, friends, and coworkers (Pitman et al. 2018). Some older adults sooth their pain by finding meaning in the death or working to spare others from similar suffering. For instance, when Joseph Biden was vice president under President Barack Obama, he led the launch of the 2016 Beau Biden Cancer Moonshot Initiative effort, a sweeping bipartisan initiative to increase funding for cancer research, in honor of Joe's son Beau, who died at age forty-six of brain cancer (Agus, Jaffee, and Van Dang 2021).

The death of one's parent, in stark contrast, is an expected transition that most people experience long before reaching old age. National data show that 99 percent of persons ages sixty-five and older have lost at least one parent, and 91 percent have lost both parents. Just 3 percent of older adults have a living father, while 8 percent have a living mother (Scherer and Kreider 2019). The personal impact of late-life parental death depends on how intertwined the two generations were, with the loss felt most strongly by those who were living with or were the primary caregiver to their aged parent(s) (Wolff and Kasper 2006). Bereaved adult children may feel anxious or depressed immediately after the death, but these symptoms typically lessen within six months. Adult children tend to report greater upset following maternal rather than paternal death (Umberson and Chen 2004) and when they had an emotionally warm rather than strained or distant relationship with their parent (Hayslip, Pruett, and Caballero 2015). The death of one's last surviving parent is a pivotal moment, as the surviving child(ren) are now the oldest generation of the family and bear the responsibilities that accompany that position (Marshall, 2004). Some bereaved children, even in old age, report distress over being an "orphan." Yet this transition also may bring an unexpected benefit. Siblings may grow closer, as they develop new traditions and routines to make up for those previously kept up by their parents, such as family holiday celebrations (Moss and Moss 1989), Siblings who had strained relationships may make amends as they grieve together over their parent's death and support one another as they manage their own challenges of aging, including illness, cognitive decline, and spousal caregiving (Hays, Gold, and Pieper 1997; Khodyakov and Carr 2009).

Sibling relationships are often the longest tie one has, so the death of a sibling can be a profound transition (Robinson and Mahon 1997). Sibling death is especially painful for unmarried, childless, or socially isolated older adults who relied most heavily on their sisters and (to a lesser extent) brothers for practical and emotional support (Freedman 1996; Steptoe et al. 2013). Because most siblings are close in age and spent their formative years together, the death of one sibling may make the others acutely aware of their own mortality. The death also can represent the loss of a role model, a missing link to family and personal lineage, and a loss of security because their sibling was someone they depended on in times of need (Steptoe et al. 2013). Despite the emotional toll associated with sibling loss, some bereaved adult siblings report a greater sense of meaning in life, heightened personal strength, an awareness and enthusiasm about new possibilities, and in the case of deaths from stigmatized causes like HIV or suicide, a greater sensitivity to others who may be suffering (Wright 2016).

The death of a friend is a common occurrence for older adults. While many report sadness and loneliness after the loss of their closest friends, these losses tend to have a relatively modest impact on older adults' everyday lives, because friends and acquaintances tend not to provide daily help or caregiving. Friends may be a cherished source of companionship and recreation, but they are rarely called on to help with medication, meals, or rides—leaving these tasks to spouses, children, and siblings (Cantor 1979). The death of one friend also may strengthen ties with other friends in their social circle, as older adults seek solace among one another, reminisce, and celebrate the life of their late friend (Roberto and Stanis 1994).

## Social Isolation and Loneliness

Angie Sinopoli was once the energetic and animated matriarch of a large close-knit family in New York. Loved dearly by her children and grandchildren, Angie relied on them for help when dementia started to jumble her thoughts and erase her memories. Her youngest son, Steven, was especially dedicated, visiting her home and cooking her dinner every evening. After Angie had a few bad falls, her children—nervous for her safety—moved her to a nursing home in early March 2020 (*New York Times* 2020). Just days later, the nursing home implemented a ban on visitors to protect its residents from the coronavirus, which was newly ravaging the northeast. When the December holidays arrived at the end of 2020, Angie had gone a full nine months without a single visit from her family. She became despondent and her once rich vocabulary became nearly nonexistent, with Angie using only a dozen or so words. A bright spot came on Christmas Day, when Steven dropped off photographs at the nursing home for the nurse to share with her. The nurse later texted Steven that Angie clutched onto the photos and would not let go.

The pain of loneliness and social isolation was never so apparent as during the pandemic, when the nightly news showed images of older adults looking wistfully through their windows at their family members on the other side. It's not just nursing home residents who were isolated and lonely. The National Poll on Healthy Aging carried out in June 2020 found that 41 percent of older adults reported that they lacked companionship, compared to just 34 percent prior to the pandemic. More than half (56 percent) said they felt isolated, and 46 percent had less than weekly contact with family, friends, or neighbors. These rates are roughly twice that detected two years earlier, prior to the pandemic. Lonely older adults and those with limited social contact during the pandemic also reported less exercise and restless sleep, as well as heightened symptoms of depression (Malani et al. 2020). While the pandemic cast a bleak spotlight on isolated older adults, social gerontologists have long known that chronic loneliness harms one's memory, mental and physical health, and lifespan (Shankar et al. 2011).

Old age is not synonymous with loneliness, however. Most surveys show that loneliness peaks among people in their teens and early twenties, and declines through midlife and the retirement years, before spiking among the oldest-old (Luhmann and Hawkley 2016). These ups and downs reflect the ways social activities and roles change with age. Recent retirees in their sixties and seventies often are young and healthy enough to spend their newfound free time with friends and family, hobbies. and volunteer activities that expand their social circles. As older adults reach their eighties, nineties, and even older, the deaths of friends and family, and the diminished capacity to travel, volunteer, or participate in social activities—especially during the pre-vaccine days of the COVID-19 pandemic—may render one isolated and vulnerable. Yet loneliness doesn't refer simply to the number of people in one's family or friendship circle, or the frequency of visits. Loneliness also encompasses the feeling that one's interpersonal needs are going unmet.

Loneliness has two dimensions, emotional and social, which we can think of as labels for *feeling* alone versus *being* alone. Emotional loneliness refers to a lack of intimacy or depth in one's relationships. An older adult who sits silently with their spouse at the breakfast table, or who has a chilly relationship with their children might feel a sense of "utter aloneness" even when surrounded by others (Weiss 1973: 21). By contrast, social loneliness refers to dissatisfaction with the number of people in one's social network and the frequency of visits or interactions (Dykstra 1995). The two types of loneliness often go hand in hand; widowed older adults, those living alone, or those living far away from friends and families report high levels of both types of loneliness (de Jong Gierveld and Havens 2004). Yet marriage isn't a cure-all for emotional loneliness: 25 percent of married older adults report emotional loneliness, with rates even higher for those whose spouses are chronically ill, who have an unfulfilling (or nonexistent) sexual relationship, and whose marital conversations are strained or terse (de Jong Gierveld et al. 2009). Men tend to report more loneliness and isolation than women, a consequence of their different relationship styles. Women give more emotional support to friends and family, and receive more in return, whereas men rely primarily on their spouse for their social and emotional needs (Luhmann and Hawkley 2016).

Loneliness and social isolation are serious public health concerns. The problem is so serious that in 2018, British prime minister Theresa May appointed the United Kingdom's first minister of loneliness, charged with leading national policies and programs to protect against isolation. Social isolation is linked with poor sleep, heart problems, elevated blood pressure, depressive symptoms, compromised immune function, and cognitive decline, each of which can hasten death (Hawkley and Cacioppo 2010). Experts predict that both emotional and social loneliness will become even more pressing social concerns as the large Baby Boom cohort enters old age. Baby Boomers are more likely than their parents' generation to divorce, stay single for life, have fewer children, and live miles away from their children (Manning and Brown 2012). Gerontologists coined the terms *elder orphans* and *solo agers* to describe older adults who don't have a spouse or romantic partner, have outlived both parents, and either have no children or maintain very limited contact with their children.

Demographers project that as many as one in five older adults are elder orphans or at risk of becoming one in the coming decades (Carney et al. 2016). Social isolation and loneliness are harmful in and of themselves, yet they also make older adults vulnerable to other dangers, especially victimization and mistreatment.

## Elder Abuse and Mistreatment

Respect and benevolence toward the oldest members of society is a hallmark of many cultures. In many of the five hundred Native American nations in the United States, tribal elders are respected for their life experience and wisdom, as they pass down lessons and language to the younger generations. Koreans and some Korean Americans celebrate older adults' milestone birthdays with big celebrations, like *hwangap* (age sixty), *chilsoon* (age seventy) or *palsoon* (age eighty), in honor of the older honoree's longevity. We'd like to believe that all societies treat their eldest members with the respect, kindness, and dignity afforded to younger people. Yet news headlines and statistical data tell us that elder mistreatment is all too common, hurting those who may already be vulnerable, dependent, or socially isolated.

Elder abuse and mistreatment can take five different forms: physical abuse, sexual abuse, emotional or psychological abuse, financial exploitation, and neglect. Physical abuse refers to any violent act that causes bodily pain or impairment, such as hitting, force-feeding, or inappropriate use of physical restraints or medication. Sexual abuse is nonconsensual intimate contact, or sexual contact when the older adult is incapable of giving consent. Emotional abuse is a sweeping category covering any act causing psychological anguish, such as threats, insults, or humiliation. Neglect is a common yet difficult-to-detect behavior that refers to a caretaker's failure to meet the older adult's basic needs; this includes depriving them of adequate food and water, willfully preventing the older adult from getting necessary medical care, not keeping them clean and well-groomed, allowing their home to fall into a state of filth or disrepair, or keeping the older adult socially isolated. Financial exploitation involves the mismanagement, misuse, or theft of an older adult's money or assets for personal gain. An estimated 10 percent of all older adults in the United States have experienced some form of abuse, with two-thirds of abuse happening at the hands of a spouse or child (National Council on Aging 2021).

The COVID-19 pandemic intensified all forms of family violence including elder abuse, with some studies showing that rates nearly doubled since prior to the pandemic (Chang and Levy 2021). Some older adults were stuck at home with stressed-out family caregivers who lashed out physically or emotionally (Makaroun et al. 2020). Older adults, anxious about their health and finances, also were targeted by scam artists posing as representatives from the Centers for Disease Control and Prevention offering for-fee nasal swabs, or governmental officials offering to "rush" their CARES (Coronavirus Aid, Relief, and Economic Security) Act stimulus checks, for an upfront fee (Han and Mosqueda 2020). Because the pandemic essentially shut down public gathering places like senior centers and houses of worship, older adults had few people with whom to confide about these hurtful and embarrassing experiences. The demise of public life also meant that fewer "eyes and ears" in the community noticed and reported signs of abuse. A shortage of home health aides and visiting nurses also meant that many older adults lacked a helper who would notice and report bruises and scrapes, or who could offer emotional support (Chang and Levy 2021).

The pandemic intensified and raised awareness of elder abuse, but mistreatment and exploitation were a serious problem long before the pandemic shutdowns. The varieties of mistreatment suffered by older adults have expanded in recent years, as technology creates new platforms for the unscrupulous to prey on their victims. Telemarketers have scammed lonely older adults like Richard Guthrie, a ninety-two-year-old World War II veteran and widower, who was tricked into disclosing his banking and personal information by a fraudulent firm that raided Guthrie's account of all his savings. A devastated Guthrie recalled, "Since my wife passed away, I don't have many people to talk with. I didn't even know they were stealing from me, until everything was gone." Social media and networking sites have fueled a new industry of abuse—romance scams that bilk lonely widows and widowers of their fortunes. A seventy-six-year-old widow from Rhode Island refinanced her home, emptied her bank account, and sent more than $660,000 to the handsome man who friended her online. Although her virtual friend claimed to be "General Mathew

Weyer," stationed with the US Army in Afghanistan, there was no General Weyer; his image and words were concocted by a multinational internet fraud ring (Span 2020). Guthrie and the lonely widow are not alone. The Federal Trade Commission estimates that 10 to 15 percent of older adults each year are the victims of consumer fraud (Shadel and Pak 2017).

It's not just older adults' bank accounts that are raided. Their bodies and dignity also are preyed upon, often by the people entrusted with their care. In the past decade, some home health aides and nursing home assistants have made a game out of taking humiliating photos and videos of older adults and posting these images on the internet. In 2016, the Centers for Medicare and Medicaid Services (CMS) started to discipline nursing homes whose workers did so (Ornstein and Huseman 2016). This federal crackdown occurred after the national news reported that a nursing assistant in New Jersey posted a photo of a nursing home resident's genitals on Facebook. And two aides at a Wisconsin assisted living facility uploaded to Snapchat a collection of photos showing older residents undressing, sitting on the toilet, defecating, or vomiting. These cruel acts of betrayal were just two of the dozens of infractions detected (Ornstein and Huseman 2016). Viral abuse is not the only form of mistreatment that happens at nursing homes. As many as one in fourteen formal complaints filed against nursing home staff focus on neglect or mistreatment of its residents, whether by staff or fellow residents (Roberto and Hoyt 2021). An estimated one in five nursing home residents has been mistreated by a fellow resident (referred to as R-REM, or resident-to-resident elder mistreatment) while one in four is physically or emotionally mistreated by staff.

While these shameful acts have sparked national outrage and triggered disciplinary actions, it is the less sensationalist, more private forms of abuse that are most common and most difficult to combat. Elder abuse occurs most frequently at the hands of those closest to older adults, especially their spouses, adult children, grandchildren, and other relatives. Because older adults often are dependent upon the people mistreating them, they are reluctant to report these incidents to authorities for fear that their abusers will retaliate (Roberto 2016). More than half of all emotional abuse and sexual abuse incidents, and three-quarters of physical mistreatment cases are perpetuated by family members (Acierno et al. 2010). That's why statistics on abuse and mistreatment are so difficult to obtain and confirm; older victims may be frightened to report their mistreatment or may not know whom to report to. Some are reluctant to tell their physicians or social workers because they fear their confidentiality will be breached. Others feel ashamed and embarrassed, or they may convince themselves that the mistreatment was justified because they were making demands on their abuser. For members of historically marginalized groups, these obstacles are even more intimidating. Some LGBTQ older adults are reluctant to report abuse, for fear that their abuser will divulge their sexual identity, or because they anticipate being dismissed or disrespected by formal service providers (Goldsen 2016). Undocumented immigrants fear contacting the legal authorities who could help them, nervous that they or their abuser could be deported (Ploeg et al. 2013).

Experts claim that "elder abuse knows no boundaries—older adults of all ages, genders, races, incomes and cultures experience abuse" (Roberto 2016:377). Older adults from all backgrounds are at risk of elder mistreatment, with rates slightly higher among women than men, oldest-old versus young-old adults, and Black and Latinx elders versus whites. Part of the reason for these disparities is that women, oldest-old, and ethnic minority older adults are more likely to suffer from poor cognitive and physical health, and social isolation—conditions that put them at a greater risk of abuse (Acierno et al. 2010). As cognitive capacities diminish, older adults become less capable of managing their financial affairs and may show impaired judgment or increased reliance on so-called "helpers" who take advantage of them (MetLife Mature Market Institute 2011). That was the case with Marvel Comics legend and *Spiderman* creator Stan Lee, who was bilked out of millions of dollars as his health and mental sharpness faded at the end of his life. Nearly half of all older adults with dementia or severe cognitive impairment have experienced emotional abuse, physical abuse, or neglect (Wigelsworth et al. 2010). Some older adults with dementia become physically and verbally aggressive toward their caregivers, who may respond by shouting at or insulting them, withholding food, or physically restraining them. Some overwhelmed caregivers may threaten to move the dementia patient into a nursing home or to stop providing care—threats that can be frightening to the patient (Cooper et al. 2009). The vast majority of beleaguered caregivers do not hurt their family members; to the contrary, caregivers are often victimized when their loved one develops dementia and the accompanying loss of impulse control (Brandl and Raymond 2012).

Social isolation makes older adults easy prey for abuse (Acierno et al. 2010). People with large or supportive networks of friends, family, and neighbors have someone they can turn to for help and assurance. The more eyes and ears older adults have focused on them, the more people can help detect early signs of abuse and intervene as needed (Schafer and Koltai 2014). Abuse and isolation can form a vicious circle. Older adults in abusive situations have fewer friends and confidantes because their abuser prevents them from maintaining those ties, and this isolation perpetuates the cycle of abuse (J. Williams et al. 2016). Geographically isolated older adults also have difficulty finding virtual support or information, whether through email, social networking sites, or websites like AARP or the National Center on Elder Abuse (NCEA). More than half of rural-area residents lack high-speed broadband, something that residents of urban areas take for granted.

## The Strains of Caregiving

Nearly everyone will be a caregiver at some point. Whether delivering chicken soup to a bedridden friend, picking up prescription medications for an ill parent, or helping a frail spouse shower and get dressed each morning, an estimated fifty-three million US adults provided care to a family member or friend in 2020 (AARP and National Alliance for Caregiving 2020). Caregiving is different from merely lending a helping hand; it is help given expressly because a loved one has a physical, psychological, or cognitive limitation. That's why so many older adults are caregivers; their friends, siblings, and spouse are their age-peers, and with advanced age comes an increased risk of conditions that limit one's capacity to function independently. While one in five US adults overall are currently caring for a loved one, more than one-third of adults ages sixty-five and older are caregivers.

Caregiving brings a sense of purpose, mastery of new tasks, and the satisfaction of helping loved ones (National Academies of Sciences, Engineering, and Medicine 2016). At the same time, intensive or long-term caregiving can be emotionally stressful and physically overwhelming,

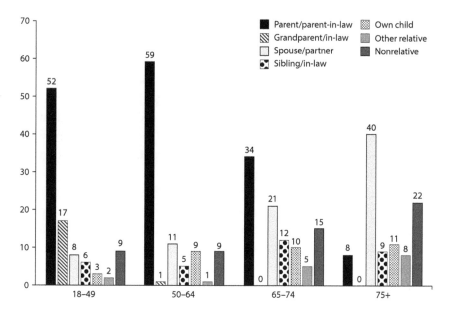

*Figure 19.* Percentage of US adults providing care to specific family members, by age of caregiver, 2020. SOURCE: AARP and National Alliance for Caregiving (2020).

especially for older adults managing their own health problems. Caregiving duties often are round-the-clock. About three-quarters of caregivers live with the person they're caring for, and nearly all live within thirty minutes, meaning that caregiving is a constant part of everyday life (Wolff et al. 2018). As figure 19 shows, 40 percent of caregivers ages seventy-five and older are helping their spouse; spousal caregiving is especially time and labor intensive because the healthier spouse tends to be solely responsible for the ailing spouse's care.

Younger caregivers tend to assist a parent or grandparent, which is less time intensive, especially when they live apart or other siblings pitch in. Caregivers in the United States report providing thirty hours per week, on average, with caregivers ages seventy-five and older putting in thirty-four hours a week on average—just one hour short of a full-time job (AARP and National Alliance for Caregiving 2020). Because older caregivers tend to be retired or living on limited incomes, they also are less likely than their younger (or employed) counterparts to have the means to pay for help. Caregivers ages seventy-five and older have fewer unpaid helpers; the friends and siblings they might otherwise turn to are also very old and may be too ill to pitch in (National Alliance for Caregiving, AARP, and Public Policy Inst. 2015). Caregiving spells tend to be long, because medical technologies have extended the duration (although not necessarily the quality) of life for chronically ill older adults, especially those with dementia. In 2020, the average duration of a caregiving spell was 4.5 years, with roughly one-third of caregivers in the role for five or more years (AARP and National Alliance for Caregiving 2020).

One particular type of caregiving is especially stressful: caring for a loved one with Alzheimer's disease or related dementias (ADRD), a condition that becomes more common with advancing age. An estimated sixteen million Americans, mostly older adults themselves, are dementia caregivers. The challenges are immense and persistent (Alzheimer's Association 2021). The average dementia patient lives with the condition for about seven years, yet some live as many as twenty years. Dementia caregivers provided about forty-eight hours of care per week in 2015, compared to just twenty-four hours weekly for other caregivers (Wolff et al. 2018).

Caring for a dementia patient is very stressful because the care recipient's behavior can change dramatically, altering the nature of their relationship. As the dementia patient's mental capacities diminish, they may leave the burners on the gas stove turned on and walk away or wander outside of the family home without warning—triggering panic in their caregivers. Others may yell, bite, throw things, curse, or behave in a sexually inappropriate way. Some may sit still as if in a coma, barely registering an eye movement, causing some caregivers to harbor guilty thoughts like "maybe he'd be better off dead" (Etters, Goodall, and Harrison 2008:125). About 60 percent of dementia caregivers rate their emotional stress as high or very high, and 40 percent suffer from depressive symptoms. The main reason why dementia caregivers place their loved one in a nursing home is that they feel they cannot provide adequate care and are fearful for their own safety (Etters et al. 2008).

The strains of caregiving for loved ones can be especially onerous for women, who provide more hours of care and for longer spells (AARP and National Alliance for Caregiving 2020). Women spend an average of 6.1 years—nearly 10 percent of their adult lives—caregiving, whereas men spend 4.1 years, or 7 percent of their adult lives giving care (National Academies of Sciences, Engineering, and Medicine 2016). The specific tasks performed also vary by gender, with women doing the most time- and labor-intensive tasks.

Researchers classify caregiving tasks into assistance with Activities of Daily Living (ADLs) and Instrumental Activities of Daily Living (IADLs). The former includes help with basic activities that need to be accomplished each day, like eating, getting dressed, bathing, and going to the bathroom (Katz 1983). The latter includes more complex activities such as cooking, driving, using the telephone or computer, shopping, and keeping track of bills and finances. Women are more likely than men to provide help with both ADL and IADL tasks, although the gender gap is a bit narrower for IADLs (Qualls 2021). A racial divide in caregiving also is evident. Black older adults spend more time in caregiving than do whites, and often take on this role at younger ages, helping their loved ones with basic daily tasks for long stretches of time (Pinquart and Sorensen 2005). Part of the reason is that Black people, on average, suffer more numerous, frequent, and earlier onset health problems than their white counterparts and thus require care at younger ages (Laditka and Laditka 2001).

Intensive caregiving can take a serious toll on older adults' well-being, with most studies showing greater harms to physical health than emotional health. Caregiving can be all-consuming, so caregivers may have less time or motivation to exercise, prepare and eat healthy meals, sleep eight hours a night, take their daily vitamins and medications, and go to the doctor regularly (Collins and Swartz 2011). Many older caregivers, especially women, neglect or minimize their own health worries, which they view as less important or serious than the health concerns of the person they're caring for. One study of dementia caregivers found that nearly one-third neglected to take their own medications, and half did not keep their own doctors' appointments (Wang et al. 2015). Some stressed-out older caregivers may try to sooth their nerves by turning to cigarettes, alcohol, or unhealthy comfort foods—behaviors that may increase their risk of lung disease, liver problems, obesity, or diabetes. Physically strenuous care increases the risk of musculoskeletal injuries, backaches, muscle strain, scrapes, and bruises. Walking up and down the stairs carrying meals to their loved one's bedroom, lifting the patient, helping them to get on and off the toilet, and assisting with bathing and showering are difficult tasks for small, frail, or arthritic older adults (National Academies of Sciences, Engineering, and Medicine 2016). The need for caregiver supports is one of the most pressing policy concerns facing the United States and most wealthy nations worldwide, a concern we revisit in chapter 5.

*Ageism*

Ageism, or the stereotyping of and both blatant and subtle discrimination against people because of their age, is not new. As far back as the 1780s, older adults were disparaged as "old fogeys" or "old coots," and were seen as lacking the mental capacities and physical strength to make meaningful contributions to society (Fleming et al. 2003a). Ageism has not disappeared. So-called "humorous" greeting cards proclaim that after a certain birthday, an "old guy" is "officially permitted to: scratch his butt in public, drive forever with his left blinker on, pass gas in a crowded elevator, mumble incoherently to himself, snore like a chain saw, . . . and fall asleep with absolutely no warning." COVID-19 has sparked new insults, like hashtags that refer to the pandemic as the #boomerremover, and the emergence of phrases like "boomer doomer," "coffin dodgers," and "sacrifice the weak" (Brooke and Jackson 2020; Lichtenstein 2020; Morrow-Howell et al. 2020).

It's not just media pundits or insensitive teens with a Twitter account who are maligning and demoralizing older adults; sometimes the culprits are family, friends, service providers, and even the health professionals who care for older adults. Well-meaning caregivers often slip into "elderspeak" or an infantilizing language and tone when speaking to older adults. A sing-song voice, overly loud or slow explanations, simplistic language, and seemingly friendly greetings like "how are you today, young lady?" are regarded as condescending and demeaning by older adults and gerontologists alike (Leland 2008). Although silly greeting cards and the occasional "sweetie" dropped into conversation may seem harmless, these subtle yet pervasive slights are hurtful. If older adults hear ageist jokes and jabs often enough, they may start to believe them, and this internalization can trigger negative feelings like neediness and depression. Psychologist Becca Levy (2003) discovered that simply exposing older adults to words and messages associated with ageist stereotypes, like the words *frail, forgetful,* or *feeble,* can lessen older adults' memory skills and inten-sify their stress levels.

Ageism—whether condescending words from one's pharmacist or hav-ing a driver's license wrested away by an overprotective adult child—can threaten older adult's mental health (Yuan 2007). Ageism, like any "ism" such as racism or sexism, is painful and can rob people of opportunities, self-worth, and dignity (Kessler, Mickelson, and Williams 1999). Studies of older nursing home patients have found that they start behaving in a more dependent manner when the nursing staff treats them as if they are children (Pasupathi and Löckenhoff 2002). Ageism also prevents some older adults from getting essential medical treatment. Older adults are less likely than younger people to be referred for the psychiatric or neu-rological assessments they need because doctors view their symptoms of sadness or forgetfulness as a "normal" part of getting old, rather than a medical condition that requires treatment (Karel, Gatz, and Smyer 2012).

Ageism also harms near-retirement-age older adults—by derailing or stalling their efforts to find work, triggering financial insecurities and anxiety. Women and those of lower socioeconomic status (SES) are particu-larly vulnerable to ageism in the workplace. Given the high value placed on youthful beauty and a slender physique among women, older women are more likely than their male peers to face discrimination in hiring, especially in jobs like sales that require interacting with customers and clients (Neumark, Burn, and Button 2017). Ageism is especially hard to avoid for those of lower SES because they tend to "look old" prematurely (Rexbye et al. 2006). Wrinkled skin, stooped shoulders, gray hair, and tooth loss render people prime targets for ageism, although these physical signs of aging tend to appear earlier for those who have experienced persistent strains like economic insecurity, unhealthy behaviors like smoking, and physical exhaustion (Gunn et al. 2009). Cosmetic treatments that can turn back time, like hair coloring, facials, and Botox, may be out of financial reach (or deemed low priorities) for older adults with more pressing fi-nancial needs.

Older job seekers may have a hard time finding work, a pattern that worsened during the economic turndown triggered by the COVID-19 pandemic. In 2015, job seekers over age fifty-five took thirty-six weeks on average to find a new job, compared to just twenty-six weeks for workers under age fifty-five. These patterns intensified during the pandemic, as cash-strapped employers first downsized their highest-paid (oldest) workers, while other employers were reluctant to hire a worker they believed was at heightened risk of getting sick on the job (Monahan et al., 2020). As a result, between April and September 2020, older workers ages fifty-five and older were 17 percent more likely than workers ages thirty-five to fifty-four to lose their jobs, and they were less likely to find new work. The prospects of losing a job and staying unemployed are worse for those who are Black, female, or lacking a college degree, contributing to widening economic inequalities (Davis et al. 2020).

Social relationships—including loving marriages, devoted children and grandchildren, and rich friendships—are essential sources of happiness, connectedness, and support. At the same time, these ties also can be a source of strain, sadness, and even physical harm. The bleaker side of social relationships like loss, loneliness, abuse and mistreatment, exhausting caregiving demands, and ageism are especially likely to befall those who already are the most physically frail and socially isolated. In these ways, social ties are both a product of and contributor to cumulative (dis)advantages over the life course.

# 4 Health and Well-Being

When people are asked to name their biggest fears about growing old, health concerns sit at the top of the list. More than two-thirds of US adults say that "poor health" and "memory loss" are their most serious concerns. "Losing one's independence" and "financial insecurity" lag only slightly behind (Sterrett et al. 2017). It's not surprising that people dread sickness and senility. Poor health can dampen nearly every aspect of life. Getting out of bed in the morning is a struggle for the 46 percent of older men and 54 percent of older women with arthritis (Federal Interagency Forum on Aging-Related Statistics 2020). A peaceful night's sleep is an elusive goal for the 50 percent of older Americans who toss and turn at bedtime, or struggle to fall back asleep in the middle of the night. Sleep problems are an unfortunate consequence of age-related health issues including medication side effects, difficulty breathing, aches and pains, and older men's frequent need to get out of bed and use the bathroom (Sleep Foundation 2020). Health problems are frustrating and even depressing because they jeopardize older adults' independence, making them reliant on family for help with once-simple tasks like showering, getting dressed, cooking dinner, and getting groceries. Physical health and functioning influence how often older adults leave their homes, visit with friends and family, attend

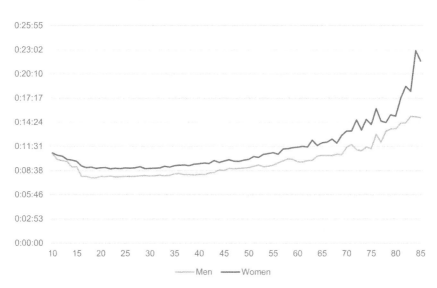

*Figure 20.* World record completion times for 5K races, by age and sex. NOTE: A 5K race is 3.1 miles. SOURCE: Association of Road Racing Statisticians (2021).

religious services, volunteer, or participate in activities that give them a sense of purpose and joy.

Are health declines an inevitable part of aging? The answer is yes and no. Old age is linked with biological changes that make it more difficult to carry out one's favorite activities, whether sleeping soundly through the night, running half-marathons, or quickly shouting out correct answers to questions on *Jeopardy*. Even elite athletes slow down with old age. As figure 20 shows, the world records for running 5K races (about 3.1 miles) get slower with age; elite runners in their eighties take twice as long as those in their twenties (Association of Road Racing Statisticians 2021). Still, running a mile in eight minutes (men) or twelve minutes (women) at age eighty-five is no small feat, and reveals the wide variation in late-life health.

The number, severity, and timing of physical, mental, and cognitive health problems are shaped by complex biological factors like genetics and social factors like whether one has access to a regular health care provider, nutritious foods, clean air and water, and safe living conditions. This chapter provides an overview of how and why older adults experience declining health, describes some of the most common late-life health concerns, and identifies the mechanisms linking sociodemographic characteristics like socioeconomic status (SES) and race to later-life health. An important theme is that health problems don't emerge suddenly in old age; rather, they are the end result of advantages and disadvantages that accumulate since birth. The COVID-19 crisis provided a dramatic example, revealing how inequalities in where we live, the jobs we hold, and our access to health care set the stage for whether one enjoys a long and healthy life or dies prematurely after a bout of suffering.

## BIOLOGICAL PERSPECTIVES ON AGING AND HEALTH: A BRIEF OVERVIEW

Senescence is a fact of life. With advancing age, biological changes can bring on physical and cognitive declines. Weakening immune systems can leave older adults vulnerable to infections like COVID-19 and pneumonia. Blood vessels may lose elasticity, and this hardening of the arteries raises the risk of heart disease and stroke. These two conditions, in turn, may reduce blood supply to the brain, causing memory loss and difficulties with thinking and problem solving. Diminishing lung capacity means that a once easy climb up the stairs leaves some older adults breathless. Gray or white hair, wrinkled skin, less crisp vision and hearing, and aching joints are inevitable aspects of aging. Many biological theories of aging have been developed to explain why disease and disability become more common with age, including perspectives that emphasize "wear and tear" on the body over time, and cellular aging models that focus on the weakening of our cells' capacities to divide and replicate over time.

Many biological changes are a normal part of life, yet the pace and intensity of these declines are linked to social factors. There's some truth to claims like "all this stress is making my hair go gray"![1] Most biological models of aging recognize—whether explicitly or implicitly—that social and environmental factors can speed up or slow down biological aging (Shanahan and Hofer 2005). Stressors like physically strenuous jobs, exposure to systemic racism and xenophobia, neighborhood crime, and troubled or abusive relationships can "get under our skin" and undermine the functioning of major organ systems.[2] Four biological approaches help us understand why and how our bodies age: cellular aging, oxidative stress, immune system, and genetic perspectives.

*Cellular aging approaches* rest on the premise that telomere length shortens with age, and this progressive shortening can increase our risk of poor health (Sanders and Newman 2013). Telomeres are the caps at the end of each strand of DNA, similar to the plastic caps that protect the end of our shoelaces.[3] Without the protection of telomeres, cells will gradually age and die. This general process of telomere aging is accelerated by social stress and adversity (Epel et al. 2004). For instance, researchers have discovered that Black older adults who reported more frequent experiences of everyday discrimination or "microaggressions" such as being treated as if they were not smart, evidenced shorter telomere lengths (Liu and Kawachi 2017).

*Oxidative stress models* propose that age-related disease results when the body's balance of pro-oxidants and antioxidants tilts to favor pro-oxidants, which can damage healthy cells. Antioxidants, by contrast, are chemical compounds that can prevent cell damage. (That's why nutritionists encourage us to eat berries and other antioxidant-rich foods). These imbalances increase the risk of neurodegenerative diseases such as dementias, cancers, heart and blood vessel disorders, heart failure, heart attack and inflammatory diseases (Romano et al. 2010). Oxidative stress is linked to social factors. For example, adults who had experienced family violence, poverty, and parents' substance abuse during childhood show higher levels of oxidative damage, which can erode physical and mental health decades into the future (Horn et al. 2019).

*Immunosenescence* refers to changes in immune system functioning that occur with advancing age. With each passing year, our T cells become less effective at fighting antigens, which are the toxins and viruses that invade our bodies and require immune responses. That's why octogenarian COVID patients were more than twenty times as likely as patients in their fifties and early sixties to die of the virus (CDC 2021a). Older adults also have less capacity to fight off other viruses, recover more slowly once they get sick, and have poorer responses to medications and vaccinations meant to fight infection. As we learned with COVID-19, older adults with social and economic disadvantages were most vulnerable. Black, Latinx, and indigenous older adults were more likely to die of COVID-19 relative to their white peers at every age (Rossen et al. 2020). Older adults who had dropped out of high school decades earlier are more than twice as likely as their college-educated peers to have an unhealthy immune response (Noppert et al. 2020).

But what about genetics? Do "good genes" slow down the pace of biological aging, and forestall disease and death? Centenarians like Australian artist Guy Warren certainly think so. Guy, and many other adults in their eleventh decade attribute their longevity to "good genes and good luck" (McDonald 2021). Researchers working on projects like the Georgia Centenarian and New England Centenarian studies agree that exceptionally long-lived people have clear genetic advantages, but genes are just one part of the story.[4] An influential editorial in the *New England Journal of Medicine* argued that genetics explain about 30 percent of how long we live, and social circumstances like hazardous working conditions, behavioral patterns like whether we drink, smoke, or eat unhealthy foods, and environmental exposures like neighborhood pollution, account for 60 percent (Schroeder 2007). Access to health care, like whether we have health insurance or access to a regular care provider explains the final 10 percent (see figure 21).

Genes undeniably affect our risk of particular diseases, but the strength of genetic influences diminishes with age as our minds and bodies are exposed to decades of social and environmental forces that intensify or weaken a genetic predisposition. Genes shape key aspects of who we are— our eye and hair color, height, and risk of some diseases, especially those that emerge early in life like juvenile (Type I) diabetes and early-onset Alzheimer's disease. However, most diseases that we first experience at older ages have more modest heritability; heritability refers to the proportion of risk for a particular trait or disease that is accounted for by our genes (Ware and Faul 2021). While juvenile diabetes is estimated to have a 50 to 80 percent heritability factor, diseases that strike in midlife or old age have lower heritability, with estimates of 30 to 50 percent for heart disease, hypertension, and prostate cancer—meaning that 50 to 70 percent is explained by nongenetic factors (Jia et al. 2019).

The simplest explanation for the diminishing power of genes is that with each passing year, adults are exposed to more and more contextual influences that can overpower one's genetic predisposition (Oliynyk 2019). Smoking two packs of unfiltered cigarettes a day for decades increases the odds of lung cancer, even for those without a genetic risk. Years of healthy

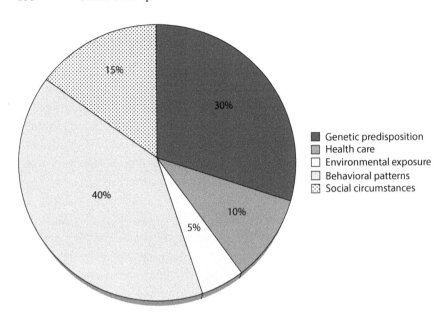

*Figure 21.* Factors contributing to premature death. SOURCE: Schroeder (2007).

living, by contrast, can mute or even turn around a genetic predisposition. One study found that older adults who had a high genetic risk of heart disease *and* who maintained a healthy lifestyle (that is, they exercised regularly, didn't smoke, ate a low-fat low-salt diet, and kept a recommended body weight) had a risk of heart disease that was just half that of their counterparts who had a high genetic risk yet had unhealthy habits (Khera et al. 2016). Studies carried out in the "gene x environment" tradition offer compelling evidence of how social, environmental, and behavioral factors can mute or amplify genetic tendencies.

A STATISTICAL SNAPSHOT OF LATE-LIFE HEALTH

Researchers have produced volumes of data showing the proportion of people who experience particular health problems, and how these patterns differ by age, sex, race, socioeconomic status, and more. This section presents statistical snapshots of some of the most common physical, cognitive, and mental health conditions reported by US older adults, and highlights subgroup differences where data are available, setting the foundation for our discussion of why these disparities exist, and why they're so hard to eradicate.[5]

*Life Expectancy*

Life expectancy, or how long members of a population live, is one of the most important indicators of the health of a society. As we learned in the introduction, life expectancy in the United States climbed dramatically over the past century. A baby boy born in 1900 could expect to live to age forty-six on average, while a baby girl could expect to live until age forty-eight. In 2020, newborn baby girls and boys are projected to live until ages seventy-six and eighty-one, respectively. While at first blush this seems a "good news" story, the United States encountered a dismal turning point in 2015. As figure 22 shows, 2015 marked the first time in nearly a century that life expectancy started to decline. Since the 2015 turning point, it has continued to fall, with the most pronounced declines for those with low levels of education and income—leading to ever-widening inequalities in health and longevity (Venkataramani, O'Brien, and Tsai 2021). Life expectancy in the United States. now lags behind other high-income nations like Japan and Switzerland by nearly five years (Woolf, Chapman, and Lee 2021). This "bad news" scenario emerged before COVID-19 was on our radar and cannot be blamed solely on the pandemic (although the pronounced life-expectancy drops in 2020 and 2021 can be). Rising rates of "deaths of despair" from opioid overdose and suicide, and deaths from obesity-related causes like heart disease and diabetes also played a major role (Case and Deaton 2020). People with less education and lower income, and who work in physically dangerous jobs have had a mortality disadvantage over the past century, but these disparities have widened due to the sharp and recent rise in "deaths of despair" which disproportionately affect lower-income and less-educated persons (Bosworth 2018).

Figure 22 also reveals persistent gender gaps in life expectancy at birth, such that US women live about five years longer than men. Race and ethnic gaps also are persistent; Hispanics live about three years longer than whites, and whites live about five years longer than Blacks on average.

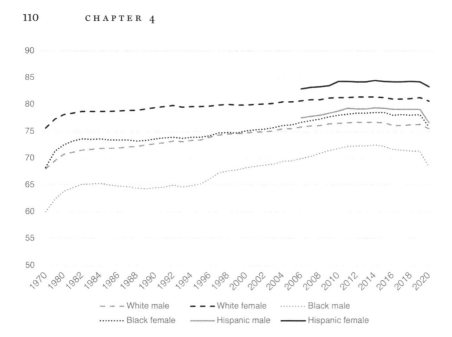

*Figure 22.* Life expectancy at birth, by race/ethnicity and sex, 1970–2020. SOURCES: Medina, Sabo, and Vespa, 2020.

Life expectancy at birth reflects mortality risk at every stage of life. Males and Black people are more likely than females and whites to succumb to complications at birth; die prematurely from adolescent or young adult accident, suicide, homicide, or substance use; and experience midlife conditions like heart disease. Recognizing that life expectancy at birth is driven by early-life mortality, researchers interested in late-life health use a second indicator: life expectancy at age sixty-five, or the average number of additional years a sixty-five-year-old can expect to live. Figure 23 shows life expectancy at age sixty-five by sex, race, and Hispanic ethnicity. This chart, like figure 22, reveals persistent gender and race differences such that women at age sixty-five can expect to live slightly longer than their male counterparts, with advantages of two years among whites, and three years among Blacks and Hispanics. Black-white gaps are two to three years, whereas Hispanics fare slightly better than both Blacks and whites. A sixty-five-year-old Hispanic man can expect to live until age eighty-four whereas his female counterpart can expect to live until age eighty-seven.

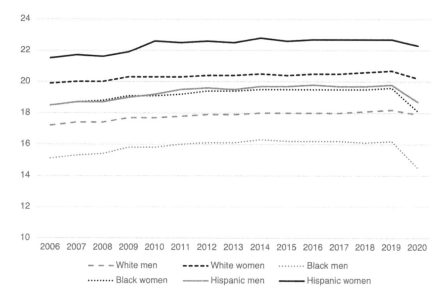

*Figure 23.* Life expectancy at age sixty-five, by race/ethnicity and sex, 2006–2020. SOURCE: Arias et al. (2021); Federal Interagency Forum on Aging-Related Statistics (2020).

Some astute readers may be perplexed, asking questions like: why are race and gender differences in life expectancy so much smaller at age sixty-five than at birth? And why is life expectancy at birth around eighty for women and seventy-six for men, yet the data plotted in figure 23 suggest that a sixty-five-year-old woman can expect to live another twenty years on average, and a sixty-five-year-old man can expect to live another eighteen years? Why are these life expectancies at sixty-five so much higher than the life expectancies at birth plotted in figure 22? The answers to these questions reflect a process that demographers call *selective survival.* People who survive until age sixty-five may have protective traits or advantages that make them different from their peers who died before age sixty-five. This is especially the case for men and Blacks; the genetic and socioeconomic advantages that helped them to withstand and survive potential threats during childhood and adulthood also help them to survive until their eighties and beyond (Markides and Machalek 2020).

*Physical Health and Functioning*

Physical health is a broad category, encompassing illnesses, chronic conditions, and symptoms. It also reflects levels of disability, or the ways that health limits our capacity to remain active and engaged. While these different dimensions are closely intertwined, each provides an important new piece of information as we strive to understand the well-being of older adults.

CAUSE OF DEATH

The age at which people die is an important indicator of the health of a society. However, researchers also focus on the *causes of death*, as this information guides public health goals like paying for end-of-life medical treatments, projecting future care needs of patients, and understanding why some subgroups—whether women, or immigrants, or farmers—are at a heightened risk of certain diseases or tragedies like suicide. Of the 3.4 million Americans who died in 2020, 74 percent were ages sixty-five and older.[6] Throughout the first two decades of the twenty-first century, the five leading causes of death to older adults have consistently been heart disease, cancer, chronic lower respiratory diseases like emphysema and bronchitis, stroke, and Alzheimer's disease. These five conditions typically account for three-quarters of all deaths to persons ages sixty-five and over. However, in 2020 COVID-19 emerged as the third leading cause of death (Ahmad and Anderson 2021).

Heart disease has been the most common cause of death among older adults for more than three decades, accounting for more than 25 percent of deaths. However, death rates from heart disease and the related condition of stroke have dropped dramatically since 1981, as shown in figure 24. These declines partly reflect lifestyle changes, like a major decline in smoking rates since the 1950s. Medical advances also play a major role. Improved treatments for cardiovascular disease mean that a heart attack is no longer a death sentence. Around 1950, nearly 40 percent of heart attack victims died either on the spot or from complications that followed. By 2010, fewer than 10 percent of heart attack patients died, thanks to the development of beta-blockers and medical advances like effective angioplasty (Levy et al. 2002). Deaths from Alzheimer's disease, the fifth

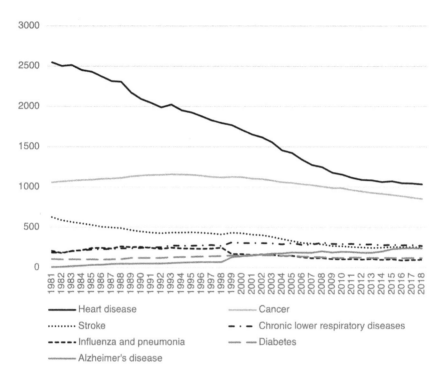

*Figure 24.* Death rates among adults ages sixty-five and over by leading causes of death, 1981–2018. NOTE: Rates are deaths per 100,000 population. ICD-9 codes used prior to 1999, ICD-10 classifications used thereafter. SOURCE: Arias et al. (2021); Federal Interagency Forum on Aging-Related Statistics (2020).

leading cause of death, have increased over the past four decades, due in part to the rising numbers of oldest-old and centenarians. Some researchers believe that official counts actually *underestimate* the number of persons who die of Alzheimer's because death certificates tend to show the immediate condition that killed an older adult, such as pneumonia or heart failure, rather than a long-term underlying condition (Stokes et al. 2020).

Cancer has consistently ranked as the second most common cause of death for older adults since the mid-twentieth century. The risk of cancer increases with age; the median age of any cancer diagnosis is sixty-six years, with a range of sixty-two for breast cancer to seventy-one for lung cancer (National Cancer Institute 2021).[7] Cancer can undermine older adults' quality of life; treatments like radiation or chemotherapy (and its side effects, like nausea) cause physical and emotional distress. The word *cancer* often is viewed as a death sentence, so older patients may become depressed and anxious (Blank and Bellizzi 2008). Most older adults with cancer also have at least one other health condition that requires care; for instance, many lung cancer patients also have COPD (chronic obstructive pulmonary disorder), while age-related conditions like high blood pressure and arthritis are common among cancer patients regardless of the tumor site (Williams et al. 2016). Researchers have documented race and socioeconomic disparities in cancer mortality, although these gaps vary based on the site of cancer and how amenable the cancer is to treatment. The main explanations for these mortality differentials are access to early screening, detection, and treatment for cancers like breast and colorectal. We revisit these themes later in the chapter.

CHRONIC HEALTH CONDITIONS

Chronic conditions are symptoms and illnesses that last one year or longer and require ongoing medical attention. People with these conditions typically take regular medications, seek treatments, and in some cases, limit or adjust their daily activities to accommodate their symptoms. The risk of chronic health conditions increases with age, and two-thirds of older adults have more than one condition, a phenomenon referred to as *comorbidity* (two conditions) or *multimorbidity* (three or more conditions). Figures 25a and b show the proportion of men and women (25a) and white, Black, and Hispanic older adults (25b) who reported any of eight common conditions. Hypertension (high blood pressure) is by far the most common, affecting just over half of men and women. Arthritis, a condition marked by pain, swelling and stiffness in the joints, is second most common, with women more likely than men to report symptoms (54 versus 46 percent). Women also are slightly more likely to report asthma (14 versus 9 percent); asthma is a lung disease that makes it hard to breathe easily. Conversely, men are more likely to report heart disease (35 versus 24 percent) and diabetes (25 versus 19 percent); diabetes occurs when the pancreas is no longer able to make insulin. If not treated properly, diabetes can lead to serious health complications including heart disease, blindness, kidney failure, and leg amputations (CDC 2020).

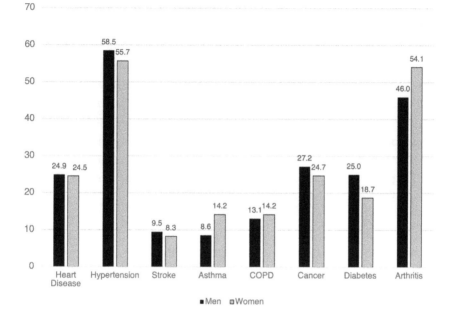

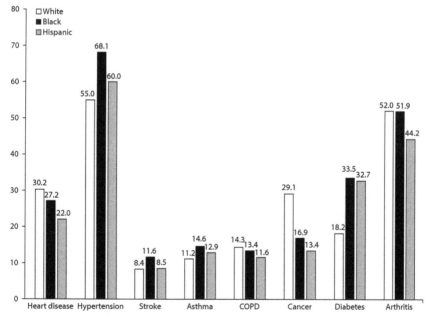

*Figure 25a–b.* Percentage of adults ages sixty-five and over with selected chronic conditions, by sex and race/ethnicity, 2018. SOURCE: Federal Interagency Forum on Aging-Related Statistics (2020).

Figure 25b shows race differences in several chronic conditions, most notably hypertension, diabetes, and asthma. More than two-thirds of older Blacks (68 percent) and more than half (60 percent) of Hispanics reported high blood pressure, compared to just 55 percent of whites. Similarly, Black and Hispanic older adults are more likely than whites to have diabetes (34 versus 18 percent). These gaps reflect risk factors like obesity and diet, consequences of limited access to health-enhancing amenities in neighborhoods. However, whites are more likely to report having cancer, a pattern that reflects whites' slightly higher age. As we shall see later in the chapter, whites have higher rates of some cancers but are less likely to die, due to their earlier detection and treatment.

DISABILITY

The illnesses, injuries, and biological changes that older adults experience may result in disability, which affects one in four older adults. *Disability* refers to any condition of the body or mind that makes it more difficult to do certain activities and interact with the world around us (Verbrugge 2020). People of any age can have a disability, whether temporary or permanent. A sports injury might have temporarily affected your ability to walk quickly and without pain. Many of us have less than perfect eyesight, and would have difficulty reading, driving, or watching TV without our glasses, contact lenses, or laser eye surgery. For older adults, however, the number and intensity of activity-limiting conditions is high, and encompasses impaired vision, hearing, mobility, cognition, and self-care. Mobility and vision impairments are dangerous because they can increase older adults' risks of falls. In an average year, one in four older adults falls, with 20 percent of these falls resulting in a broken bone (often a hip fracture) or a major head injury. Understanding the social patterning and consequences of disability can guide workplace accommodation practices, public spending on long-term care, and the design of homes and the built environment so that they meet older adults' needs.

Figure 26 shows the proportion of older adults with each of five disabilities, by age, sex, and race. Mobility limitation, or difficulty with movement, is most common, with 12 percent of persons ages sixty-five to seventy-four, 17 percent of those seventy-five to eighty-four, and one-third of those ages eighty-five and older reporting that they have "a lot" of

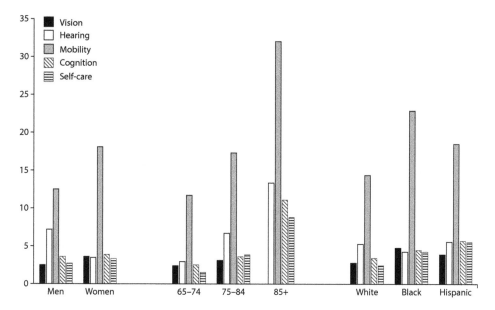

*Figure 26.* Percentage of adults ages sixty-five and over with specific disabilities, by age, race, and sex, 2018. NOTE: Disability is defined as "a lot" or "cannot do/unable to do" when asked about difficulty with seeing, even if wearing glasses (vision); hearing, even if wearing hearing aids (hearing); walking or climbing steps (mobility); remembering or concentrating (cognition); and self-care, such as washing all over or dressing (self-care). SOURCE: Federal Interagency Forum on Aging-Related Statistics (2020).

difficulty or "cannot" walk or climb stairs. Women have higher rates than men, due to the fact that women live longer and thus are older than men on average. They also are more likely to have arthritis, which can limit movement. Sensory impairments, which encompass difficulty seeing and hearing, are relatively rare, although they become more common with advancing age. Part of the reason why these rates are low is that most older adults use assistive devices like eyeglasses or a hearing aid, which boost their capacity to see and hear. Likewise, the proportion unable to perform self-care, such as dressing and washing, is low because most older adults have someone to assist them. Race disparities exist, such that a higher proportion of Blacks and Hispanics (relative to whites) report difficulty with their sight, mobility, cognition, and self-care.

Disability researchers want to know whether older adults are adding more "years to their life" or "more life to their years." Are older adults' later years filled with activity and social engagement, or impairment and isolation? To answer this question, researchers first determine how much difficulty older adults have doing ADLs and IADLs. Recall from chapter 3 that ADLs include dressing and other basic daily activities, and IADLs include complex activities like managing medications (Katz and Akpom 1976). Using information on older adults' capacity to perform ADLs and IADLs, researchers have constructed a new measure called *active life expectancy* (ALE) or *disability-free life expectancy*. This measure indicates the proportion of an older adult's years that are relatively healthy versus the proportion marked by disability (Manton Gu, and Lowrimore 2008). This is an important statistic because it tells us whether illness and disability are packed into a short time period at the very end of life, or whether older adults struggle for years with disability, requiring services and supports for long stretches of time. Most evidence suggests that more advantaged older adults have shorter periods, whereas less advantaged older adults experience longer time periods of disability, compromising their independence and quality of life (House, Lantz, and Herd 2005). The typical sixty-five-year-old can expect that about 55 percent of their future years will be disability-free, about 40 percent will have some disability, and the remaining 5 percent will be spent in long-term care (Crimmins, Zhang, and Saito 2016).

ORAL HEALTH

Oral health, or the state of our teeth and gums, is an important yet frequently overlooked component of older adults' health. Healthy teeth and gums affect our capacity to smile, speak clearly, and chew food. Dental problems can prevent older adults from finding paid work, given the social stigma associated with missing or decaying teeth (Moore and Keat 2020). Some readers may wonder why dental health is important for older adults. After all, timeworn stereotypes tell us that older adults are toothless, soaking their dentures in a glass on the nightstand at the end of the day. The notion that "older adults don't have teeth" is now wholly outdated. Thanks to innovations like community water fluoridation and improvements in hygiene throughout the twentieth century, most older adults are keeping at

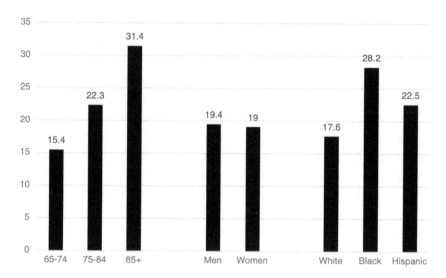

*Figure 27.* Percentage of adults ages sixty-five and over with no natural teeth, by age, sex, and race/ethnicity, 2018. NOTE: "No natural teeth" refers to the proportion who indicate that they have lost all of their upper and lower natural (permanent) teeth. SOURCE: Federal Interagency Forum on Aging-Related Statistics (2020).

least some of their natural teeth until very advanced ages. However, older adults who are financially disadvantaged, who lack health insurance, and who are members of racial or ethnic minority groups are at the greatest risk of tooth loss. Figure 27 shows the proportion of US adults ages sixty-five and older who are edentulous, meaning they have no natural teeth. This proportion rises with age; those ages eighty-five and up are more than twice as likely as those ages sixty-five to seventy-four to have no teeth (31.4 vs. 15.4 percent). Black and Hispanic elders are more likely than whites to have no teeth (28.2 and 22.5 percent versus 17.6 percent). The CDC (2021b) finds that more than one-third of high school dropouts ages sixty-five and older but just 9 percent of those with some college are edentulous.

These disparities are largely the result of early life influences like regular access to dental care, and whether one smoked, drank alcoholic and sugary beverages, and maintained a healthy diet during their younger years (Gerontological Society of America 2017). Socioeconomic disparities also reflect the fact that Medicare, the federal health insurance program for older adults, does not currently include dental benefits.[8] Once older adults retire and lose their employer-provided health insurance, only those who can afford to buy dental insurance or who can pay for their care out-of-pocket tend to see a dentist regularly. Regular dental visits are especially important for older adults because of their vulnerability to tooth decay (also known as caries). Nearly two-thirds have periodontal disease including sore or bleeding gums, which makes it painful to brush and care for their teeth (Kramarow 2019). Older adults with dementia cannot easily brush their teeth and may require professional assistance. Many prescription and over-the-counter medications reduce older adults' production of saliva; a parched "dry mouth" increases the risk of cavities. Older adults who can't afford to have their tooth decay treated or to get properly fitting dentures may suffer from nutritional deficits. For people with tooth pain or missing teeth, it's easier to eat soft foods rather than crisp healthy foods like fresh vegetables. Embarrassment about missing teeth and bad breath may keep some older adults from socializing with friends and families, compounding their social isolation (Gerontological Society of America 2017).

*Neurocognitive Health*

One of the most pervasive myths of aging is that "all old people are senile." Ageist birthday cards recycle tired jokes about older people "mumbling incoherently" to themselves, as we saw in chapter 3. And when President Joe Biden tripped on the steps while boarding Air Force One in 2021, former President Donald Trump (just four years Biden's junior), sniped "he didn't know where the hell he was." Although our brains change as we age, neurocognitive disorders like Alzheimer's disease and related dementias (ADRD) are not a "normal" or inevitable part of aging (Livingston et al. 2017). Just 11 percent of US adults ages sixty-five and over are diagnosed with ADRD, and the CDC estimates that as many as 40 percent of US dementia cases can be delayed or prevented. Social, environmental, and lifestyle changes are just as important as biomedical interventions.[9] A high-quality education and intellectually complex jobs, living in a neighborhood with clean air and access to state-of-the-art treatments for heart disease, and an active lifestyle can delay cognitive declines (Karlamangla et al. 2009).

Our neurocognitive abilities, or our capacity to think, reason, and re-member, are multifaceted, such that some decline while others remain sta-ble or even improve with age. One dimension, *fluid intelligence*, refers to our capacity to think quickly and use flexible reasoning when solving new problems. This kind of problem solving relies on innovation and creativity, rather than accumulated knowledge or life experience. We use our fluid intelligence when solving puzzles, learning a new technology, or wrestling with unfamiliar ideas. Fluid intelligence tends to peak in our late twen-ties, before starting to slowly decline (Cacioppo and Freberg 2012). These declines partly reflect biological factors, like age-related neurological changes. Yet they also reflect social factors, like the opportunities afforded to older adults. If older people are deprived of opportunities to think cre-atively and innovate, whether on the job or at home, their problem-solving skills may wane (Cavanaugh and Blanchard-Fields 2018).

*Crystallized intelligence*, by contrast, refers to knowledge acquired through life-long learning. This includes things like a rich vocabulary, knowledge of history and literature, wisdom gleaned from life experience, and recollections of major events. Psychologists generally agree that crys-tallized intelligence improves as we age, peaking in our sixties and seven-ties, and starting to decline only in advanced old age, with the onset of memory problems (Hartshorne and Germine 2015). Crystallized and fluid intelligence are highly correlated, meaning that people who are high on one also tend to be high on the other, in part because education is key to both aptitudes (McDonough et al. 2018).

Dramatic declines in reasoning and memory, common symptoms as-sociated with dementia, don't appear overnight. Rather, gradual declines occur over an extended time period. Mild cognitive impairment (MCI) is an early stage of memory loss, accompanied by declining language and spatial perception capacities. These initial changes may be serious enough that family and friends notice and worry, yet they are mild enough that they don't impair one's ability to carry out everyday activities. Signs of MCI might be things like misplacing car keys, needing frequent remind-ers about upcoming appointments, asking the same questions over and over again, struggling to remember the first name of an old friend or dis-tant relative, and reacting more slowly than usual. According to the Alz-heimer's Association (2021), 12 to 18 percent of US adults ages sixty and older have MCI. For some, the symptoms are short-lived, perhaps due to anxiety or the side effects of a new medication. For others, however, these symptoms progress, leading to dementia.

Dementia is often thought of as a single disease, but it encompasses a range of conditions—just as "heart disease" can include conditions like high blood pressure and congestive heart failure. Dementia generally entails the loss of memory, language, problem-solving, and other thinking abilities that are severe enough to interfere with daily life. These changes also can affect emotions, making people erratic and angry, potentially threatening their personal relationships. Alzheimer's disease is the most common type of dementia, accounting for 60 to 80 percent of all cases (Alzheimer's Association 2021).

The risk of poor neurocognitive health, like the risk of poor physical health, varies widely across race and socioeconomic groups, as shown in figure 28. This figure shows the proportion of participants ages sixty-five and over in the National Health and Aging Trends Study (NHATS) with a "probable dementia diagnosis." This measure includes persons who reported a diagnosis of dementia either by self or proxy (i.e., a family member who answered survey questions for the older adult); or who scored poorly on a cognition test. These tests include questions assessing memory, like recalling ten words that the interviewer recently read to them, and one's orientation, like being able to name the current date. Figure 28 shows that the risk of a probable dementia diagnosis increases with age. While less than 5 percent of adults ages sixty-five to seventy-four have a probable diagnosis, this rate climbs to 10 percent among those ages seventy-five to eighty-four, and 25 percent among those ages eighty-five and above. Men and women show generally similar patterns, yet disparities are evident on the basis of education and race. Rates are generally similar regardless of whether one is a high school or college graduate, yet high school dropouts (i.e., those with fewer than twelve years of education) fare much worse than high school graduates. Blacks and Hispanics are at greater risk than whites, especially at older ages. Just one in five oldest-old whites (ages eighty-five and older) has probable dementia, compared to 40 percent of Black and 35 percent of Latinx oldest old (ASPE 2020).

Many factors increase dementia risk, including having a gene known as APOE e4, although having the gene isn't a guarantee that a person will have

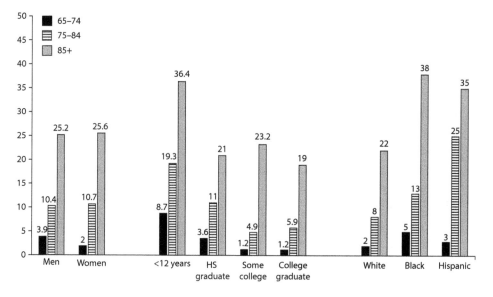

*Figure 28.* Percentage of community-dwelling adults ages sixty-five and over with a probable dementia diagnosis, by sex, education, and race/ethnicity, 2015. NOTE: Probable dementia diagnosis encompasses the following: older adults in the National Health and Aging Trends Study (NHATS) who reported a diagnosis of dementia either by self or by proxy, older adults whose proxy respondents reported a score of 2 or higher in the AD8 dementia screening interview, and older adults with impairment in at least two domains in the cognition battery were considered to have probable dementia. SOURCE: Assistant Secretary for Planning and Evaluation (2019).

the disease. Behavioral and social factors also matter, whether directly or indirectly. People who cannot afford or access nutritious foods, safe places to exercise, and healthy strategies for managing stress, are at greater risk of unhealthy behaviors like smoking, heavy drinking, an unhealthy diet, and a sedentary lifestyle. These behaviors, in turn, are linked with health conditions like diabetes, obesity, high blood pressure, and heart disease—all of which increase one's risk of neurocognitive problems (Lee et al. 2010). Higher education is linked with having mentally and socially stimulating work and hobbies, which may help older adults build their *cognitive reserve*, or the strengthened connections among brain cells they can draw on if their memory or reasoning ability begins to diminish (Wilson et al. 2019).

*Mental Health*

Another common misperception about aging is that "old people are sad, lonely, and depressed." While old age is filled with troubling experiences like health declines and the deaths of friends and family, older adults typically have mental health on par with or better than younger persons, with this advantage disappearing only at very advanced ages. Mental health is a broad category that encompasses many different symptoms, including depression, anxiety, anger, suicidal thoughts, loneliness, grief, and other negative emotions, as well as serious mental illnesses such as schizophrenia, substance use disorder, or bipolar disorder.[10] Depression is one of the most common (and commonly studied) dimensions of mental health; roughly one in six US adults has ever been diagnosed with depression. Depression refers to emotional and behavioral symptoms that persist for two or more weeks, including sadness, hopelessness, self-critical thoughts, lost interest in one's usual activities, low energy, difficulty concentrating, sleep troubles, and in some cases, suicidal thoughts. Figure 29 shows the proportion of US adults ages eighteen and older who reported any depressive symptoms in the past two weeks, as well as the proportion who reported mild, moderate, or severe symptoms. Young adults ages eighteen to twenty-nine are more likely than their midlife and older counterparts to have reported any symptoms (21 versus 17 to 18 percent). The age groups do not differ significantly with respect to moderate or severe symptoms, although persons ages sixty-five and over are slightly less likely than young adults to report such symptoms.

A more fine-grained analysis among older adults shows that depression risk increases after age sixty-five, because each passing year brings more physical and cognitive health problems, which can cause distress. Figure 30 shows that persons in their late fifties have substantially higher rates of clinically relevant depressive symptoms, relative to retirement-age persons. However, after age sixty-five, the proportion with clinically relevant symptoms increases from around 10 and 14 percent among men and women ages sixty-five to sixty-nine, to roughly 12 and 18 percent among those ages eighty-five and over, respectively. At every age, women are more likely than men to report depressive symptoms. However, it would be incorrect to conclude that men don't get depressed. Experts attribute

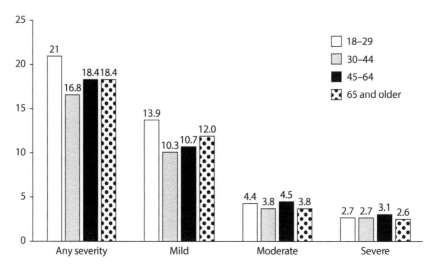

*Figure 29.* Percentage of adults ages eighteen and over with depressive symptoms in the past two weeks, by severity and age group, 2019. SOURCE: Villarroel and Terlizzi (2019).

this gender gap to men's reluctance to divulge their symptoms to a doctor or survey interviewer. Especially for older men, who were raised in an era when being strong, silent, and invincible was the masculine "ideal," admitting symptoms like crying and loneliness may seem like a sign of weakness. That's a key reason why men ages sixty-five to seventy-four have suicide rates four times higher than their female peers, and men ages seventy-five and older are roughly ten times as likely as same-age women to kill themselves (National Institute of Mental Health 2021): they bottle up their feelings and conceal their suffering from others until it becomes unbearable.[11]

Socioeconomic disparities in depression also are well documented. Regardless of whether SES is measured in terms of income, education, assets, or a composite measure, researchers consistently find that older adults with fewer socioeconomic advantages have roughly twice the rates of depression as their more advantaged counterparts (Saraceno, Levav, and Kohn 2005; Richardson et al. 2020). It seems painfully obvious to say that older adults who grew up in poverty have less education and income, held poorer-quality jobs, and live in rundown or crowded homes in poor

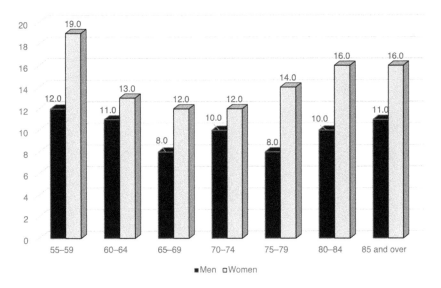

*Figure 30.* Percentage of adults ages fifty-five and over with clinically relevant depressive symptoms, by age and sex, 2018. SOURCE: Federal Interagency Forum on Aging-Related Statistics (2020).

neighborhoods are more susceptible to symptoms of sadness and demoralization. However, despite a long history of racial oppression in the United States, Black and Latinx older adults are less likely than their white peers to report depressive symptoms. The reasons are unclear. Some researchers point to the coping resources of ethnic and racial minorities in the United States, such as strong and supportive family ties, the solace provided by formal religion and prayer, and a resilience developed through overcoming prejudice and discrimination earlier in life (Mouzon 2013). Yet other research suggests that mental health problems may be stigmatized in Black and Latinx communities, so people may be reluctant to disclose their symptoms to a health care provider or family caregiver (Shellman, Granara, and Rosengarten 2011). This latter explanation is troublesome, as it means that racial and ethnic minorities (just like men) may not receive the therapies they need (Harris, Edlund, and Larson 2005).

Depression affects a relatively small fraction of older adults, yet it is a major public health concern because it puts older adults at risk of other problems like social isolation, elder abuse, and financial exploitation

(Roepke-Buehler, Simon, and Dong 2015). Depressed older adults may not follow doctor's orders, such as taking daily medications, and may not keep up with self-care—neglecting to eat, bathe, or groom regularly (Di-Matteo, Lepper, and Croghan 2000). Their relationships also may become strained, and they may reject the well-intended efforts of potential care-givers (Mechanic and McAlpine 2011). As a result, depression is linked with a seven- to ten-year reduction in life span (Chesney, Goodwin, and Fazel 2014).

Late-life depression is a consequence of social and biological factors. The loss of important social roles, like retirement after a lifetime of enjoy-able work, the deaths of loved ones, social isolation, experiences of ageism, and exhausting caregiving can leave an older adult emotionally depleted. Physical health problems also are a major source of depression. Cardio-vascular disease damages our brain's capacity to regulate our emotions, making us vulnerable to depression and sadness (Mather 2012). Medica-tions commonly prescribed to older adults, like anti-hypertension drugs, beta blockers, and some cancer medications can have side effects that in-crease one's risk of depressive symptoms.

Physical health problems including arthritis, cancer, dementias, dia-betes, heart disease, lung disease, musculoskeletal conditions, and vision impairments also bring two sets of daily challenges that can harm mental health: symptom management and activity limitations. *Symptom manage-ment,* or daily efforts to manage one's illness and medications, takes time and energy away from other enjoyable activities like get-togethers with friends and family, or relaxing quietly at home. Time-use studies show that older adults with health problems spend an average of two hours per day on health-related activities like taking medications, testing their blood sugar levels, and injecting insulin shots (Jonas, Ibuka, and Russell 2011). They also spend an average of two and a half hours receiving care, on those days when they see a health care provider. That includes travel to and from the clinic (thirty-five minutes), waiting in the doctor's office or ER (forty-seven minutes), and receiving care (seventy-two minutes). The stress of driving, waiting, dealing with insurance company red tape, the disruption to one's daily routines and activities, and the inescapable reminder of one's physical declines can trigger feelings of sadness, anxiety, and hopelessness (Clark et al. 1991).

Activity limitation refers to the ways that health problems reduce one's capacity to lead a full, independent, and satisfying life. Health problems that limit mobility, hearing, seeing, and communicating can compromise one's ability to read, participate in family conversations, and navigate one's physical environment with ease. These obstacles can reduce older adults' feelings of competence and independence (Wolf 2016). Activity limitations also create new stressors, like worrying about falling in one's home, moving to a long-term care facility, or coordinating a team of family caregivers who may be reluctant to help or who may disagree about their duties (McPherson et al. 2007). These struggles are intensified for older adults who can't afford assistive devices like hearing aids or walkers, or who don't have family or friends to lend a hand.

## DISPARITIES IN LATE-LIFE HEALTH AND WELL-BEING

Health disparities, or differences in physical, mental, or cognitive health across population subgroups, are found at every age.[12] As we have seen throughout this chapter, socioeconomic disparities exist along nearly every health outcome (House 2015). Consider the following statistics. High school dropouts die about fifteen years younger than those with a graduate degree. Laborers like roofers or janitors die about eleven years younger than professional workers like doctors, lawyers, or accountants (Singh and Lee 2021). The richest 1 percent of men live about fifteen years longer than the poorest 1 percent, while the comparable gap for women is ten years (Chetty et al. 2016).

SES gaps are so consistent across health outcomes—from dementia to depression to diabetes to disability—that sociologists Bruce Link and Jo Phelan (1995) have called socioeconomic resources a "fundamental cause" of health and longevity. Higher SES encompasses benefits like money, education, knowledge, power, and access to helpful social connections that protect one's health no matter what the specific disease. Each dimension of SES brings its own distinctive health benefits. Education is associated with higher levels of health literacy, the development of cognitive reserves, and a greater understanding of and compliance with doctor's orders. Higher incomes help us buy health-enhancing products and services like homes in neighborhoods with walking paths, clean air, and safe drinking water. White-collar jobs allow us to sit in comfortable offices, whereas blue-collar work can pose physically hazardous working condition (Carr 2019). Some researchers argue that the association between SES and health reflects a process called *social selection*, meaning that poor health in early life limits one's options for higher education and rewarding professions. Overall, evidence is more compelling for the process referred to as *social causation*, whereby low SES is a contributor to rather than a consequence of poor health (Warren 2009).

Race also matters. In the United States, Blacks have a greater risk of illness, disability, and death from nearly all causes relative to whites, with the two main exceptions of suicide and skin cancer. Latinx older adults enjoy lifespans that are longer than their white counterparts, a pattern referred to as the "Hispanic paradox" (Goldman 2016). Despite their longer lifespans, however, Hispanics are more likely than whites to have chronic diseases such as diabetes and hypertension (Odlum et al. 2020). Fewer studies focus on Asian and Native American older adults, although the data generally show that Asians fare as well as whites, whereas Native Americans are at a greater risk of nearly all health outcomes and have much lower life expectancy. Racial disparities were especially apparent during the COVID-19 pandemic., Black adults ages sixty-five to seventy-four were five times as likely as their white or Asian counterparts to die of the virus, whereas Latinx persons were four times as likely to succumb (Ford, Reber, and Reeves 2020; CDC 2021). Black-white health disparities narrow but persist for most health outcomes even after SES is controlled statistically; that means that even if Black and white older adults had the same levels of education, occupational status, or earnings, Blacks would still have a higher risk of illness and death than whites (Phelan and Link 2015).

A well-established explanation for the persistence of Black-white gaps, even when socioeconomic status is controlled statistically, is called Minorities' Diminished Return (MDR). This perspective shows that each year of education or dollar of income brings fewer health gains to Black Americans relative to their white counterparts (Assari 2018). This disheartening phenomenon is vividly illustrated in a classic study that compared older white physicians who graduated from Johns Hopkins University Medical School in the 1950s and 1960s, and Black physicians who graduated from

Meharry Medical College during the same era. When they reached their sixties and seventies, the Black physicians had double the rates of diabetes and hypertension relative to the white doctors (Thomas et al. 1997). Why did the Black doctors have poorer health than their white counterparts with the exact same degree and job? One plausible explanation is that upward social mobility may lead African Americans to largely white neighborhoods and workplaces, where they experience the strains of racism, tokenism, and discrimination. Efforts to overcome these obstacles, by working as hard as possible, may engender frustration and strain one's cardiovascular health (James 1994). Black adults' more modest health gains also reflect a long-standing history in the United States of systemic racism in education, employment, banking, housing, and health care, as well as other stressors associated with being a visible minority (Rothstein 2017; Williams, Lawrence, and Davis 2019).

Another well-documented yet surprising pattern is the "Hispanic paradox" or "Latino mortality advantage" (Goldman 2016). Recall that Hispanics live considerably longer than whites, despite their lower levels of education, income, and wealth, as well as less access to health-enhancing supports like health insurance and safe, white-collar jobs (Markides and Eschbach 2005). Given these economic disadvantages, why do Hispanics enjoy such long lives? Researchers point to three main factors. First, the people who migrate to the United States from Mexico, Central America, and South America may have better health than their counterparts who remain in or return to their home country. Migration can be a grueling process, so the strongest and healthiest are the ones who make the move and remain in the United States. Second, immigrants, and especially first-generation Hispanic immigrants, have healthier lifestyles than native-born Americans, including lower rates of smoking. Third, the social support one receives from their family and community upon arrival to the United States can help people to take good care of themselves and their children.

*Explaining Late-Life Health Disparities: Three Mechanisms*

Older adults can't swallow a pill or undergo a surgery that magically erases the long-term impacts of early nutritional deficits, poverty, systemic racism, subpar health care access, or living in a neighborhood with high levels of pollution and few grocery stores. That's why disparities persist despite older adults' near-universal access to health care through Medicare, the national health insurance program for US older adults.[13] While access to health care is critically important as older adults seek treatments and medication for chronic illnesses, it cannot undo the physical, mental, and cognitive health assaults that have accumulated over the life course. The next sections elaborate on three mechanisms—stress, health behaviors, and access to care—that contribute to later-life disparities in health and well-being.

STRESS EXPOSURE

Stress is any type of occurrence that causes physical, emotional, or psychological strain. It is a normal and expected part of life, no matter how old we are. College students preparing for final exams, lawyers preparing for a big trial, and first-time parents awaiting the arrival of their child lament that they're stressed out. Stress comes in several forms (Carr 2014). It may be an *acute event*, like the death of a loved one or a major surgery, or an ongoing and *chronic strain*, like a troubled marriage, working for an unreasonable boss, or walking nervously through an unsafe neighborhood every evening. Years of exposure to acute and chronic stressors can overwhelm one's cardiovascular, immune, and central nervous systems and bring about disease and premature death. Many ethnic minorities and others who have fewer socioeconomic resources have higher levels of stress exposure at every point in their lives, placing them at greater risk for health problems (Turner and Avison 2003).

Stress harms us by raising our levels of cortisol, also known as the "stress hormone." When we encounter a sudden stressor, such as a near-miss traffic accident, or hearing footsteps close behind us as we walk down a deserted street, our cortisol levels rise. Small increases in cortisol levels are protective in the short-term; they boost our memory and immune function and give us the adrenaline rush needed to escape from imminent danger. However, when we live under conditions of constant stress, such as persistent worries about paying for medications or caring for an ailing spouse, we have prolonged high levels of cortisol in the bloodstream. These elevated cortisol levels increase the risk of high blood pressure, weaker immune responses, slower healing from injuries or illness, and decreases in bone density and muscle tissue. High cortisol levels also increase our risk of abdominal adiposity (or belly fat), which is linked with health problems like heart attack and stroke (Carr 2014).

We all know someone who has experienced seemingly insurmountable stressors in life yet lives until a ripe old age. How is that possible? Just as people differ with respect to the number and types of stressors they face, they also differ with respect to the tools they have to cope with stress. These tools, called *coping resources*, may include the social support we receive, the material resources we can access, and our own traits and skills, such as creative problem solving and optimism. As we saw in chapter 3, social ties uphold our well-being. Family and friends can provide practical support, like rides to a doctor's appointment; material support, like help paying for a prescription medication; and emotional support, like love and comfort when one's spouse or partner dies. Our thought processes also affect how we cope. People with lower levels of education tend to feel a greater sense of hopelessness and fatalism, and they may resign themselves to a stressful and unhealthy situation rather than try to change it. For instance, older patients with low levels of education tend to view cancer as an inevitable death sentence and may reject early screening and treatment as exercises in futility (Freeman 1989). This acquiescence may be a realistic reaction to the obstacles they've encountered earlier in life, but it also prevents them from trying to fix or escape unhealthy situations (Taylor and Seeman 1999).

HEALTH BEHAVIORS

Health behaviors are another mechanism contributing to race and socioeconomic disparities in health, and gender differences in mortality risk. An influential article in the *New England Journal of Medicine* concluded that health behaviors account for as much as 40 percent of premature death (Schroeder 2007). Smoking, drinking, drug use, a sedentary lifestyle and a high-fat, high-salt diet increase the risk of conditions like lung cancer, cirrhosis of the liver, arthritis, dementia, obesity, diabetes and more. These behaviors also can trigger a vicious cycle, generating more stress and unhealthy behaviors. Heavy drinkers may lash out at family members, and their guilt drives them to drink even more to sooth their pain. While some mood-enhancing behaviors like drinking, smoking, and comfort foods calm one's nerves in the short-term, the long-term health consequences can be dire.

Health behaviors vary by socioeconomic status and race (Pampel, Krueger, and Denney 2010). For example, smoking rates are twice as high among older adults living beneath the federal poverty line versus those living at 200 percent or more of the poverty threshold (14 percent versus 7 percent). Obesity, a function of a high-calorie diet and sedentary lifestyle, is more common among Black versus white older adults, and those with fewer versus more socioeconomic resources (Ford et al. 2011). Older adults living in low-income neighborhoods cannot easily access healthy and affordable foods at their local grocery stores or farmers' markets. Access issues are compounded by the fact that fast food corporations, soda and snack food companies, cigarette manufacturers, and alcohol distributors explicitly target Blacks, inner-city, and low-income populations in their marketing campaigns (Cruz 2015). Older adults living in rundown or crowded neighborhoods also may lack safe places to walk and get basic exercise.

ACCESS TO CARE

Access to health care providers and the services and medications they offer is critical to maintaining good health. However, affordable high-quality health care is out of reach to many Americans, setting them on a course toward poor health in old age. Older adults' near-universal access to health care through Medicare may be "too little too late" for those with physical, neurocognitive, or mental health problems that emerged earlier in life. Late detection of health problems can be deadly. That's one reason why white and Black women are equally likely to be diagnosed with breast cancer, but Black women are more likely to die; they tend to be diagnosed at later stages, when their cancer is less amenable to life-saving treatments (Yedjou et al. 2019). Quality of care also matters. African American older adults are less likely than whites to have state-of-the-art health care facilities near their homes, and are more likely to receive care at crowded high-volume hospitals where quality of care may be compromised (Williams and Jackson 2005)

Health insurance is the main path to receiving both *preventative care* to ward off disease, and *curative care* to treat illness once it strikes. However, health insurance historically has been provided by employers in the United States, meaning that health benefits have been a privilege afforded to full-time workers, or those married to full-time workers. In 2010, shortly before the implementation of the Affordable Care Act (ACA), 70 percent of working-age Americans received health insurance through their employers. Those who are too young to work, too old to work, or out of work often rely on public insurance programs. Low-income adults are eligible to receive health insurance through Medicaid, older adults through Medicare, and children through state-based Children's Health Insurance Programs (CHIP) if their parents earn too much to qualify for Medicaid. Roughly one in five older adults who are Medicare beneficiaries have an income that is low enough to also qualify them for Medicaid, a status referred to as *dual eligible.*

Unfortunately, this piecemeal system left 18 percent of Americans under age sixty-five (46.5 million) uninsured in 2010, a fraction that dipped to 10 percent (26.7 million) by the end of 2015, thanks to the implementation of the ACA under President Barack Obama (Tolbert, Orgera, and Damico 2020). However, the proportion uninsured climbed back up to 10.9 percent (28.9 million) by 2019. Lower-income Americans, especially Black and Latinx families, are most likely to be uninsured because the costs of coverage are prohibitive, even under ACA. In 2019, just 7 to 8 percent of whites and Asians under age sixty-four were uninsured, compared to 11 percent of Blacks, 20 percent of Hispanics, and 22 percent of Native Americans (Tolbert et al. 2020).

Lack of health insurance is an important contributor to late-life health disparities, but even those who are insured are not guaranteed that they'll receive timely and high-quality medical care. Insurance does not necessarily mean access. Medicaid recipients may have difficulty finding a doctor who will take them as a patient; some doctors will not see them because the reimbursement received for treating Medicaid patients is roughly half that received from private insurance (Lopez et al. 2020). Reimbursement refers to the payment that a hospital, doctor, diagnostic facility, or other health care provider receives from insurance companies for providing care to a patient. While 90 percent of health care providers will accept a new patient with private insurance, just 71 percent will take a new Medicaid patient (Holgash and Heberlein 2019). Even when doctors do accept Medicaid patients, those patients may fall to the end of the queue, waiting longer to get appointments and referrals because private pay and employer-insured patients are considered higher priority. Sometimes a Medicaid recipient will find a provider who will take them on as a new patient, only to discover that they cannot easily travel to the far-away office or medical center. As a result, Medicaid patients who must travel long distances to their providers may receive delayed diagnoses and treatment for diseases like breast cancer (Carr 2019).

Physical distance isn't the only obstacle to care; social distance also matters. Some lower-income patients report feeling uneasy with doctors, worrying that they will be looked down upon or judged for being on Medicaid or seeking care at a Federally Qualified Health Center (FQHC) which serves low-income patients (Stuber et al. 2000). Black Americans have a history of mistrust toward the health care system, rooted in travesties like the Tuskegee trial, in which physicians allowed Black men to die from untreated syphilis, as part of a scientific study. This lingering distrust was cited as a reason why some Blacks were hesitant to receive the COVID-19 vaccine, contributing to their higher rates of illness and death (Bajaj and Stanford 2021).

Medicare also has limitations that prevent older adults from accessing care. Medicare recipients often are surprised to learn that some treatments and services they need are excluded under the standard benefits provided by Medicare Parts A and B. These two parts of Medicare, which are essentially "free" for eligible older adults, partially cover basics like inpatient care in a hospital or nursing home, hospice care, medical tests, surgery, and doctor's visits. However, other services that older adults need are provided by Parts C and D, each of which charges a monthly premium. Part C covers hearing aids and glasses, which are essential for older adults' functioning and social engagement. Part D, also known as Medicare's prescription drug coverage, helps pay for medications not covered under parts A or B. Even though the federal government pays 75 percent of medication costs for Part D, the patient is still left to pay premiums, copays, and deductibles. Medications prescribed to Alzheimer's patients can run from $200 to $400 per month, so partial coverage may put these drugs out of reach to older adults who lack a financial cushion.

Some older adults like super-centenarian Hester Ford have "good genes and good luck," healthy behaviors, and meaningful work and family ties that promote long and healthy lives. But how long one lives, the illnesses one suffers from, and the chances of surviving an illness once diagnosed, are stratified by socioeconomic status and race. Medicare is not sufficient to erase these persistent gaps, heightening the need for what sociologist James House (2015:xvii) calls "nonhealth policies . . . that shape the conditions of life and work, especially among the half or so of our population who live and work in disadvantaged conditions and whose health is consequently affected." Well-designed policies are key to enhancing the health and well-being of older adults, as chapter 5 shows.

# 5  Aging Policy Issues

DOMESTIC AND INTERNATIONAL PERSPECTIVES

"The silver tsunami is coming!" News headlines about population aging often have an ominous tone, likening the rapidly growing sixty-five-and-over population to natural disasters like a "silver tsunami" or "gray tidal wave." This apocalyptic imagery suggests that the rising number of older adults worldwide will overwhelm the economy, health care systems, family caregivers, and more, just as a giant ocean wave destroys everything in its path. But these sensationalist warnings perpetuate the ageist notion that older adults are a problem to be solved, rather than a resource that can strengthen families and societies. Older adults are workers, volunteers, caregivers, innovators, entrepreneurs, taxpayers, and keepers of family memories and traditions. Think about the three million older adults in the United States caring for their grandchildren. Or infectious disease expert Anthony Fauci, who at age eighty led the United States through the COVID-19 pandemic. Or eighty-two-year-old Dawn Harris-Martine, the owner of a Harlem bookstore who launched a bookmobile for low-income children in 2021. Or Betty White, who was a beloved comedian and TV actor up until her death at age ninety-nine, even hosting Saturday Night Live at age eighty-eight. The extent to which older adults contribute to society depends, in part, on the opportunities afforded them and social policies that protect their health, functioning, economic security, and social integration.

This chapter shows how social programs and policies can help the United States and other nations address the needs of rapidly aging populations. It begins with a global snapshot of population aging, to place the United States in an international context. I then describe three types of social policies that are critical to aging societies: *economic policies* like public pensions, *health care policies* like publicly funded health insurance, and *family and caregiver policies*, like family caregiver supports or programs to attract and retain paid caregivers. Current US policies have well-known limitations; millions of older adults (especially women) still live in poverty, despite near-universal Social Security coverage, and stubborn race and socioeconomic disparities in health and longevity persist, despite near-universal Medicare coverage. Innovative social programs from other nations provide models for how the United States might meet the needs of older adults and their families (Reinhardt 2019). The chapter concludes by underscoring the enormous benefits of public investments in older adults—investments that can improve the quality of life for all members of society.

## GLOBAL POPULATION AGING: A STATISTICAL SNAPSHOT

The United States is a graying society, yet nearly all nations—especially in Asia and Europe—are aging even more rapidly, due to declining fertility and mortality rates throughout the late twentieth and early twenty-first centuries. In 2020, roughly 727 million people worldwide were ages sixty-five and older, and this number is projected to more than double by 2050, topping 1.5 billion. While 9 percent of the global population was over age sixty-five in 2020, that share will jump to over 16 percent in 2050. This means that one out of every six people on the planet will be an older adult in the year 2050 (United Nations 2020). Most will be women, consistent with the US trend described as the *feminization of old age*. On a global scale, women account for 55 percent of those ages sixty-five and older and 62 percent of those ages eighty and older, owing to their life expectancy advantage. As a result of population aging, nearly every nation in the world must wrestle with the question: how do we support and celebrate our oldest members?

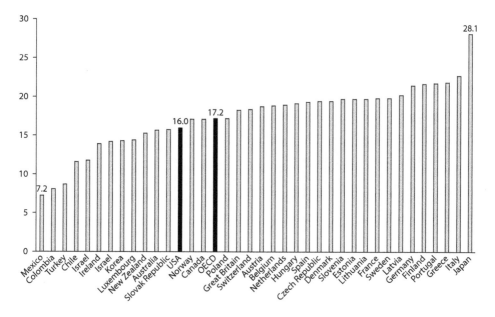

*Figure 31.* Percentage of population ages sixty-five and over for selected OECD nations, 2018. SOURCE: Organisation for Economic Co-operation and Development (OECD) (2021a).

Finding answers to this question is most urgent in the world's oldest nations. Figure 31 shows the proportion age sixty-five and older in more than three dozen nations (Organisation for Economic Co-operation and Development [OECD] 2021a). These proportions range from under 10 percent for countries in Latin America (e.g., Mexico, Colombia), to 28 percent in Japan. Most nations in North America and Europe range between 15 and 20 percent. Several southern European countries, most notably Italy, Greece, and Portugal, are even higher, with more than one-fifth of their residents over age sixty-five. By 2050, this fraction is expected to top one-third. Japan leads the world in population aging; by the year 2050, a remarkable 39 percent of its residents will be older adults, and other Asian nations will experience comparable patterns.

Another way of capturing global population aging is with an old-age dependency ratio, a concept presented in the introduction.[1] This refers to the number of people ages sixty-five and older relative to the number of working-age persons ages twenty-five to sixty-four (or vice versa),

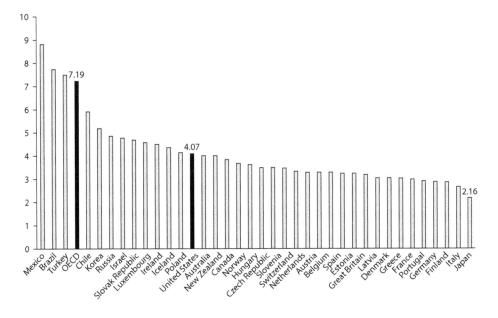

*Figure 32.* Ratio of persons ages twenty-five to sixty-four relative to persons ages sixty-five and over, for selected OECD nations, 2015. SOURCE: OECD (2017).

as shown in figure 32. In 2015, OECD nations had an average of about 3.6 working-age persons per every person aged sixty-five or older. This ratio is expected to drop to 1.87 by the year 2050. The comparable decline in the United States is from 4.1 (in 2015) to 2.48 (2050). In Japan, the most extreme case, the ratio is projected to dip from 2.2 in 2015 to just 1.3 in 2050. Other nations in Asia and southern Europe are projected to reach levels nearly as low as Japan's by 2050. Dependency ratios are important markers for policy makers because they provide an indirect (albeit imperfect) indicator of the potential support available for older adults. The most pressing policy challenges for the twenty-first century are ensuring adequate financial support for older adults' public pensions and health care, and addressing the dire shortage of both family and paid caregivers. Solutions are predicated, in part, on the availability of working-age persons, whether as direct caregivers or as taxpayers contributing to the public safety net.

PUBLIC POLICIES

*Economic Security*

Poverty among older adults—especially older women—is a global concern. As older adults' health worsens, their capacity to work for pay diminishes. In low-income nations where manual labor and farming jobs can outnumber desk jobs, employment is not an option for physically frail older adults. Household income drops upon a person's own or a spouse's retirement, yet the need for costly health care and medications increases, causing some older adults to use up all or most of their savings. Some nations, most notably in Scandinavia, provide income security through generous social programs, yet these nations are the clear minority. As the number of older adults increases worldwide, the number who are poor will increase as well, unless innovative income support programs are implemented. Yet old age poverty is not inevitable. Just 3 percent of older adults in Denmark, Iceland, and the Netherlands live in poverty, demonstrating that well-designed programs can have dramatic positive effects.

Poverty rates for OECD nations are presented in figure 33. OECD rates are calculated differently from the US poverty statistics presented earlier in the book. The OECD rates refer to the proportion of persons over age sixty-five whose income is less than half the median household income for the total population. According to this metric, 23 percent of US older adults live in poverty, which is roughly the midpoint between the single-digit rates in most northern European nations and the astonishing 43 percent statistic for South Korea. South Korea is an interesting anomaly; it is a quite wealthy nation, and its cultural values emphasize *filial piety*—a devotion to one's parents and grandparents. However, its old-age pension program offers meager benefits that have not kept pace with inflation over the past two decades (Jun 2020). As a result, many older Koreans now must work in menial jobs like street cleaners or live with their kin.[2]

It is difficult to calculate poverty rates in low-income nations because data are not readily available; however, the United Nations estimates that rates are as high as 80 percent in Sub-Saharan African nations like Namibia. The main reason for high old-age poverty is the lack of government-funded (public) or worker and employer-funded (private) pensions, leaving older adults dependent on their families—who also may be at risk of poverty and

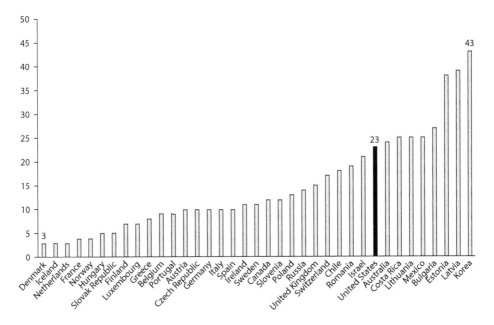

*Figure 33.* Poverty rate, persons ages sixty-five and over, for selected OECD nations, 2018. SOURCE: OECD (2021c).

thus unable to support their aged relatives. Lower-income nations provide either no or inadequate publicly funded income security for older adults. Workers in low-income nations often hold jobs in the informal economy, such as farming, and do not receive a private pension. While more than 90 percent of older adults in North America receive either a public or private pension, just 17 percent in sub-Saharan Africa, 30 percent in the Middle East, 37 percent in North Africa, 47 percent in Asia, and 56 percent in Latin America have a pension (United Nations 2016).

While the United States fares relatively well on a global scale, its overall poverty rate conceals vast disparities. Older women, and especially Black and Hispanic women, and those with low levels of education, poor-quality jobs, and poor health are at a high risk of old-age poverty. Many of the reasons for these disparities were described in chapter 2, which showed that the three legs of the retirement income stool (i.e., Social Security, private pensions, savings, and interest income) were less secure for women, Blacks, Hispanics, and those from economically disadvantaged backgrounds. That's part of the reason why roughly five million US older adults live in poverty, despite receiving monthly Social Security payments. For those with sparse savings, no employer-provided pension, and little if any interest from investments, the modest benefits of Social Security are not sufficient to cover their living expenses.

A further reason why Social Security is not sufficient to eradicate poverty, especially among women, is that the program design is based on an outdated notion of families and gender roles. Benefits rules advantage couples who maintained a traditional homemaker/breadwinner marriage, and those whose marriages ended by widowhood rather than divorce. By contrast, those in dual-earner households and divorced persons are disadvantaged. For instance, a widow is entitled to 100 percent of her late spouse's benefits (i.e., survivor benefits) if the couple was married for at least nine months, whereas a divorced person is entitled to just half of her former spouse's benefit—and only if the couple was married for ten or more years. Given rising rates of divorce over the past six decades, and the rise in women's participation in the labor force, the structure of Social Security benefits will need to change to reflect the reality of US families in the twenty-first century (Carr 2020). Change is possible, however, and the Social Security Administration can revise their policies to reflect contemporary family lives. For instance, in late 2021, the Social Security Administration revised their policies to ensure that older adult same-sex couples could receive survivor benefits upon one partner's death, even if they were not married. This change recognized that long-time companions in same-sex unions did not have the right to legally marry in all fifty states until 2015 (Bernard 2021).

Policy makers in the United States continue to debate whether and how to best provide income security for older adults. The Netherlands offers an effective model; its public pension program is consistently rated as one of the best in the world, lifting nearly all older adults out of poverty (Jensen et al. 2020). The workings of any public pension plan are complex, but experts point to one main factor that distinguishes the stellar Dutch program from the United States. In the Netherlands, people are required to save for their pension, as soon as they are employed, whereas in the United States, it is a "choice" to do so. However, choices are constrained by structural obstacles. Many US workers cannot afford to contribute a fraction of every paycheck to their pension, or they are reluctant to bear the risk of contributing to a pension that may have an uncertain future.

In the Netherlands, most workers have a defined-benefit (DB) pension plan, whereas US workers tend to participate in defined-contribution (DC) plans. Recall from chapter 2 that DB plans are generally a safer investment for workers. They are funded by employers and employees, and provide retirees with lifetime annuities based on how long they've been with their employer and their salary. DC plans, by contrast, are tax-deferred savings accounts like 401K plans that provide tax and savings incentives to both employers and employees to set aside money for retirement.[3] The payout to retirees is determined by the amount of money contributed to the plan and the rate of return on the money invested over time. The future value of DC accounts, like savings accounts, depends both on fluctuations of the market and the worker's skill in investing their funds wisely. A bad investment decision can wipe out a worker's future retirement income. Moreover, lower-income workers with immediate financial concerns may not have the cushion needed to contribute generously to their pension (US Government Accountability Office 2016).

Economists have proposed that employers could automatically enroll workers in retirement plans rather than have workers "opt in." Employers also could provide a savings credit, or the government could provide a federal match for retirement savings accounts to help lower-income adults amass a nest egg for their retirements (Haas Institute 2016). Some policy experts have proposed boosting older adults' monthly income by raising Social Security benefits for low-income Americans. This program, referred to as a minimum benefit plan (MBP), would provide older adults with a monthly benefit guaranteed at 100 percent of the poverty line. The details of the program are complex, but the upshot is that by focusing on the neediest older adults, disparities in late-life economic security could be addressed (Herd et al. 2018). There are no easy or perfect solutions, and debates over how to provide for the large cohort of Baby Boomers will continue to vex policy makers and taxpayers alike.

*Health Care*

The COVID-19 pandemic took a devastating toll on health worldwide, with older adults dying from the virus at higher rates than any other age group. Most nations saw their life expectancy worsen between 2019 and 2021, yet the United States had a much steeper dip than its peer nations (Woolf et al. 2021). This isn't the first time the United States has lagged behind other nations in terms of longevity. A 2017 study in the prominent journal *The Lancet* showed that Asian nations topped the list of thirty-five countries, with Korea boasting life expectancies of ninety-one and eighty-four for women and men, respectively. The United States, by contrast, was mired in the bottom tier alongside less wealthy Eastern European nations like Poland and the Czech Republic (Kontis et al. 2017). Data from OECD nations in 2018 show similar patterns, with the United States lagging behind most wealthy nations in Europe and Asia. As figure 34 shows, the East Asian nations of Japan and Korea, and western and southern European nations of Spain, France, Switzerland, and Italy have among the highest life expectancies in the world, while the United States fares about the same as lower-income nations like Brazil and Poland.

The United States also lags behind its peers in Asia, Australia, Canada, Europe, and New Zealand on other health indicators. A recent international survey found that US older adults were most likely to have three or more chronic health conditions (36 percent) and to report problems getting health care due to cost (23 percent). Fewer than 20 percent of older adults in New Zealand, Switzerland, Norway, the Netherlands, and other wealthy nations reported multiple chronic conditions, and in most European nations fewer than 10 percent (and just 3 percent in Sweden) said that they couldn't afford health care. Older adults in the United States also were most likely to say that they couldn't afford nutritious meals, had not filled a prescription, stopped taking required medications, or skipped a doctor's visit because they couldn't afford it. Roughly one-quarter of all US older adults said they had made a health sacrifice due to cost, compared to fewer than 5 percent in France, Norway, Sweden, and the United Kingdom (Osborn et al. 2017).

How is it possible that the United States, widely regarded as the world's richest and most powerful nation, lags behind more than a dozen high-income nations with respect to older adults' health and longevity?[4] The answers are complex, yet experts point to several explanations (Reinhardt 2019). First, the United States has relatively low government spending on social services like education, housing, nutrition, and anti-poverty programs—all factors contributing to poor health and premature mortality, as

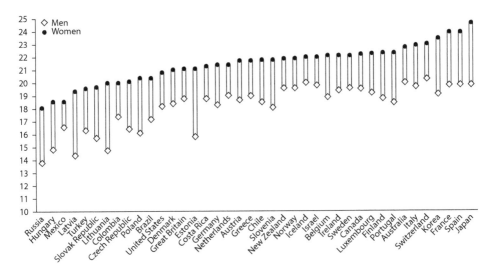

*Figure 34.* Life expectancy at age sixty-five by sex for selected OECD nations, 2018.
SOURCE: OECD (2021b).

we saw in chapter 4. Second, sweeping societal problems like gun violence, homicide, opioid addiction, and obesity are more common in the United States than in its peer nations, and contribute to the premature deaths of Americans, especially among economically disadvantaged populations. Third, the United States lacks a universal health care system, leaving millions of working-age adults without access to affordable care, setting the stage for late-life health problems and premature mortality. Although low-income Americans receive health insurance through Medicaid, many struggle to find health care providers who will accept their insurance. Federally qualified health centers (FQHCs) often have long waits for appointments. Some lower-middle-class families fall through the cracks, earning too much to qualify for Medicaid yet unable to afford insurance premiums even though the Affordable Care Act has made health care more accessible to all (Kontis et al. 2017).

Health policy experts praise Taiwan's single-payer health care system as one of the most effective in the world and a potential model for the United States (Reinhardt 2019). A *single-payer system* refers to a government-run national health insurance plan that covers everyone. In Taiwan, everyone is insured through the National Health Insurance Administration (NHIA) and receives an ID card as proof of coverage. Patients can insert their card into a chip reader, and their medical record will be pulled up. Although the system does not cover every possible condition or treatment, it does cover the main types of care that most people need: hospital care, primary care, prescription drugs, and traditional Chinese medicine. Co-pays are required when patients go to the emergency room, see their doctor, or fill a prescription, but the amounts paid out-of-pocket are generally low (the equivalent of ten to fifteen dollars). The system also recognizes disparities; lower-income patients can get a break on payment, while wealthier patients can take out additional private insurance to pay for those services not covered by NHIA. The system is funded primarily by contributions from workers and their employers, publicly generated revenues from income taxes, and tobacco and lottery surcharges (Cheng 2020).

The Taiwanese system resembles the proposed "Medicare for All" plans that some progressive Democrats support. Although there may not be political will for a publicly funded plan to give health care coverage to all US adults, support is emerging for policies that would lower the age at which Americans can buy into Medicare at a reasonable cost, with most proposals setting the age at fifty or fifty-five (Marans 2017). The enactment of such plans could be life altering for the 75 percent of US adults ages fifty-five to sixty-four with at least one chronic health condition, or the millions of pre-retirement-age adults suffering from depression, anxiety, or substance use (Federal Interagency Forum on Aging-Related Statistics 2020). It would also lessen their financial burden. Adults ages fifty-five to sixty-four pay an average of $1,500 each year on out-of-pocket medical expenditures, along with insurance premiums that are roughly three times higher than those for younger adults (Health Care Cost Institute 2020).

Other proposals under consideration, including some under President Biden's American Rescue Plan, would focus on making health care more comprehensive and affordable for Medicare recipients. Proposals include issuing a cap on out-of-pocket expenses and negotiating lower prescription drug prices. Although these policy changes would not have a major impact on national life expectancy, they would help older adults to save money on their medication costs—all promising avenues for incremental increases in older adults' well-being.

Yet many scholars, activists, and policy makers believe that publicly funded health insurance is just one small step toward improving population health and longevity (House 2015). As chapter 4 showed, lack of access to health care only accounts for 10 percent of premature mortality in the United States, whereas social, behavioral, and environmental factors account for 60 percent (Schroeder 2007). Consequently, public investments should target the social determinants that place Black, Hispanic, and economically disadvantaged persons at greater risk of health problems at every age. This solution would require generous investments in early education, housing, nutrition, air quality, criminal justice reform, and other factors that undermine the well-being of low-income and minoritized communities. Some experts have called for Medicare and Medicaid benefits that cover things like air conditioners for people with asthma, home-delivered meals for those who are immunocompromised, and investments in co-housing or other creative housing approaches for socially isolated persons with depression (Fulmer et al. 2021). The goal of such programs is not only to extend life, but also to ensure a higher quality of life.

*Family and Caregiver Policies*

Who will care for older adults when they become too ill, frail, or mentally unable to care for themselves? The challenges of direct caregiving are immense for societies with a high proportion of oldest-old adults, persons with dementia, and those with multiple health conditions who may require intensive or round-the-clock care. Older adults who reside with family members often are the best situated, as they live with people who can look after them and provide basic assistance. Living arrangements vary widely throughout the globe, such that older adults in nations with a "collectivist" orientation that emphasizes family and community are most likely to co-reside, whereas those in more individualistic nations like the United States are more likely to live alone (Pike and Bengtson 1996).

While cultural values like filial piety partly guide living arrangements, economic factors also are a driving force. In the wealthy nations of North America and Europe, people tend to have fewer children with whom they might live. Government-supported pensions, housing subsidies, and health care benefits make it more affordable for older adults to live on their own, should they choose to do so. In lower-income countries, by contrast, multigenerational families may live together so that they can pool their financial resources and share household and caregiving tasks (United Nations 2020). Low-income countries, as we saw earlier, provide few or no governmental benefits to older adults. Opportunities for paid work also may be scarce, so older adults must rely on their families to provide a safety net. Older adults living in wealthier countries also tend to have better health and few functional limitations. As a result, they are more likely to live alone or with a spouse, as they are capable of maintaining a household on their own.

Figure 35 shows living arrangements of older men and women in 2019, by region. Worldwide, living with extended family (dark gray segment of bar) is the most common arrangement for people ages sixty and older, with nearly 40 percent living in this household type, and another 10 percent (dotted segment) living with an adult child. Living with one's spouse or partner (white segment) is the second most common experience (31%), followed by living alone (16%, black segment). However, there is wide variation in each of these patterns. Women in Europe and North America have higher than average rates of living alone, whereas men in these regions are more likely to live with a spouse. Older adults in sub-Saharan Africa and Asia, especially women, are most likely to live with extended family or an adult child (Pew 2019).

Living arrangements vary widely by region, yet nearly every nation in the world shares one commonality when it comes to elder care: family members shoulder the lion's share of responsibility. Unpaid family members serve as an unsung army of direct care providers. Time-intensive caregiving can overwhelm caregivers' physical and mental health. This work also takes a financial toll. Especially in places like the United States, with few public supports for caregivers, working-age family caregivers (especially women) cut back on paid work and see their earnings and pensions diminish in the process. The AARP (2020) estimates average income losses of five thousand dollars annually in the United States, with women especially vulnerable to these losses. Caregivers also bear direct costs, like paying for home modifications (e.g., putting a ramp in an aged parent's house), food, cleaning supplies, toiletries, and other purchases for the care recipient. Even small expenses can add up, like the gas, tolls, and parking fees for

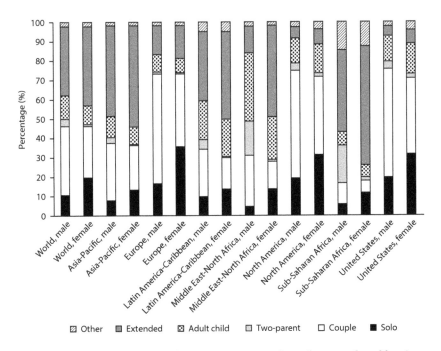

*Figure 35.* Living arrangements of persons ages sixty and over by sex and world region, 2019. SOURCE: Pew Research Center (2019).

driving an aged relative to their medical appointments. That's why an estimated 25 percent of family caregivers in the United States take out loans or credit card debt to meet their caregiving roles, with 10 percent reporting that they're unable to meet their own monthly expenses (AARP 2020).

Recognizing the struggles of family caregivers, in 2021 the Biden administration unveiled new programs to help support caregivers and older adults living on their own who require assistance. As part of the American Rescue Plan for Older Americans Acts, funding was dedicated to the National Family Caregiver Support Program, which helps family and informal caregivers pay for in-home supports such as respite care and training. Funding for home-delivered or "grab and go" meals give family caregivers a break from meal preparation, while increased support for Home and Community-Based Services (HCBS) provides funds to help older adults with household chores, shopping, transportation, and other services that would otherwise fall to family members. Some state governments, primarily in "blue" Democrat-led states, also provide supports. California, Massachusetts, New Jersey, New York, Rhode Island, and Washington, as well as the District of Columbia, offer paid family-leave public insurance programs that enable workers to receive a fraction of their regular pay while on leave to care for family members (AARP 2019).

Community-based programs like the Village movement also provide support to older adults living on their own in the community. This membership-based initiative launched in 2002, with the goal of "neighbors helping neighbors." Older adults pay dues and also volunteer—offering rides, computer training, home repairs, meal preparation, gardening, and grocery shopping to other members. The modest dues, usually five hundred to a thousand dollars per year, also help to pay staff members who coordinate services through platforms like a website and "concierge" hotline. One of the best parts of the model is the social events and social support that help older adults to stay connected and engaged. More than three hundred Village programs now exist throughout the United States, mostly in urban and suburban neighborhoods. Participation in the Villages program improves older adults' quality of life, strengthens their social ties, and increases their self-confidence (Graham, Scharlach, and Kurtovich 2018). These supports were especially important during the peak of the COVID-19 pandemic, with most Village sites providing virtual classes, social events, and more for their members (Galucia et al. 2021).

Older adults without family, who can't access Village services, or whose care needs are too complex for family caregivers may require paid assistants. Yet paid caregivers are in dangerously short supply, a crisis that was exacerbated by COVID-19. The pandemic left many care workers exhausted, demoralized, and anxious to find other work. In 2020, about 4.6 million Americans were employed as direct care workers, including home health aides, nursing assistants, and personal care workers. According to the Bureau of Labor Statistics (2021), home health aides and personal care workers top the list of occupations expected to grow over the next decade, with more than 1 million new job openings projected by 2029. Yet this statistic is a dramatic *underestimate*, as it counts only those caregivers hired by companies; if the estimate also includes caregivers hired directly by families and patients, more than 7 million workers are needed by 2026 (Paraprofessional Healthcare Institute 2021). Despite this desperate need for care workers in the United States, the pay is dismal—just $27,000 per year or about $13.50 per hour. Immigrant and ethnic minority women make up the majority of care workers, and about 15 percent live in poverty. It's hard to entice new employees to a job that is exhausting, stressful, sometimes physically dangerous, low-paying, and lacking pathways to advancement or upward mobility (Osterman 2017).

How can this crisis be managed? Increasing paid caregiver wages, while ideal, isn't realistic. Middle- and working-class families who pay caregivers directly can't afford higher wages. Home health agencies cover roughly three-quarters of their workers' wages through Medicaid and Medicare, which already face daunting financial constraints. Potential enticements might include providing training and opportunities for advancement as "universal workers," or direct care professionals who learn skill sets that give them flexibility to work in different care sites (home health, nursing homes, etc.). Other possible solutions include recruiting experienced family caregivers into paid caregiver jobs or encouraging retired health care providers to volunteer or work part-time as direct care providers. Experts also propose changing immigration policy to welcome more paid caregivers to the United States. Expanding guest worker programs and making more visas available for elder caregivers—just as cultural exchange visas are available to au pairs who care for children under age eighteen—can help expand the pipeline of paid caregivers (Stone and Bryant 2021).

The United States may require other novel solutions, enlisting everyday citizens to help meet the care needs of ever-rising numbers of older adults. Japan, the world's oldest nation, has been a pioneer in developing community-based programs to help care for older adults, especially their growing ranks of dementia patients. In 2015, Japan implemented its National Campaign of Dementia Supporter Caravan, a "total community" approach that enlists everyday citizens to help support dementia patients and their caregivers. Volunteers attend a ninety-minute informational and training session and then receive a bright orange bracelet or bib that signifies they're a member of a neighborhood patrol. They walk around neighborhoods, check in on those in need of home visits, distribute flyers describing dementia support services, and help dementia patients who might have wandered off from their homes. As of 2019, an astounding ten million Japanese had completed the training. These street patrol volunteers are not a substitute for trained nursing personnel, and some dementia patients are uncomfortable with the volunteers, yet they meet a critical and escalating need (Aihara and Maeda 2021).

One of the most intriguing innovations for addressing the caregiver shortage is the use of robots. Although the word *robot* conjures up images like Pixar's WALL-E, in reality, these robots resemble more ordinary (and less futuristic) devices, like the Roomba vacuum cleaner or voice-activated assistants like Siri and Alexa. Japan has led the way in the use of robots for elder care, with the government investing in the development of inventions like an electric-boosted mobility aid that an older adult can grasp onto when walking. Other innovations include a "butler robot" that can fold laundry and wash dishes. Some nursing homes are relying on humanoid robots like "Pepper," which can play games, sing, and communicate with older adults, retaining important information like their names and other biographical details (Lufkin 2020). These innovations are not a perfect substitute for personal care from a trusted human caregiver, yet they do fill critical gaps and are increasingly embraced by older adults in Japan.

Americans have been reluctant to embrace robots, although the pandemic has heightened the recognition that technology can be an important lifeline, especially for homebound people. A 2017 survey found that while 70 percent of adults believe that robot caregivers would ease the burden of elder care, just 40 percent say they would ever consider using them. However, during the COVID pandemic, long-term care facilities throughout the United States increased their reliance on robots, while some local departments of elderly affairs distributed robotic pets to homebound older adults, who felt less alone as they cuddled their new electronic (yet surprisingly lifelike) cats and dogs (Samuel 2020). Despite this potential, high-tech innovations and robots—like other scientific advances—might be out of reach to economically disadvantaged older adults (Link and Phelan 1995).

## OLDER ADULTS AS A GLOBAL RESOURCE

Population aging is driving nations to devise inventive strategies for providing income security, health care, and caregiving supports to older adults and their families. Public expenditures on "old age" programs are not a zero-sum game; money invested in older adults can help *all* members of society. Older adults who are financially secure; in good physical, emotional, and cognitive health; and socially integrated are a valuable resource who can share their knowledge, wisdom, and skills with younger generations. The most high-profile example is The Elders (2021), a powerful coalition of older adults who are working together to advance global peace and human rights. Formed by an eighty-nine-year-old Nelson Mandela in 2007, its 2021 leadership council includes seventy-seven-year-old Mary Robinson, the first woman president of Ireland; seventy-seven-year-old Ban Ki-Moon, the former UN secretary-general and South Korean foreign minister; and eighty-two-year-old Ellen Johnson-Sirleaf, a Nobel Peace laureate, former president of Liberia, and Africa's first women to be elected head of state. When Mandela established the Elders, he explicitly recognized what a team of older adults with "almost 1,000 years of collective experience" could bring to the table, working on persistent global challenges including climate change, HIV/AIDS, global poverty, and war.

World peace is a lofty goal for anyone to achieve, regardless of age. But older adults of all backgrounds are capable of giving back to their communities on a smaller scale, provided they are given the opportunities and supports to do so. For instance, in the United States, federally funded volunteer programs like AmeriCorps place older volunteers in public schools and other community settings. More than two thousand older volunteers in more than twenty cities participate in the AARP Foundation Experience Corps, a tutoring program serving more than thirty thousand children in struggling elementary schools. Volunteers put in an average of six to fifteen hours per week, and their efforts pay off; program assessments find a 60 percent improvement in their young pupils' critical literacy skills. During the COVID-19 pandemic, the AARP Experience Corps pivoted, and trained its older volunteers to serve as virtual tutors to low-income children doing distance learning in their homes (AARP 2020). Many programs, most notably AmeriCorps provide small cash stipends to lower-income volunteers, recognizing that these small incentives may go a long way to keeping older adults socially engaged.

Older adults are one of the United States' (and the world's) most valuable yet unsung resources. A pre-pandemic federal study documented that more than twenty-one million US adults ages fifty-five and older contributed more than three billion hours of service to their communities in 2015 (Corporation for National Community and Service 2016). The study valued these contributions at seventy-seven billion dollars per year. Older volunteers perform many different tasks, based on their interests and skills, such as collecting and distributing food donations for local food drives, fundraising for or providing professional and managerial assistance to nonprofits, or visiting with lonely homebound seniors, whether virtually or face-to-face. Older adults of all backgrounds can give back to their community, to the extent their time, energy, and physical health allow, and in the process, they are helping younger generations to achieve their potential.

# Conclusion

This book opened with the question: what will your life look like at age seventy-five? When answering that question, you might have thought about your genes or family history, or you may have considered your health habits, such as your diet and exercise routines. The social and economic advantages you've had, like the chance to attend college, or the benefits you might enjoy in the future, such as a supportive romantic partner, a good job with health insurance, and enough money to buy a home in a safe neighborhood, also matter. As you have learned throughout this book, our health, financial security, personal relationships, and quality of life in old age are a product of the cumulative advantages and disadvantages we've experienced. Gender, race, ethnicity, and socioeconomic status also shape the opportunities (or obstacles) we face, the stressful situations we encounter, and the structural and personal resources we draw on to manage or overcome those stressors.

Historical forces also matter. As C. Wright Mills famously observed in *The Sociological Imagination* (1959), human lives reflect our own personal biography and the historical contexts we inhabit. Older adults in the year 2050 will differ from today's older adults in many ways, most notably their ethnic and racial diversity. More than half of all Americans under age eighteen are now Black, Hispanic, Asian, or Native American, according to the

2020 Census, meaning that in another five to six decades, whites will account for a minority of older adults (Frey 2021). Social, cultural, economic, and political shifts also will transform how old age is experienced by the tail end of the Baby Boom cohort now approaching their retirement years, and the Generation X, Millennial, and Generation Z cohorts that follow. It's easy to imagine that long-term care facilities in 2050 will pipe in music by Nirvana and Beyonce, rather than Frank Sinatra and The Andrews Sisters, and that Minecraft will replace Yahtzee in the public game room. As we envision what old age might look like in the future, we have many reasons for optimism. People growing up in the 1960s and later have attained higher levels of education than the generations before them. They have benefited from modern medical and pharmaceutical breakthroughs and have breathed in fresher air and less pollution thanks to the Clean Air Act of 1970 (Thompson 2020). Each generation also is more tech-savvy— using the latest app or website for practical information, advice, and social networks to help manage life's challenges (Pruchno 2019). Generations growing up in the years since the Civil Rights, feminist, and LGBTQ pride movements have legal rights and opportunities that were unimaginable in earlier decades (although the dream of full equality is yet to be realized).

Yet other indications point to a less rosy and more bifurcated future, with successive cohorts witnessing an ever-widening gap between the haves and have nots. Future older adults who are fortunate enough to occupy the very top rung of the economic ladder might enjoy concierge medical care, luxury housing, and a team of home health aides and high-tech robots who provide daily care. Those on the lower rungs may be especially vulnerable to physical health problems, poverty, and social isolation. Technological innovations and public investments in education and health care may disproportionately benefit those who can best access and exploit these breakthroughs, further widening the chasm between those whose later years are "golden" and those living with financial precarity (Link and Phelan 1995).

## PREDICTING THE FUTURE

Predicting the future is a risky enterprise, as unforeseen events like a pandemic, war, or baby boom can alter the course of history. With this caveat, three contemporary phenomena may have an especially powerful impact on how today's young and midlife adults might experience old age: (1) rising economic inequality; (2) climate change; and (3) threats posed by obesity, opioid addiction, and COVID-19. While these sweeping influences will touch the lives of almost everyone, the most economically vulnerable will be at greatest risk.

## Rising Economic Inequality

Rising economic inequality refers to a widening gap between the income and wealth levels of the most elite, typically those in the top 1 or 5 percent, versus everyone else. Since the late 1960s the average household income of the richest 5 percent of Americans has increased, with an especially steep climb since the 1980s. At the same time, middle- and low-income households have seen modest or no income growth, as shown in figure 36. Put simply, the rich are getting richer while everyone else is stagnating. Other wealthy nations like Canada, France, Germany, and Japan also have seen rising income inequality over the last five decades, yet nowhere has this trend been as dramatic as the United States (Piketty 2014). The soaring fortunes of the wealthy and dwindling fortunes of the middle and working classes are a result of social and economic trends like globalization, disappearing manufacturing jobs, and the decline of labor unions. However, most experts attribute rising inequality to economic and tax policies dating back to the 1980s Reagan era that favor the rich. Cuts to corporate, capital gains, estate, and gift taxes have reduced jobs, lowered wages, and weakened the national safety net (Piketty 2014). Economic inequality puts goods and services like medications, groceries, housing, and home health aides out of reach for older adults with modest incomes, as their wealthier peers drive up demands and costs (Piketty 2014). Social inequalities also fuel demoralization, political apathy, resentment, diminishing social cohesion and trust, and widening health disparities (Wilkinson and Pickett 2009).

Inequality can undermine one's chances for upward economic mobility, or doing better financially than one's parents. Economist Alan Krueger (2015) calls this the "Great Gatsby effect," such that people are less likely to be upwardly mobile if they grow up in eras when income inequality is high. That's why birth cohorts who grew up in the 1980s and later, like the

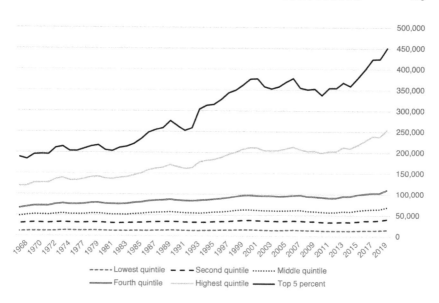

*Figure 36.* Mean household income by income quintile, 1967–2019. NOTE: Values reported are 2019 dollars. Categories refer to the income limits for each quintile and the top 5 percent of US households. SOURCE: US Census Bureau (2019b).

Millennials, may have divergent destinies, based on their socioeconomic background. Many Millennials entered college during the 2000s when tuition prices were ballooning (Center on Budget and Policy Priorities 2019).[1] Students from wealthy families could rely on their parents to pay their tuition and provide the social connections needed to secure desirable summer internships and lucrative jobs after graduation. Middle- and lower-income students, by contrast, worked part-time jobs to help cover their ever-rising tuition. After graduation, many felt they needed graduate degrees to secure a good job with benefits, given a competitive labor market. At the same time, demand for housing spiked in the desirable cities where Millennials were seeking work. Those from modest backgrounds took out school loans and mortgages, and they are now strapped with record levels of debt and relatively little in savings (Cramer et al. 2019). However, many received relief from Biden's 2022 student loan forgiveness program.

Historical bad luck also has created challenges for Millennials. Those who graduated college during the economic downturn of 2007–9 found slim job prospects, with unprecedented numbers working in the gig economy—taking temporary or freelance jobs that do not provide benefits or pensions. That's part of the reason why Millennials are delaying marriage and childbearing until they feel financially secure. Demographers predict that rising numbers may forsake marriage and children all together (Brown 2017). Some who choose to be single and childfree have happy and fulfilling lives, yet others may find they lack an important source of caregiving and support as they approach old age.

For these reasons, the retirement years are looking bleak for many of today's young and midlife adults. According to a 2020 survey of more than one thousand adults, each generation is more pessimistic than their predecessors about their economic security after retirement (Doonan and Kenneally 2021). An astounding 78 percent of Millennials anticipate that they will need to work past their "normal" retirement age in order to have enough money for retirement, compared to just over half of Gen Xers and Baby Boomers, and one-third of Silent Generation members. Nearly three-quarters of Millennials and 60 percent of Gen Xers say they're concerned that they "won't have a financially secure retirement," compared to just 43 percent of Boomers. While the ultra-rich one-percenters may be spared these concerns, the majority of Millennials and Gen Xers may have to work into their seventies and beyond. It is unclear whether the economic fallout of the COVID-19 pandemic will diminish or boost the long-term financial security of today's young and midlife adults. The 2021 economic crisis, ironically, opened up promising career doors for young people like twenty-five-year-old Mark Wray. Wray lost his job at a movie theater but entered a training program that led to a position as an online mortgage lender—tripling his earnings along the way. Major employers, desperate for workers, are starting to increase wages, offer training programs and tuition benefits, and provide pensions and health insurance—a trend that may bode well as these now-young workers reach old age (Lohr 2021).

*Climate Change*

Greta Thunberg is an outspoken environmental activist and one of the most influential members of Generation Z. As a teenager in 2019, she raised worldwide awareness of the perils of climate change, especially for

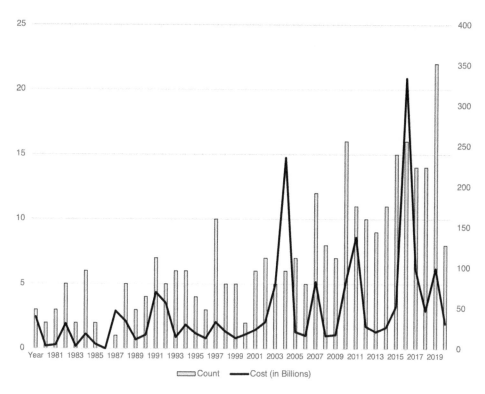

*Figure 37.* Total number and annual cost (in billions) of billion-dollar climate and weather events, 1980–2021. NOTE: Dollar values are adjusted for annual Consumer Price Index (CPI) increases. SOURCE: National Centers for Environmental Information (2021).

her generation and those to come, telling policy makers, "We deserve a safe future. And we demand a safe future." Thunberg rightly worries that the long-term future could be bleak. The number and intensity of climate-related natural disasters have increased over the past four decades, as shown in figure 37. The number of catastrophic "billion-dollar" disasters (shown in figure 37) is expected to continue rising—unless social policies and human behavior shift dramatically (Smith 2021).[2] Increases in greenhouse gases in the atmosphere boost temperatures. Rising temperatures trigger more and deadlier natural disasters including droughts, hurricanes, cyclones, and heatwaves. Melting glaciers and ice caps can lead to rising sea levels—making coastal flooding more severe when storms hit shore. Over the past two decades, the United States has witnessed tragedies like Hurricane Katrina, which destroyed parts of New Orleans and the surrounding Gulf Coast in 2005, taking an estimated eighteen hundred lives. In the fifteen years that followed, Hurricane Sandy ravaged the east coast, Hurricane Maria left Puerto Rico in ruins, wildfires devastated California and the Pacific Northwest, and a torrent of tornados, mudslides, floods, droughts, and blizzards have struck worldwide (Smith 2021).

The life-altering impacts of natural disasters and extreme temperatures are dangerous for older adults, especially those already suffering from poor health or poverty. That's why intensifying natural disasters may pose a particular threat to future cohorts of older adults. People ages sixty-five and older now make up 17 percent of the overall US population, yet they consistently account for anywhere from one-half to three-quarters of all deaths following natural disasters (Brunkard, Namulanda, and Ratard 2008). More than two-thirds of all those who died from causes related to Hurricanes Katrina and Maria were people ages sixty-five and older. More than half of the 117 who succumbed to Hurricane Sandy were older adults. The average age of the 739 people dying of heat-related causes during Chicago's 1999 heatwave was seventy-five (Jenkins et al. 2014). While some were already ill, others were relatively healthy yet succumbed to powerful environmental factors. Hurricane victims drowned in their own homes, unable or afraid to evacuate—especially if they had nowhere to go, or no one to help them move. In 2017's Hurricane Irma, fourteen South Florida nursing home residents, ages seventy-one to ninety-nine, died of heat-related causes after the facility's air conditioning failed (Gabler, Fink, and Yee 2017). Heatwaves and extreme cold can be deadly for older adults, who are vulnerable to hypothermia and hyperthermia.

Environmental threats disproportionately affect residents of low-income neighborhoods that lack the infrastructure and supports needed to withstand the crisis. The 1995 Chicago heatwave was especially deadly to low-income older Blacks, who couldn't afford working air conditioners or were reluctant to open their windows and doors, wary of neighborhood crime (Klinenberg 2002). Houston's poorest residents suffered greatly in Hurricane Harvey. The city's low-income neighborhoods are in flood-prone areas and near industrial facilities, which are the site of chemical spills triggered by storm damage (Krause and Reeves 2017). Despite this devastation, there are glimmers of hope. At a 2021 global climate summit, the United States committed to cut greenhouse gas emissions in half by 2030. A late 2020 international survey found that 64 percent of people consider climate change a "global emergency" (Mocatta and Harris 2021). As more policy makers and voters heed the warning of Greta Thunberg, the planet may be safer for older adults in 2030 and beyond.

### Health Crises: From COVID to Opioids

Three contemporary health crises—obesity, opioid abuse, and COVID-19—may have long-term impacts for future cohorts of older adults, threatening their physical and mental health, functioning, and family lives. The toll may be especially severe for Blacks, Hispanics, and those from low-income backgrounds, contributing to ever-widening disparities. Obesity rates worldwide have doubled since 1980, with the United States faring worst of all high-income nations. The United States has been characterized as an "obesogenic environment," where cheap, fast, unhealthy food is available at all hours, and our busy lives and built environment discourage physical activity. In 2020, a record 40 percent of US adults and 20 percent of teens and children were classified as obese (Warren, Beck, and Delgado 2020). Millennials and members of Generation Z are more likely than their parents' generations to be overweight or obese, with far-reaching impacts that can extend for years if not decades. High body weight harms physical health and can take an emotional toll, making one vulnerable to insults, teasing, and poor self-esteem. Dozens of studies show that childhood and adolescent obesity is linked to poorer performance in school, lower rates of college attendance, more frequent workplace discrimination, and lower earnings, as well as health problems including diabetes and metabolic syndrome, high blood pressure, heart disease, some cancers, sleep apnea, and ultimately a short-ened life span (Kelsey et al., 2014).

The obesity crisis has evolved over the past four decades, yet the ravages of the opioid epidemic are more recent and dire. Opioids are a drug classification that includes prescription pain relievers, heroin, and synthetic opioids such as fentanyl; they are highly addictive, and their misuse can be lethal. US deaths from opioid overdose nearly tripled between

2002 and 2015. In 2020, more than ninety-two thousand Americans died of drug overdoses, roughly two-thirds from opioids or heroin (Hedegaard et al. 2021). Deaths are just one indicator of the epidemic's reach; millions of Americans are struggling with their own or a loved one's addiction. In 2019, 1.6 million had an opioid addiction problem, and 10 million had misused opioids, meaning that they took them without a doctor's prescription, or took more than they were prescribed.

Most experts blame these dramatic spikes on pharmaceutical companies, who assured the medical community that patients would not become addicted. Physicians and dentists began prescribing them at a greater rate, for everything from wisdom teeth removal to sports injuries. As more prescriptions were doled out, more people started to use and misuse them, ultimately becoming addicted. The problem got so bad so quickly that in 2017, the Department of Health and Human Services declared the opioid epidemic a national emergency and many health care providers dramatically cut back on or stopped prescribing the medications. Sadly, the crisis has continued and intensified during the COVID-19 pandemic, as stress and social isolation have led people to self-medicate. Meanwhile, quarantines and lockdowns during the crisis stages of the pandemic prevented users from getting the treatments (like naloxone) and medical help they needed (American Medical Association 2021).

The opioid epidemic may have long-term effects, threatening the quality of life for future generations of older adults. Opioid addiction, especially among young adults, can derail their work and family lives, increasing their chances of imprisonment, unemployment, lost earnings, and unstable romantic partnerships (e.g., Birnbaum et al. 2011). The harms of addiction also spiral out to affect families, especially the late Boomer and Gen X parents of young adults struggling with addiction. In poor and rural white communities, the opioid crisis is taking the lives of young adults who would be future caregivers for their Boomer and Gen X parents. Even well-off parents are draining their bank accounts to pay for pricy (and seldom effective) rehab programs for their young adult children. That's what happened to fifty-something Denise Mariano and her husband, who depleted their retirement savings and two of their children's college funds of roughly $375,000, to help their twenty-seven-year-old son overcome addiction (Kapadia 2019). New evidence provides some good news; rates of opioid use and misuse among children and teens started to decline in the late

2010s, as policy makers and the medical community have cracked down on the use of these drugs. Although the future is uncertain, rising awareness of and public health initiatives to fight addiction hold great promise.

The future also is uncertain regarding the long-term impacts of COVID-19 for today's young and midlife adults. One thing is certain: low-income, Black, and Hispanic communities have been especially vulnerable to the virus. However, it is not clear what the long-term health effects are. Some epidemiologists say that "long haulers" will have symptoms that continue to undermine their health and well-being, like fatigue, headaches, shortness of breath, a persistent cough, heart damage, neurologic problems, depression, and anxiety.[3] These symptoms could undermine one's capacity to work and save for retirement, rendering patients dependent on disability payments. But as the rapid development and rollout of effective vaccines taught us in 2021, scientists worldwide are working to quickly develop effective therapies and treatments, providing hope for people living with long-term COVID-19 effects.

The adage "change is the only constant in life" applies to the case of population aging. As we have seen throughout this book, many aspects of growing old—especially biological changes—are an inevitable aspect of the aging process. Yet many others are tightly tied to ever-changing factors, including public policies like Social Security and Medicare, cultural beliefs regarding the talents and capacities of older adults, technological innovations like assistive devices and medications, social trends including rising levels of education and shifting family forms, and demographic changes that have altered the gender, race, and age composition of the sixty-five-and-over population in the United States and worldwide. Through processes of cohort replacement, old age will look very different in 2060 than it does today. Sweeping social phenomena like rising economic inequality, climate change, and current health epidemics pose potentially devastating challenges to future cohorts of older adults, yet there are ample reasons for optimism. The large Millennial and Generation Z cohorts will make up roughly half of eligible voters by the year 2028, and they can use their voting muscle to advocate for greater economic and racial equality, protective environmental policies, and health care for all (Brownstein 2020). Such efforts will be a critical step toward ensuring that future generations from all backgrounds can enjoy good health, physical comfort, meaningful personal relationships, a sense of purpose, and dignity in old age.

# Notes

INTRODUCTION

1. Iris Westman passed away on January 3, 2021, and Hester Ford died on April 17, 2021.

2. Population pyramids are typically based on data obtained from censuses or registries. As of 2022, the US Census did not provide an option to identify oneself as outside the male/female gender binary such as transgender or non-binary. As the number of persons identifying as non-binary increases worldwide, statistical practices are expected to evolve accordingly (Wilson and Meyer 2021).

CHAPTER 1. HISTORICAL AND CONTEMPORARY
PERSPECTIVES ON AGING

1. By contrast, in 2019, among US adults ages seventy-five and older, just 6 percent of men and 19 percent of women lived with a relative other than a spouse, such as an adult children or sibling (US Census Bureau 2019). For full data, see: https://www.census.gov/data/tables/time-series/demo/families/adults.html.

2. The IAT shows a computer screen image such as a photo of an older adult or a teenager, or words such as *old* and *young*. Study participants quickly click their computer mouse on either the positive word or negative word presented side by side on the screen. For instance, they might see a photo of an older man and

then have the option to quickly click on a positive word like *strong* or a negative word such as *weak*. After proceeding through this task for several images associated with old age versus youth, the study participant receives a score indicating whether they hold implicitly positive or negative views toward older adults. The IAT captures subconscious beliefs about age, gender, race, sexual orientation, and so on (Cunningham, Preacher, and Banaji 2001).

3. Ample data confirm that Generation X, born in the mid-1960s through early 1980s, and the Millennial cohort born in the 1980s and 1990s lag far behind where Baby Boomers were when they were young. An analysis of Survey of Consumer Finance (SCF) data found that the average level of homeowner equity today (in 2016 dollars) is around $150,000 for older adults, but just a fraction of that ($55,000) for adults in their thirties and forties (Cortright 2017). Similarly, a Federal Reserve study compared the 2016 wealth levels of households headed by persons born in the 1930s through the 1980s (Kurz, Li, and Vine 2018). Households headed by someone born post-1960 fared worse than those born earlier, and householders born in the 1980s fared worst of all. In 2016, the Millennials' median net worth was 34 percent lower than what past trends would predict for their age group, while Gen Xers were 18 percent behind the wealth levels of those born in the 1930s through 1950s.

4. The social, economic, and political history of public and private pensions is a vast topic, and one that is beyond the scope of this brief chapter. For further information on the history of private pensions see Clark et al. (2003) and for a history of Social Security see Schieber and Shoven (1999).

5. The Johnson administration also ushered in legislation opposing age-based discrimination, although the earliest policies were not sufficient to erase ageism in hiring. When Congress drafted the Civil Rights Act of 1964, it was reluctant to include age as a protected category. President Lyndon B. Johnson's labor secretary Willard Wirtz studied the experiences of older workers and concluded that they were being denied opportunities for "useful activity which constitutes much of life's meaning" (Lipnic 2018). The 1965 study *The Older American Worker: Age Discrimination in Employment*, dubbed *The Wirtz Report*, was the inspiration for the 1967 passage of the Age Discrimination in Employment Act (ADEA), which forbade employment discrimination against anyone ages forty to sixty-five. However, it did not go so far as to ban discrimination against workers over sixty-five or to abolish mandatory retirement, limiting older adults' engagement with society and capacity to earn (Lipnic 2018).

6. Basic Medicare benefits exclude dental, vision, hearing, and long-term care services. As a result, older adults must bear the costs, which may be prohibitive to those on a limited income. In 2016, the average Medicare beneficiary spent $5,500 on out-of-pocket medical expenditures, with women, persons aged eighty-five and older, those in poorer health, and those without supplemental insurance paying even more (Cubanski et al. 2019).

7. A full discussion of the many theories used to understand aging are beyond the scope of this brief chapter. Contemporary research in aging also is shaped by psychological theories including socioemotional selectivity theory (Carstensen 1992), selective optimization with compensation theory (Baltes and Baltes 1990), and successful aging perspectives (Rowe and Kahn 2015) as well as critical perspectives including critical gerontology (Holstein and Minkler 2007), feminist gerontology (Calasanti 2004), and political economy approaches (Minkler and Estes 2019).

8. Some scholars have argued that gaps between the advantaged and disadvantaged become *smaller* over time due to the "age as leveler" effect. This perspective argues that people with the most serious adversities in early life are especially likely to die prematurely. Those who survive those difficulties yet go on to live a long life may have genetic, psychological, or interpersonal benefits that help them to have a particularly long and healthy old age. To put it more bluntly, "age as leveler" proponents believe the gap between the haves and have nots narrows over time, because those with the most difficult lives have already died off (Dupre 2007).

## CHAPTER 2. WHO ARE OLDER ADULTS TODAY?

1. We focus on men and women only because very limited data are available on transgender persons. One analysis of data from the Behavioral Risk Factor Surveillance System (BRFSS) estimated that just 0.5 percent of persons aged sixty-five or older identified as transgender, a fraction slightly lower than among persons ages twenty-five to sixty-four (0.6%) and the same as ages eighteen to twenty-four (0.5%) (Flores et al. 2016).

2. Detailed information on the process through which immigrants become naturalized are described by the US Citizenship and Immigration Services, https://www.uscis.gov/citizenship/learn-about-citizenship/citizenship-and -naturalization.

3. Gifts, veterans' payments, and other sources make up a fifth income source, although just 5 percent of older adults rely on these (Federal Interagency Forum on Aging-Related Statistics 2020).

## CHAPTER 4. HEALTH AND WELL-BEING

1. Zhang and colleagues (2020) found that the stress hormone noradrenaline, also known as norepinephrine, is key to stress-induced hair graying. By injecting noradrenaline under the skin of unstressed mice, the researchers were able to cause melanocyte stem cell loss and hair graying.

2. A full discussion of biological models of aging is beyond the scope of this book. For a straightforward review of biological theories of aging, see Leonard Hayflick's (1994) *How and Why We Age*, and for a compendium of recent research see Musi and Hornsby (2021).

3. Trivia buffs know that the actual ends of our shoelaces are called "aglets."

4. For further information on the data, methods, and findings from the Georgia Centenarian Study, see Poon et al. (1992). Regularly updated information on the New England Centenarian Study can be found at http://www.bumc.bu.edu /centenarian/.

5. For a full compendium of population-level data on older adults' health in the United States, see the Federal Interagency Forum on Aging-Related Statistics (2020) https://agingstats.gov/docs/LatestReport/OA20_508_10142020.pdf. For data on other nations, see the Ageing Data portal established by the World Health Organization (WHO) in 2020. https://www.who.int/data/maternal -newborn-child-adolescent-ageing/ageing-data.

6. The proportion of 2020 decedents who are age sixty-five or older is slightly higher than in prior years, as older adults were especially vulnerable to COVID-19 deaths. Of the three hundred seventy-eight thousand COVID deaths in 2020, 81 percent were persons ages sixty-five and older.

7. A discussion of the biological reasons for the link between cancer and aging is beyond the scope of this chapter. For an excellent review, see Campisi (2013).

8. In 2021, Congress debated whether to add dental, vision, hearing, and other benefits to regular Medicare coverage, as part of the Build Back Better Bill. Unfortunately, the expansion was not ultimately supported (Sanger-Katz 2021).

9. The causes of dementia are not fully understood, and that's part of the reason why a cure remains elusive—despite the FDA's 2021 approval of the controversial new medication Biogen's Aduhelm. For a discussion of the debates regarding the efficacy of Aduhelm, see Mahase (2021).

10. A discussion of all mental health symptoms as well as major mental health disorders with a strong genetic basis, such as schizophrenia, are beyond the scope of this book. For a helpful overview of more serious mental illnesses and disorders in later life, see Zarit and Zarit (2011).

11. Suicide rates are calculated as the number of deaths by suicide per 100,000 people. In 2019, the suicide rate for women ages sixty-five to seventy-four and ages seventy-five and over were 5.9 and 4.3 per 100,000, respectively. Among their male counterparts, the comparable rates were a remarkable 26.4 and 39.9, respectively.

12. Although socioeconomic disparities in health are present at every age, they tend to be narrowest at young ages when people are most biologically robust (childhood, adolescence, and early adulthood) or most vulnerable (infancy and very old age). Disparities are widest during midlife and early old age (House et al. 2005).

13. Residents of the United States, including citizens and permanent residents, are eligible for premium-free Medicare Part A if they have worked at least

ten years in jobs where they or their spouses paid Medicare payroll taxes and are at least sixty-five years old. Legal immigrants who are age sixty-five or older who do not have this work history can purchase Medicare Part A after residing legally in the United States for five years continuously. Legal immigrants (noncitizen permanent residents) under age sixty-five with disabilities also may qualify for Medicare, but typically they first must meet the same eligibility requirements for SSDI (disability benefits) that apply to citizens, which are based on work history, paying Social Security taxes on income, and having enough years of Social Security taxes accumulated to equal between five and ten years. New immigrants are not eligible for Medicare regardless of their age. Once immigrants meet the residency requirements, eligibility and enrollment works the same as it does for others (Kaiser Family Foundation 2021).

### CHAPTER 5. AGING POLICY ISSUES

1. Some would argue that "old-age dependency ratio" is a misnomer. Certainly, old age is not synonymous with "dependency." Many older adults work for pay and are financially and residentially independent, providing economic and practical support to others. Likewise, rising numbers of persons ages twenty-five to sixty-four are not employed, whether due to a disability, family responsibilities, or challenges in finding work.

2. South Korea provides a fascinating case of how older adults can be impoverished, despite living in a wealthy and technologically advanced nation. For a fuller discussion of this complex case, see Ku and Kim (2020).

3. The proportion of all workers in private industry with access to a pension varies widely by socioeconomic status. Overall, about 67 percent of US workers have access to some kind of pension plan, with 52 percent having access to a DC plan only. While 82 percent of workers in the highest income quartile have access to a pension, just 42 percent of those in the lowest quartile have access to one, with nearly all (39 percent) having access to a DC only (Bureau of Labor Statistics 2021a).

4. In 2021, the gross domestic product (GDP) of the United States topped $21 trillion. The second highest was China, at $14.3 trillion. While the US GDP is roughly 33 percent higher than that of China, the US population is less than one-quarter of China's (331 million versus 1.4 billion), according to World Bank data (2021).

### CONCLUSION

1. Between 2008 and 2018, the average tuition at four-year public colleges increased by 37 percent. After taking scholarships and grants into account, the net

costs to students and their families increased by 24 percent (Center on Budget and Policy Priorities 2019).

2. According to National Centers for Environmental Information (2021), as of August 2021, the United States had sustained 298 weather and climate disasters since 1980 in which overall damages/costs reached or exceeded $1 billion (including CPI adjustment to 2021). The total cost of these 298 events exceeded $1.975 trillion.

3. Research is evolving on COVID-19 "long haulers," although regular updates are provided by the Centers for Disease Control and Prevention (CDC 2021c).

# References

Achenbaum, W. Andrew. 2020. *Old Age in the New Land: The American Experience since 1790.* 2nd ed. Baltimore: Johns Hopkins University Press.

Acierno, Ron, Melba A. Hernandez, Ananda B. Amstadter, Heidi S. Resnick, Kenneth Steve, Wendy Muzzy, and Dean G. Kilpatrick. 2010. "Prevalence and Correlates of Emotional, Physical, Sexual, and Financial Abuse and Potential Neglect in the United States: The National Elder Mistreatment Study." *American Journal of Public Health* 100(2):292–97.

Adams, Bert N. 1999. "Cross-Cultural and U.S. Kinship." Pp. 77–91 in *Handbook of Marriage and the Family*, edited by M. B. Sussman, S. K. Steinmetz, and G. W. Peterson. Boston: Springer.

Administration for Community Living. 2020. "2019 Profile of Older Americans." https://acl.gov/aging-and-disability-in-america/data-and-research/profile -older-americans, accessed October 12, 2020.

Agus, David B., Elizabeth M. Jaffee, and Chi Van Dang. 2021. "Cancer Moon-shot 2.0." *The Lancet Oncology* 22(2):164–65.

Ahmad, Farida B., and Robert N. Anderson. 2021. "The Leading Causes of Death in the US for 2020." *JAMA* 325(18):1829–30.

Aihara, Yoko, and Kiyoshi Maeda. 2021. "National Dementia Supporter Programme in Japan." *Dementia* 20(5):1723–28. doi.org/10.1177/14713012209 67570.

Allan, Graham. 1998. "Friendship, Sociology and Social Structure." *Journal of Social and Personal Relationships* 15(5):685–702.

Almack, Kathryn, Jane Seymour, and Gary Bellamy. 2010. "Exploring the Impact of Sexual Orientation on Experiences and Concerns about End of Life Care and on Bereavement for Lesbian, Gay, and Bisexual Older People." *Sociology* 44(5):908–24.

Alzheimer's Association. 2020. *Alzheimer's Disease Facts and Figures*. Washington, DC: Alzheimer's Association. https://www.alz.org/media/Documents /alzheimers-facts-and-figures.pdf, accessed July 11, 2020.

———. 2021. "Mild Cognitive Impairment." https://www.alz.org/alzheimers -dementia/what-is-dementia/related_conditions/mild-cognitive-impairment, accessed July 7, 2021.

American Association of Retired Persons (AARP). 2002. *The Grandparent Study 2002 Report*. Washington, DC: American Association of Retired Persons. http://assets.aarp.org/rgcenter/general/gp_2002.pdf, accessed October 9, 2020.

———. 2019. *2018 Grandparents Today National Survey*. Washington, DC: American Association of Retired Persons. https://www.aarp.org/content /dam/aarp/research/surveys_statistics/life-leisure/2019/aarp-grandparenting -study.doi.10.26419-2Fres.00289.001.pdf, accessed February 2021.

———. 2020. "AARP Foundation Experience Corps 2020–2021 School Year: A Pivot to Virtual Tutoring." AARP (November 17) https://www.aarp.org /experience-corps/about-us/virtual/, accessed August 25, 2021.

American Association of Retired Persons (AARP) and National Alliance for Caregiving. 2020. "Caregiving in the US 2020." American Association of Retired Persons (May 14). https://www.aarp.org/ppi/info-2020/caregiving-in -the-united-states.html, accessed February 1, 2021.

American Medical Association. 2021. "Issue Brief: Nation's Drug-Related Overdose and Death Epidemic Continues to Worsen." AMA (August 4). https://www.ama-assn.org/system/files/issue-brief-increases-in-opioid -related-overdose.pdf, accessed August 18, 2021.

Angel, Jacqueline L., Maren A. Jimenez, and Ronald J. Angel. 2007. "The Economic Consequences of Widowhood for Older Minority Women." *The Gerontologist* 47, 2:224–34.

Arias Elizabeth, B. Tejada-Vera, and F. Ahmad. 2021. "Provisional Life Expectancy Estimates for January through June, 2020." *Vital Statistics Rapid Release, No. 10* (February). doi.org/10.15620/cdc:100392, accessed July 7, 2021.

Assari, Shervin. 2018. "Health Disparities due to Diminished Return among Black Americans: Public Policy Solutions." *Social Issues and Policy Review* 12(1):112–45.

Assistant Secretary for Planning and Evaluation (ASPE). 2019. "Community-Dwelling Older Adults with Dementia and Their Caregivers: Key Indicators from the National Health and Aging Trends Study." https://aspe.hhs.gov

/reports/community-dwelling-older-adults-dementia-their-caregivers-key
-indicators-national-health-aging-0#acknow.

———. 2020. "Implications of Alternative Methods of Identifying Populations
with Dementia." Issue brief (February 12). https://aspe.hhs.gov/basic-report
/implications-alternative-methods-identifying-populations-dementia-issue
-brief, accessed July 7, 2021.

Association of Road Racing Statisticians. 2021. "World Single Age Records:
5 km." https://arrs.run/SA_R5K.htm, accessed July 7, 2021.

Atchley, Robert C. 1989. "A Continuity Theory of Normal Aging." *The Gerontologist* 29(2):183–90.

August, Kristin J., and Dara H. Sorkin. 2010. "Marital Status and Gender
Differences in Managing a Chronic Illness: The Function of Health-Related
Social Control." *Social Science & Medicine* 71(10):1831–38.

Bajaj, Simar Singh, and Fatima Cody Stanford. 2021. "Beyond Tuskegee—
Vaccine Distrust and Everyday Racism." *New England Journal of Medicine*
384(5):e12.

Baltes, Paul B., and Margret M. Baltes. 1990. "Psychological Perspectives on
Successful Aging: The Model of Selective Optimization with Compensation."
Pp. 1–34 in *Successful Aging: Perspectives from the Behavioral Sciences*,
edited by P. B. Baltes and M. M. Baltes. Cambridge: Cambridge University
Press.

Bartels, Virginia B., ed. 1994. "The History of South Carolina Schools." Center
for Educator Recruitment, Retention, and Advancement. https://www
.carolana.com/SC/Education/History_of_South_Carolina_Schools
_Virginia_B_Bartels.pdf, accessed July 12, 2020.

Bengtson, Vernon L., and Richard Settersten Jr., eds. 2016. *Handbook of
Theories of Aging*. New York: Springer Publishing Company.

Bennett, Kate M., Georgina M. Hughes, and Philip T. Smith. 2003. "'I Think
a Woman Can Take It': Widowed Men's Views and Experiences of Gender
Differences in Bereavement." *Ageing International* 28(4):408–24.

Berger, Roni. 1998. *Stepfamilies: A Multi-dimensional Perspective*. New York:
Haworth.

Bernard, Tara Siegel. 2021. "More Same-Sex Couples May Be Eligible for Social
Security Survivor Benefits." *New York Times* (November 2). https://www
.nytimes.com/2021/11/02/business/social-security-same-sex-survivor
-benefits.html, accessed January 20, 2022.

Birnbaum, Howard G., Alan G. White, Matt Schiller, Tracy Waldman, Jody M.
Cleveland, and Carl L. Roland. 2011. "Societal Costs of Prescription Opioid
Abuse, Dependence, and Misuse in the United States." *Pain Medicine*
12(4):657–67.

Blanck, Peter. 2001. "Civil War Pensions and Disability." *Ohio State Law Journal*
62:109–238.

Blank, Thomas O., and Keith M. Bellizzi. 2008. "A Gerontologic Perspective on Cancer and Aging." *Cancer* 112(S11):2569–76.

Blanton, Kayla. 2020. "The World's Oldest Yoga Teacher Has Died at 101—Here Were Her Secrets to a Long Life." *Prevention* (February 24). https://www.prevention.com/fitness/a31077716/tao-porchon-lynch-oldest-yoga-teacher-death/, accessed August 8, 2020.

Bonanno, George A., Camille B. Wortman, Darrin R. Lehman, Roger G. Tweed, John Sonnega, Deborah Carr, and Randolph M. Nesse. 2002. "Resilience to Loss and Chronic Grief: A Prospective Study from Pre-loss to 18 Months Post-loss." *Journal of Personality and Social Psychology* 83(5):1150–64.

Bortz, Abe. 2012. "Abe Bortz Lecture on the History of Social Security." US Social Security Administration. https://www.ssa.gov/history/bortz.html, accessed August 2, 2020.

Bosworth, Barry. 2018. "Increasing Disparities in Mortality by Socioeconomic Status." *Annual Review of Public Health* 39:237–51.

Bowlby, John. (1980). *Attachment and Loss. Vol. 3: Loss, Sadness and Depression*. New York: Basic Books.

Bowman, Cynthia Grant. 2009. "Women in the Legal Profession from the 1920s to the 1970s: What Can We Learn from Their Experience about Law and Social Change?" *Maine Law Review* 61:1.

Brammer, Richard. 1994. "A Home for the Homeless: Remembering the Pleasants County Poor Farm." *Goldenseal* (Fall). https://www.wvgenweb.org/pleasants/poor.htm, accessed August 1, 2020.

Brandl, Bonnie, and Jane A. Raymond. 2012. "Policy Implications of Recognizing That Caregiver Stress Is *Not* the Primary Cause of Elder Abuse." *Generations: Journal of the American Society on Aging* 36(3):32–39.

Bratt, Anna Sofia, Ulf Stenström, and Mikael Rennemark. 2017. "Effects on Life Satisfaction of Older Adults after Child and Spouse Bereavement." *Aging & Mental Health* 21(6):602–8.

Brooke, Joanne, and Debra Jackson. 2020. "Older People and COVID-19: Isolation, Risk and Ageism." *Journal of Clinical Nursing* 29(13–14):2044–46.

Brown, Anna. 2020. "Nearly Half of U.S. Adults Say Dating Has Gotten Harder for Most People in the Last 10 Years." Pew Research Center, August 20. https://www.pewresearch.org/social-trends/2020/08/20/nearly-half-of-u-s-adults-say-dating-has-gotten-harder-for-most-people-in-the-last-10-years/, accessed February 15, 2021.

Brown, Rebecca T., Kaveh Hemati, Elise D. Riley, Christopher T. Lee, Claudia Ponath, Lina Tieu, David Guzman, and Margot B. Kushel. 2017. "Geriatric Conditions in a Population-Based Sample of Older Homeless Adults." *The Gerontologist* 57(4):757–66.

Brown, Susan. 2017. *Families in America*. Oakland: University of California Press.

Brown, Susan L., Jennifer Roebuck Bulanda, and Gary R. Lee. 2012. "Transitions into and out of Cohabitation in Later Life." *Journal of Marriage and Family* 74(4):774–93.

Brown, Susan L., Gary R. Lee, and Jennifer Roebuck Bulanda. 2006. "Cohabitation among Older Adults: A National Portrait." *Journals of Gerontology Series B: Psychological Sciences and Social Sciences* 61(2):S71–S79.

Brown, Susan L., and I-Fen Lin. 2012. "The Gray Divorce Revolution: Rising Divorce among Middle-Aged and Older Adults, 1990–2010." *Journals of Gerontology Series B: Psychological Sciences and Social Sciences* 67(6):731–74.

———. 2022. "The Graying of Divorce: A Half Century of Change." *Journals of Gerontology: Series B*: Psychological Sciences and Social Sciences. doi.org/10 .1093/geronb/gbac057.

Brown, Susan L., I-Fen Lin, Anna M. Hammersmith, and Matthew R. Wright. 2019. "Repartnering Following Gray Divorce: The Roles of Resources and Constraints for Women and Men." *Demography* 56(2):503–23.

Brown, Susan L., and Sayaka K. Shinohara. 2013. "Dating Relationships in Older Adulthood: A National Portrait." *Journal of Marriage and Family* 75(5):1194–202.

Brown, Susan L., and Matthew R. Wright. 2017. "Marriage, Cohabitation, and Divorce in Later Life." *Innovation in Aging* 1(2):1–11. doi.org/10.1093/geroni /igx015.

Brownstein, Ronald. 2020. "The GOP's Demographic Doom." *Atlantic* (October 23). https://www.theatlantic.com/politics/archive/2020/10/millennials -and-gen-z-will-soon-dominate-us-elections/616818/, accessed July 27, 2021.

Brunkard, Joan, Gonza Namulanda, and Raoult Ratard. 2008. "Hurricane Katrina Deaths, Louisiana, 2005." *Disaster Medicine and Public Health Preparedness* 2(4):215–23.

Budiman, Abby, Christine Tamir, Lauren Mora, and Luis Noe-Bustamente. 2020. "Facts on U.S. Immigrants, 2018: Statistical Portrait of the Foreign-Born Population in the United States." Pew Research Center (August 20). https:// www.pewresearch.org/hispanic/2020/08/20/facts-on-u-s-immigrants/, accessed October 19, 2020.

Bui, Quoctrung, and Claire Cain Miller. 2018. "The Age That Women Have Babies: How a Gap Divides America." *New York Times* (August 4). https:// www.nytimes.com/interactive/2018/08/04/upshot/up-birth-age-gap.html.

Bureau of Labor Statistics (BLS). 2019. *Census of Fatal Occupational Injuries Summary, 2018*. Washington, DC: Bureau of Labor Statistics (December 17, 2019). https://www.bls.gov/news.release/pdf/cfoi.pdf, accessed October 2, 2020.

———. 2021a. "The Economics Daily, 67 Percent of Private Industry Workers Had Access to Retirement Plans in 2020" (March 1). https://www.bls.gov

/opub/ted/2021/67-percent-of-private-industry-workers-had-access-to
-retirement-plans-in-2020.htm, accessed August 30, 2021.

———. 2021b. *Fastest Growing Occupations, 2019–29*. Washington, DC: Bureau
of Labor Statistics. https://www.bls.gov/ooh/most-new-jobs.htm, accessed
August 10, 2021.

Burgess, Ernest W. 1960. *Aging in Western Societies*. Chicago: University of
Chicago Press.

Cacioppo, John, and Laura Freberg. 2012. *Discovering Psychology: The Science
of Mind*. New York: Cengage.

Cahill, Kevin E., Michael D. Giandrea, and Joseph F. Quinn. 2015. "Evolving
Patterns of Work and Retirement." Pp. 271–92 in *Handbook of Aging and the
Social Sciences*, edited L. K. George and K. Ferraro. New York: Academic Press.

Calasanti, Toni. 2004. "Feminist Gerontology and Old Men." *Journals of
Gerontology Series B: Psychological Sciences and Social Sciences* 59(6):
S305–S314.

Camerota, Steven A., and Karen Zeigler. 2019. *Immigrants Are Coming to
America at Older Ages*. Center for Immigration Studies (July 1). https://cis
.org/Report/Immigrants-Are-Coming-America-Older-Ages, accessed
October 19, 2020.

Campisi, Judith. 2013. "Aging, Cellular Senescence, and Cancer." *Annual Review
of Physiology* 75:685–705.

Cantor, Marjorie H. 1979 "Neighbors and Friends: An Overlooked Resource in
the Informal Support System." *Research on Aging* 1(4):434–63.

Carleton, Will. 1882. "Over the Hill to the Poorhouse." *Farm Ballads*. New York:
Harper and Brothers.

Carney, Maria T., Janice Fujiwara, Brian E. Emmert Jr., Tara A. Liberman,
and Barbara Paris. 2016. "Elder Orphans Hiding in Plain Sight: A Growing
Vulnerable Population." *Current Gerontology and Geriatrics Research*.
doi: 10.1155/2016/4723250.

Carr, Deborah. 2004a. "The Desire to Date and Remarry among Older Widows
and Widowers." *Journal of Marriage and Family* 66(4):1051–68.

———. 2004b. "Gender, Preloss Marital Dependence, and Older Adults' Adjustment to Widowhood." *Journal of Marriage and Family* 66(1): 220-235.

———. 2014. *Worried Sick: How Stress Hurts Us and How to Bounce Back*. New
Brunswick, NJ: Rutgers University Press.

———. 2019. *Golden Years? Social Inequality in Later Life*. New York:
Russell Sage.

———. 2020. "Families in Later Life." *Annual Review of Gerontology and
Geriatrics* 40(1):43–68.

Carr, Deborah, Kathrin Boerner, and Sara Moorman. 2020. "Bereavement
in the Time of Coronavirus: Unprecedented Challenges Demand Novel
Interventions." *Journal of Aging & Social Policy* 32(4–5):425–31.

Carr, Deborah, and Elizabeth Luth. 2019. "Well-Being at the End of Life."
    *Annual Review of Sociology* 45:515–34.
Carr, Deborah, and Heather Mooney. 2021. "Bereavement in Later Life."
    Pp. 240–54 in *Handbook of Aging and the Social Sciences*, 9th ed., edited
    by K. F. Ferraro and D. Carr. New York: Academic Press.
Carstensen, Laura L. 1992. "Social and Emotional Patterns in Adulthood: Support
    for Socioemotional Selectivity Theory." *Psychology and Aging* 7(3):331–38.
Case, Anne, and Angus Deaton. 2020. *Deaths of Despair and the Future of
    Capitalism*. Princeton, NJ: Princeton University Press.
Cavanaugh, John C., and Fredda Blanchard-Fields. 2018. *Adult Development
    and Aging*. Boston, MA: Cengage Learning.
Center on Budget and Policy Priorities. 2019. "State Higher Education Funding
    Cuts Have Pushed Costs to Students, Worsened Inequality." CBPP (Octo-
    ber 24). https://www.cbpp.org/sites/default/files/atoms/files/10-24-19sfp.pdf,
    accessed August 5, 2021.
Centers for Disease Control and Prevention (CDC). 2019. "Infant Mortality."
    https://www.cdc.gov/reproductivehealth/maternalinfanthealth/infant
    mortality.htm, accessed July 15, 2020.
———. 2020. "What Is Diabetes." (June 11). https://www.cdc.gov/diabetes/basics
    /diabetes.html, accessed July 10, 2021.
———. 2021a. "Risk for COVID-19 Infection, Hospitalization, and Death by Age
    Group." (February 18). https://www.cdc.gov/coronavirus/2019-ncov/covid
    -data/investigations-discovery/hospitalization-death-by-age.html, accessed
    April 24, 2021.
———. 2021b. "Older Adult Oral Health." (May 5). https://www.cdc.gov/oral
    health/basics/adult-oral-health/adult_older.htm, accessed July 17, 2021.
———. 2021c. "Provisional COVID-19 Deaths by Race and Hispanic Origin, and
    Age." (July 7). https://data.cdc.gov/NCHS/Provisional-COVID-19-Deaths-by
    -Race-and-Hispanic-O/ks3g-spdg, accessed July 7, 2021.
Central Intelligence Agency. 2020. "Median Age." In *The World Factbook*.
    https://www.cia.gov/the-world-factbook/field/median-age/, accessed July 5,
    2022.
Chang, E-Shien, and Becca R. Levy. 2021. "High Prevalence of Elder Abuse
    during the COVID-19 Pandemic: Risk and Resilience Factors." *American
    Journal of Geriatric Psychiatry*. Doi: 10.1016/j.jagp.2021.01.007.
Chapman, Steve. 2003. "Meet the Greedy Grandparents: Why America's Elderly
    Are So Spoiled." *Slate* (December 10). https://slate.com/news-and-politics
    /2003/12/why-america-s-elderly-are-so-spoiled.html, accessed January 5,
    2021.
Charles, Susan Turk, and Laura L. Carstensen. 2007. "Emotion Regulation
    and Aging." Pp. 307–27 in *Handbook of Emotion Regulation*, edited by
    J. J. Gross. New York: Guilford.

Cheng, Tsung-Mei. 2020. "International Health Care System Profiles: Taiwan." The Commonwealth Fund (June 5). https://www.commonwealthfund.org /international-health-policy-center/countries/taiwan, accessed August 30, 2021.

Chesney, Edward, Guy M. Goodwin, and Seena Fazel. 2014. "Risks of All-Cause and Suicide Mortality in Mental Disorders: a Meta-Review." *World Psychiatry* 13:153–60.

Chetty, Raj, Michael Stepner, Sarah Abraham, Shelby Lin, Benjamin Scuderi, Nicholas Turner, Augustin Bergeron, and David Cutler. 2016. "The Association between Income and Life Expectancy in the United States, 2001–2014." *Journal of the American Medical Association* 315(16):1750–66.

Choi, HwaJung, Robert F. Schoeni, Emily E. Wiemers, V. Joseph Hotz, and Judith A. Seltzer. 2020. "Spatial Distance between Parents and Adult Children in the United States." *Journal of Marriage and Family* 82(2): 822–40.

Chudacoff, Howard P. 1989. *How Old Are You? Age Consciousness in American Culture.* Princeton, NJ: Princeton University Press.

Clark, Noreen M., Marshall H. Becker, Nancy K. Janz, Kate Lorig, William Rakowski, and Lynda Anderson. 1991. "Self-Management of Chronic Disease by Older Adults: A Review and Questions for Research." *Journal of Aging and Health* 3(1):3–27.

Clark, Robert L., Robert Louis Clark, Lee A. Craig, and Jack W. Wilson. 2003. *A History of Public Sector Pensions in the United States.* Philadelphia: University of Pennsylvania Press.

Clausen, John A. 1995. *American Lives: Looking Back at the Children of the Great Depression.* Berkeley: University of California Press.

Clouston, Sean A. P., Dylan M. Smith, Soumyadeep Mukherjee, Yun Zhang, Wei Hou, Bruce G. Link, and Marcus Richards. 2019. "Education and Cognitive Decline: An Integrative Analysis of Global Longitudinal Studies of Cognitive Aging." *Journals of Gerontology: Series B* 75(7):e151–e160. doi.org/10.1093 /geronb/gbz053.

Cohen, Philip N. 2021. "Generation Labels Mean Nothing. It's Time to Retire Them." *Washington Post* (July 7, 2021). https://www.washingtonpost.com /opinions/2021/07/07/generation-labels-mean-nothing-retire-them/, accessed July 22, 2021.

Coleman, Joshua. 2021. *Rules of Estrangement: Why Adult Children Cut Ties and How to Heal the Conflict.* New York: Harmony.

Collins, Lauren G., and Kristine Swartz. 2011. "Caregiver Care." *American Family Physician* 83(11):1309–1317.

Connidis, Ingrid Arnet, Klas Borell, and Sofie Ghazanfareeon Karlsson. 2017. "Ambivalence and Living Apart Together in Later Life: A Critical Research Proposal." *Journal of Marriage and Family* 79(5):1404–18.

Cook, John. 2017. "How to Effectively Debunk Myths about Aging and Other Misconceptions." *Public Policy & Aging Report* 27(1):13–17.

Cooney, Teresa M., Christine M. Proulx, and Linley A. Snyder-Rivas. 2016. "A Profile of Later Life Marriages: Comparisons by Gender and Marriage Order." Pp. 1–37 in *Divorce, Separation, and Remarriage: The Transformation of Family*, vol. 10, edited by G. Gianesini and S. L. Blair. Bingley, UK: Emerald Group Publishing Limited.

Cooper, Claudia, Amber Selwood, Martin Blanchard, Zuzana Walker, Robert Blizard, and Gill Livingston. 2009. "Abuse of People with Dementia by Family Carers: Representative Cross Sectional Survey." *BMJ* 338(7694): 583–86. doi: 10.1136/bmj.b155.

Corporation for National Community and Service. 2016. *Value of Senior Volunteers to U.S. Economy Estimated at $77 Billion*. Washington, DC: CNCS (May 16). https://www.nationalservice.gov/newsroom/press-releases /2016/value-senior-volunteers-us-economy-estimated-77-billion, accessed August 26, 2021.

Cortright, Joe. 2017. "Here's What's Wrong with That 'Peak Millennials' Story." Citylab (January 24). https://www.citylab.com/equity/2017/01/flood-tide-not -ebb-tide-for-young-adults-in-cities/514283/, accessed July 5, 2022.

Cotten, Shelia. 2021. "Technologies and Aging: Understanding Use, Impacts, and Future Needs." Pp. 373–392 in *Handbook of Aging and the Social Sciences*, 9th ed., edited by K. F. Ferraro and D. Carr. New York: Academic Press.

Cramer, Reid, et al. 2019. *The Emerging Millennial Wealth Gap: Divergent Trajectories, Weak Balance Sheets, and Implications for Social Policy.* Washington, DC: New America. https://www.newamerica.org/millennials /reports/emerging-millennial-wealth-gap/, accessed July 21, 2021.

Crimmins, Eileen M., Yuan Zhang, and Yasuhiko Saito. 2016. "Trends over 4 Decades in Disability-Free Life Expectancy in the United States." *American Journal of Public Health* 106 (7): 1287–93.

Cruz, Lenika. 2015. "'Dinnertimin' and 'No Tipping': How Advertisers Targeted Black Consumers in the 1970s." *Atlantic*, June 7, 2015. Last modified 2017. Accessed July 1, 2017. https://www.theatlantic.com/entertainment/archive /2015/06/casual-racism-and-greater-diversity-in-70s-advertising/394958/.

Crystal, Stephen, and Dennis Shea. 1990. "Cumulative Advantage, Cumulative Disadvantage, and Inequality among Elderly People." *The Gerontologist* 30(4):437–43.

Cubanski, Juliette, Wyatt Koma, Anthony Damico, and Tricia Neuman. 2019. *How Much Do Medicare Beneficiaries Spend Out of Pocket on Health Care?* Kaiser Family Foundation (November 4). https://www.kff.org/medicare /issue-brief/how-much-do-medicare-beneficiaries-spend-out-of-pocket-on -health-care/, accessed August 8, 2020.

Cumming, Elaine, and William Earl Henry. 1961. *Growing Old: The Process of Disengagement.* New York: Basic Books.

Cunningham, Timothy J., Janet B. Croft, Yong Liu, Hua Lu, Paul I. Eke, and Wayne H. Giles. 2017. "Vital Signs: Racial Disparities in Age-Specific Mortality among Blacks or African Americans—United States, 1999–2015." *MMWR. Morbidity and Mortality Weekly Report* 66(17):444–56.

Cunningham, William A., Kristopher J. Preacher, and Mahzarin R. Banaji. 2001. "Implicit Attitude Measures: Consistency, Stability, and Convergent Validity." *Psychological Science* 12(2):163–70.

Cutler, David M., and Ellen Meara. 2004. "Changes in the Age Distribution of Mortality over the Twentieth Century." Pp. 333–66, in *Perspectives on the Economics of Aging.* Chicago: University of Chicago Press.

Dannefer, Dale. 1987. "Aging as Intracohort Differentiation: Accentuation, The Matthew Effect, and the Life Course." *Sociological Forum* 2(2):211–36.

Davidson, Kate M., and Graham Fennell. 2017. *Intimacy in Later Life.* New York: Routledge.

Davis, Owen, Bridget Fisher, Teresa Ghilarducci, and Siavash Radpour. 2020. "A First in Nearly 50 Years, Older Workers Face Higher Unemployment Than Mid-Career Workers." Schwartz Center for Economic Policy Analysis (October 20). https://www.economicpolicyresearch.org/jobs-report/a-first-in-nearly-50-years-older-workers-face-higher-unemployment-than-mid-career-workers, accessed February 10, 2021.

de Jong Gierveld, Jenny, Marjolein Broese van Groenou, Adriaan W. Hoogendoorn, and Johannes H. Smit. 2009. "Quality of Marriages in Later Life and Emotional and Social Loneliness." *Journals of Gerontology Series B: Psychological Sciences and Social Sciences* 64B(4):497–506.

de Jong Gierveld, Jenny, and Betty Havens. 2004. "Cross-National Comparisons of Social Isolation and Loneliness: Introduction and Overview." *Canadian Journal on Aging* 23(2):109–13.

de Jong Gierveld, Jenny, and Eva-Maria Merz. 2013. "Parents' Partnership Decision-Making after Divorce or Widowhood: The Role of (Step) Children." *Journal of Marriage and Family* 75(5):1098–113.

de Vries, Brian, Rebecca Utz, Michael Caserta, and Dale Lund. 2014. "Friend and Family Contact and Support in Early Widowhood." *Journals of Gerontology Series B: Psychological Sciences and Social Sciences* 69(1):75–84.

Dilworth-Anderson, Peggye, Beverly H. Brummett, Paula Goodwin, Sharon Wallace Williams, Redford B. Williams, and Ilene C. Siegler. 2005. "Effect of Race on Cultural Justifications for Caregiving." *Journals of Gerontology Series B: Psychological Sciences and Social Sciences* 60(5):S257–S262.

DiMatteo, M. Robin, Heidi S. Lepper, and Thomas W. Croghan. 2000. "Depression Is a Risk Factor for Noncompliance with Medical Treatment:

Meta-Analysis of the Effects of Anxiety and Depression on Patient Adherence." *Archives of Internal Medicine* 160(14):2101–07.

Doley, Rebekah, Ryan Bell, Bruce Watt, and Hannah Simpson. 2015. "Grandparents Raising Grandchildren: Investigating Factors Associated with Distress among Custodial Grandparent." *Journal of Family Studies* 21(2):101–19.

Donnelly, Rachel, Corinne Reczek, and Debra Umberson. 2018. "What We Know (and Don't Know) about the Bereavement Experiences of Same-Sex Spouses." Pp. 109–32 in *LGBTQ Divorce and Relationship Dissolution: Psychological and Legal Perspectives and Implications for Practice*, edited by A. E. Goldberg and A. Romero. New York: Oxford University Press.

Doonan, Dan, and Kelly Kenneally. 2021. "Generational Views of Retirement in the United States." National Institute on Retirement Security (July). https://www.nirsonline.org/wp-content/uploads/2021/07/Generations-Issue-Brief-F4.pdf, accessed July 24, 2021.

Duffy, Bobby. 2021. *The Generation Myth: Why When You're Born Matters Less Than You Think*. New York: Basic Books.

Dupre, Matthew E. 2007. "Educational Differences in Age-Related Patterns of Disease: Reconsidering the Cumulative Disadvantage and Age-as-Leveler Hypotheses." *Journal of Health and Social Behavior* 48(1):1–15.

Durkheim, Emile. [1897] 1951. *Suicide: A Study in Sociology*. Translated by John A. Spaulding. New York: Free Press.

Dushi, Irena, Howard M. Iams, and Christopher R. Tamborini. 2011. "Defined Contribution Pension Participation and Contributions by Earnings Levels Using Administrative Data." *Social Security Bulletin* 71 (2011): 67–77.

Dykstra, Pearl A. 1995. "Loneliness among the Never and Formerly Married: The Importance of Supportive Friendships and a Desire for Independence." *Journals of Gerontology Series B: Psychological Sciences and Social Sciences* 50B(5):S321–S329.

Elder, Glen H., Jr., ed. 1985. *Life Course Dynamics: Trajectories and Transitions, 1968–1980*. Ithaca, NY: Cornell University Press.

——. 1994. "Time, Human Agency, and Social Change: Perspectives on the Life Course." *Social Psychology Quarterly* 57(1):4–15.

The Elders. 2021. The Elders. https://theelders.org/, accessed August 28, 2021.

Ellis, Renee R., and Tavia Simmons. 2014. *Coresident Grandparents and Their Grandchildren: 2012*. U.S. Census Bureau. Washington, DC: U.S. Government Printing Office. https://www.census.gov/content/dam/Census/library/publications/2014/demo/p20-576.pdf, accessed December 25, 2020.

Elwert, Felix, and Nicholas A. Christakis. 2008. "The Effect of Widowhood on Mortality by the Causes of Death of Both Spouses." *American Journal of Public Health* 98(11):2092–98.

Epel, Elissa S., Elizabeth H. Blackburn, Jue Lin, Firdaus S. Dhabhar, Nancy E. Adler, Jason D. Morrow, and Richard M. Cawthon. 2004. "Accelerated

Telomere Shortening in Response to Life Stress." *Proceedings of the National Academy* 101(49):17312–15.

Etters, Lynn, Debbie Goodall, and Barbara E. Harrison. 2008. "Caregiver Burden among Dementia Patient Caregivers: A Review of the Literature." *Journal of the American Academy of Nurse Practitioners* 20(8):423–28.

Fairlie, Henry. 1988. "Talkin' 'Bout My Generation." *New Republic* (March 28), 19–21.

Faverio, Michelle. 2022. "Share of Those 65 and Older Who Are Tech Users Has Grown in the Past Decade." Pew Research Center (January 13). https://www.pewresearch.org/fact-tank/2022/01/13/share-of-those-65-and-older-who-are-tech-users-has-grown-in-the-past-decade, accessed January 15, 2022.

Federal Interagency Forum on Aging-Related Statistics. 2016. *Older Americans 2016: Key Indicators of Well-Being*. Washington, DC: US Government Printing Office.

———. 2020. *Older Americans 2020: Key Indicators of Well-Being*. Washington, DC: US Government Printing Office. (https://www.agingstats.gov/docs/LatestReport/OA20_508_10142020.pdf).

Ferraro, Kenneth F., and Tetyana Pylypiv Shippee. 2009. "Aging and Cumulative Inequality: How Does Inequality Get under the Skin?" *The Gerontologist* 49(3):333–43.

Fingerman, Karen, Laura Miller, Kira Birditt, and Steven Zarit. 2009. "Giving to the Good and the Needy: Parental Support of Grown Children." *Journal of Marriage and Family* 71(5):1220–33.

Fischer, David Hackett. 1978. *Growing Old in America*. New York: Oxford.

Fleming, Kevin C., Jonathan M. Evans, and Darryl S. Chutka. 2003a. "A Cultural and Economic History of Old Age in America." *Mayo Clinic Proceedings* 78: 914–21.

———. 2003b. "Caregiver and Clinician Shortages in an Aging Nation." *Mayo Clinic Proceedings* 78(8):1026–40.

Flores, Andrew R., Jody L. Herman, Gary J. Gates, and Taylor N. T. Brown. 2016. *How Many Adults Identify as Transgender in the United States?* Los Angeles: The Williams Institute. https://williamsinstitute.law.ucla.edu/wp-content/uploads/Trans-Adults-US-Aug-2016.pdf, accessed January 18, 2022.

Floyd, Frank J., Marsha Mailick Seltzer, Jan S. Greenberg, and Jieun Song. 2013. "Parental Bereavement during Mid-to-Later Life: Pre- to Postbereavement Functioning and Intrapersonal Resources for Coping." *Psychology and Aging* 28(2):402–13.

Ford, E. S., C. Li, G. Zhao, and J. Tsai. 2011. "Trends in Obesity and Abdominal Obesity among Adults in the United States from 1999–2008." *International Journal of Obesity* 35(5):736–43.

Ford, Tiffany Y, Sarah Reber, and Richard V. Reeves. 2020. "Race Gaps in COVID-19 Deaths Are Even Bigger Than They Appear." Brookings

(Tuesday, June 16). https://www.brookings.edu/blog/up-front/2020/06/16
/race-gaps-in-covid-19-deaths-are-even-bigger-than-they-appear/, accessed
July 7, 2021.

Freedman, Vicki. 1996. "Family Structure and the Risk of Nursing Home
Admission." *Journals of Gerontology Series B: Psychological and Social
Sciences* 51(2):S61–69.

Freeman, Harold P. 1989. "Cancer in the Socioeconomically Disadvantaged."
*CA: A Cancer Journal for Clinicians* 39(5):266–88.

Frey, William. 2021. "New 2020 Census Results Show Increased Diversity
Countering Decade-Long Declines in America's White and Youth Populations." Brookings Institution (August 13). https://www.brookings.edu
/research/new-2020-census-results-show-increased-diversity-countering
-decade-long-declines-in-americas-white-and-youth-populations/, accessed
August 18, 2021.

Friend, Tad. 2017. "Silicon Valley's Quest to Live Forever." *New Yorker* (April 3).
http://www.newyorker.com/magazine/2017/04/03/silicon-valleys-quest-to
-live-forever, accessed August 6, 2020.

Fry, Richard. 2020a. "Millennials Overtake Baby Boomers as America's Largest
Generation." Pew Research Center (April 28). https://www.pewresearch.org
/fact-tank/2020/04/28/millennials-overtake-baby-boomers-as-americas
-largest-generation/, accessed July 14, 2020.

———. 2020b. "The Pace of Boomer Retirements Has Accelerated in the Past
Year." *Pew Research Center* (November 9). https://www.pewresearch.org/fact
-tank/2020/11/09/the-pace-of-boomer-retirements-has-accelerated-in-the
-past-year/, accessed July 5, 2022.

Fulmer, Terry, David B. Reuben, John Auerbach, Donna Marie Fick, Colleen
Galambos, and Kimberly S. Johnson. 2021. "Actualizing Better Health and
Health Care for Older Adults: Commentary Describes Six Vital Directions
to Improve the Care and Quality of Life for All Older Americans." *Health
Affairs* 40(2):219–25.

Gabler, Ellen, Sheri Fink, and Vivian Yee. 2017. "At Florida Nursing Home,
Many Calls for Help, but None That Made a Difference." *New York Times*
(September 23). https://www.nytimes.com/2017/09/23/us/nursing-home
-deaths.html, accessed August 5, 2018.

Galucia, Natalie, Nancy Morrow-Howell, Peter Sun, Tanner Meyer, and Ying Li.
2021. "The Impact of COVID-19 on Villages: Results from a National
Survey." *Journal of Gerontological Social Work* 65(4):382–401. doi.org/10
.1080/01634372.2021.1968094.

Gans, Herbert. J. 1995. *The War against the Poor: The Underclass and Anti-
poverty Policy.* New York: Basic Books.

George, Linda K. 1993. "Sociological Perspectives on Life Transitions." *Annual
Review of Sociology* 19:353–73.

Gerontological Society of America. 2017. "Oral Health: An Essential Element of Healthy Aging." *What's Hot: Newsletter of the Gerontological Society of America.* https://www.geron.org/images/gsa/documents/oralhealth.pdf, accessed July 7, 2021.

Goldin, Claudia. 2006. "The Quiet Revolution that Transformed Women's Employment, Education, and Family." *American Economic Review* 96(2):1–21.

Goldman, Noreen. 2016. "Will the Latino Mortality Advantage Endure?" *Research on Aging*, 38(3):263–82.

Goldsen, Karen Fredriksen. 2016. "The Future of LGBT+ Aging: A Blueprint for Action in Services, Policies, and Research." *Generations* 40(2):6–15.

———. 2018. "Shifting Social Context in the Lives of LGBTQ Older Adults." *Public Policy & Aging Report* 28(1):24–28.

Graham, Carrie, Andrew E. Scharlach, and Elaine Kurtovich. 2018. "Do Villages Promote Aging in Place? Results of a Longitudinal Study." *Journal of Applied Gerontology* 37(3):310–31.

Green, Lorraine, and Victoria Grant. 2008. "'Gagged Grief and Beleaguered Bereavements?' An Analysis of Multidisciplinary Theory and Research Relating to Same Sex Partnership Bereavement." *Sexualities* 11(3):275–300.

Griffith, Derek M., Garima Sharma, Christopher S. Holliday, Okechuku K. Enyia, Matthew Valliere, Andrea R. Semlow, Elizabeth C. Stewart, and Roger Scott Blumenthal. 2020. "Men and COVID-19: A Biopsychosocial Approach to Understanding Sex Differences in Mortality and Recommendations for Practice and Policy Interventions." *Preventing Chronic Disease* 17:E63.

Grigoryeva, Angelina. 2017. "Own Gender, Sibling's Gender, Parent's Gender: The Division of Elderly Parent Care among Adult Children." *American Sociological Review* 82(1):116–46.

Guillet, Edwin C. 1963. *The Great Migration.* Toronto, ON: University of Toronto Press.

Gunn, David A., Helle Rexbye, Christopher E. M. Griffiths, Peter G. Murray, Amelia Fereday, Sharon D. Catt, and Cyrena C. Tomlin, et al. 2009. "Why Some Women Look Young for Their Age." *PloS One* 4:e8021.

Gurrentz, Benjamin. 2019. "Unmarried Partners More Diverse Than 20 Years Ago." Census Bureau (September 23). https://www.census.gov/library/stories/2019/09/unmarried-partners-more-diverse-than-20-years-ago.html, accessed February 14, 2021.

Haas Institute. 2016. *Responding to Rising Inequality Policy Interventions to Ensure Opportunity for All.* Berkeley, CA: Haas Institute. http://haas institute.berkeley.edu/sites/default/files/HaasInstitute_InequalityPolicy Brief_FINALforDISTRO_2.pdf, July 15, 2021.

Haber, Carole, and Brian Gratton. 1993. *Old Age and the Search for Security: An American Social History.* Bloomington: Indiana University Press.

Hagestad, Gunhild O. 1986. "The Family: Women and Grandparents as Kin-Keepers." Pp. 141–60 in *Our Aging Society: Paradox and Promise*, edited by A. J. Pifer and L. Bronte. New York: W.W. Norton.

Haines, Michael. 2008. "Fertility and Mortality in the United States." *EH.Net Encyclopedia*, edited by R. Whaples. Economic History Association (March 19). http://eh.net/encyclopedia/fertility-and-mortality-in-the-united -states/, accessed July 24, 2020.

Han, S. Duke, and Laura Mosqueda. 2020. "Elder Abuse in the COVID-19 Era." *Journal of the American Geriatrics Society* 68(7):1386–87. https://doi.org/10 .1111/jgs.16496.

Hannon, Joan Underhill. 1984. "The Generosity of Antebellum Poor Relief." *Journal of Economic History* 44(3):810–21.

Hannon, Kerry. 2011. "An Aging Population Means New Jobs." *Forbes* (September 26). https://www.forbes.com/sites/kerryhannon/2011/09/26/an-aging -population-means-new-jobs/#57988d157661.

Harada, Caroline N., Marissa C. Natelson Love, and Kristen L. Triebel. 2013. "Normal Cognitive Aging." *Clinics in Geriatric Medicine* 29(4):737–52.

Harris, Katherine M., Mark J. Edlund, and Sharon Larson. 2005. "Racial and Ethnic Differences in the Mental Health Problems and Use of Mental Health Care." *Medical Care* 43(8): 775–84.

Hartshorne, Joshua K., and Laura T. Germine. 2015. "When Does Cognitive Functioning Peak? The Asynchronous Rise and Fall of Different Cognitive Abilities across the Life Span." *Psychological Science* 26(4):433–43.

Havighurst, Robert J. 1963. "Successful Aging." In *Processes of Aging: Social and Psychological Perspectives*, edited by by R. H. Williams, C. Tibbits, and W. Donohue. New Brunswick, NJ: Aldine Transaction.

Hawkley, Louise C., and John T. Cacioppo. 2010. "Loneliness Matters: A Theoretical and Empirical Review of Consequences and Mechanisms." *Annals of Behavioral Medicine* 40(2):218–27.

Hayflick, Leonard. 1994. *How and Why We Age*. New York: Ballantine Books.

Hays, Judith C., Deborah T. Gold, and Carl F. Pieper. 1997. "Sibling Bereavement in Late Life." *OMEGA: Journal of Death and Dying* 35(1):25–42.

Hayslip, Bert Jr., Christine A. Fruhauf, and Megan L. Dolbin-MacNab. 2019. "Grandparents Raising Grandchildren: What Have We Learned over the Past Decade?" *The Gerontologist* 59(3):e152–e163.

Hayslip Bert Jr., Jessica H. Pruett, and Daniela M. Caballero. 2015. "The "How" and "When" of Parental Loss in Adulthood: Effects on Grief and Adjustment." *OMEGA: Journal of Death and Dying* 71(1):3–18.

Health Care Cost Institute. 2020. *2018 Health Care Cost and Utilization Report*. Washington, DC: HCCI. https://healthcostinstitute.org/images/pdfs/HCCI _2018_Health_Care_Cost_and_Utilization_Report.pdf, accessed August 20, 2021.

Hedegaard, Holly, Arialdi M. Miniño, Merianne Rose Spencer, and Margaret Warner. 2021. "Drug Overdose Deaths in the United States, 1999–2020." *NCHS Data Brief* 426:1–8.

Helppie-McFall, Brooke, Amanda Sonnega, Robert J. Willis, and Peter Hudomiet. 2015. "Occupations and Work Characteristics: Effects on Retirement Expectations and Timing." Ann Arbor, MI: Michigan Retirement Research Center, Working Paper 2015-331. https://ssrn.com/abstract=2737980 or http://dx.doi.org/10.2139/ssrn.2737980, accessed August 1, 2020.

Herd, Pamela, Melissa Favreault, Madonna Harrington Meyer, and Timothy M. Smeeding. 2018. "A Targeted Minimum Benefit Plan: A New Proposal to Reduce Poverty Among Older Social Security Recipients." *RSF: The Russell Sage Foundation Journal of the Social Sciences* 4(2):74–90.

Himes, Christine L., and Erin B. Reidy. 2000. "The Role of Friends in Caregiving." *Research on Aging* 22(4):315–36.

Holgash, Kayla, and Martha Heberlein. 2019. "Physician Acceptance of New Medicaid Patients." Health Affairs (April 10). https://www.healthaffairs.org/do/10.1377/forefront.20190401.678690/full/, accessed July 7. 2021.

Holmes, Thomas H., and Richard H. Rahe. 1967. "The Social Readjustment Rating Scale." *Journal of Psychosomatic Research* 11(2): 213–18.

Holstein, Martha B., and Meredith Minkler. 2007. "Critical Gerontology: Reflections for the 21st Century." Pp. 13–26 in *Critical Perspectives on Ageing Societies*, edited by M. Bernard and T. Scharf. Bristol, UK: Policy Press.

Hooper, Monica Webb, Anna María Nápoles, and Eliseo J. Pérez-Stable. 2020. "COVID-19 and Racial/Ethnic Disparities." *JAMA* 323(24):2466–67. doi:10.1001/jama.2020.8598.

Horn, Sarah R., Leslie D. Leve, Pat Levitt, and Philip A. Fisher. 2019. "Childhood Adversity, Mental Health, and Oxidative Stress: A Pilot Study." *PloS One* 14(4): doi.org/10.1371/journal.pone.0215085, accessed July 7, 2021.

House, James S. 2015. *Beyond Obamacare: Life, Death, and Social Policy*. New York: Russell Sage Foundation.

House, James S., Paula M. Lantz, and Pamela Herd. 2005. "Continuity and Change in the Social Stratification of Aging and Health over the Life Course: Evidence from a Nationally Representative Longitudinal Study from 1986 to 2001/2002 (Americans' Changing Lives Study)." *Journals of Gerontology: Series B*, 60: S15–S26.

Jacobson, Gretchen, Judith Feder, and David C. Radley. 2020. COVID-19's Impact on Older Workers: Employment, Income, and Medicare Spending. *Commonwealth Funds Issue Briefs* (October 6). https://www.commonwealth fund.org/publications/issue-briefs/2020/oct/covid-19-impact-older-workers-employment-income-medicare, accessed July 5, 2022.

James, Sherman A. 1994. "John Henryism and the Health of African-Americans." *Culture, Medicine and Psychiatry* 18(2):163–82.

Jenkins, J. Lee, Matthew Levy, Lainie Rutkow, and Adam Spira. 2014. "Variables Associated with Effects on Morbidity in Older Adults Following Disasters." *PLoS Currents* 6(December 5). doi: 10.1371/currents.dis.0fe970aa1 6d51cde6a962b7a732e494a.

Jensen, Svend E. Hougaard, Jukka Lassila, Niku Määttänen, Tarmo Valkonen, and Ed Westerhout. 2020. "The Top Three Pension Systems: Denmark, Finland, and the Netherlands." *Journal of Retirement* 8 (2)76–82.

Jia, Gengjie, Yu Li, Hanxin Zhang, Ishanu Chattopadhyay, Anders Boeck Jensen, David R. Blair, Lea Davis, et al. 2019. "Estimating Heritability and Genetic Correlations from Large Health Datasets in the Absence of Genetic Data." *Nature Communications* 10(1):1–11.

Johnson, Richard W., and Claire Xiaozhi Wang. 2017. "What Are the Top Jobs for Older Workers?" Urban Institute (December). https://www.urban.org /sites/default/files/publication/95011/what-are-the-top-jobs-for-older -workers_0.pdf, accessed October 6, 2020.

Johnson, Sara B., Robert W. Blum, and Jay N. Giedd. 2009. "Adolescent Maturity and the Brain: the Promise and Pitfalls of Neuroscience Research in Adolescent Health Policy." *Journal of Adolescent Health* 45(3):216–21.

Jonas, Daniel E., Yoko Ibuka, and Louise B. Russell. 2011. "How Much Time Do Adults Spend on Health-Related Self-Care? Results from the American Time Use Survey." *Journal of the American Board of Family Medicine* 24(4):380–90.

Jones, Maggie. 2022. "The Joys (and Challenges) of Sex after 70." *New York Times* (January 12). https://www.nytimes.com/2022/01/12/magazine/sex-old -age.html, accessed January 15, 2022.

Jun, Hankyung. 2020. "Social Security and Retirement in Fast-Aging Middle-Income Countries: Evidence from Korea." *Journal of the Economics of Ageing* 17(October). doi/10.1016/j.jeoa.2020.100284.

Kail, Ben Lennox, and Dawn C. Carr. 2020. "Structural Social Support and Changes in Depression during the Retirement Transition: "I Get by with a Little Help from My Friends." *Journals of Gerontology: Series B* 75(9): 2040–49.

Kaiser Family Foundation. 2019. "State Population Distribution by Age." State Health Facts. https://www.kff.org/other/state-indicator/distribution-by-age /?currentTimeframe=0&sortModel=%7B%22colId%22:%22Location%22, %22sort%22:%22asc%22%7D, accessed July 11, 2020.

———. 2021. "Can Immigrants Enroll in Medicare?" Enrollment Information for People New to Medicare. https://www.kff.org/faqs/medicare-open -enrollment-faqs/can-immigrants-enroll-in-medicare/, accessed July 7, 2021.

Kapadia, Resma Kapadia. 2019. "Addiction: The New Retirement Threat." *Barrons* (March 22). https://www.barrons.com/articles/addiction-the-new -retirement-threat-51553287281, accessed August 20, 2021.

Karel, Michelle J., Margaret Gatz, and Michael A. Smyer. 2012. "Aging and Mental Health in the Decade Ahead: What Psychologists Need to Know." *American Psychologist* 67(3):184–98.

Karlamangla, Arun S., Dana Miller-Martinez, Carol S. Aneshensel, Teresa E. Seeman, Richard G. Wight, and Joshua Chodosh. 2009. "Trajectories of Cognitive Function in Late Life in the United States: Demographic and Socioeconomic Predictors." *American Journal of Epidemiology* 170 (3):331–42.

Katz, Michael B. 1996. *In the Shadow of the Poorhouse: A Social History of Welfare in America*. New York: Basic Books.

Katz, Sidney. 1983. "Assessing Self-Maintenance: Activities of Daily Living, Mobility, and Instrumental Activities of Daily Living." *Journal of the American Geriatrics Society* 31(12):721–27.

Katz, Sidney, and C. Amechi Akpom. 1976. "A Measure of Primary Sociobiological Functions." *International Journal of Health Services* 6(3):493–508.

Kawachi, Ichiro, Norman Daniels, and Dean E. Robinson. 2002. "Health Disparities by Race and Class: Why Both Matter." *Health Affairs* 24(2): 343–52.

Kelsey, Megan M., Alysia Zaepfel, Petter Bjornstad, and Kristen J. Nadeau. 2014. "Age-Related Consequences of Childhood Obesity." *Gerontology* 60(3):222–28.

Kessler, Ronald C., Kristen D. Mickelson, and David R. Williams. 1999. "The Prevalence, Distribution, and Mental Health Correlates of Perceived Discrimination in the United States." *Journal of Health and Social Behavior* 40(3):208–30.

Khera, Amit V., Connor A. Emdin, Isabel Drake, Pradeep Natarajan, Alexander G. Bick, Nancy R. Cook, Daniel I. Chasman, Usman Baber, Roxana Mehran, Daniel J. Rader, Valentin Fuster, Eric Boerwinkle, Olle Melander, Marju Orho-Melander, Paul M Ridker, and Sekar Kathiresan. 2016. "Genetic Risk, Adherence to a Healthy Lifestyle, and Coronary Disease." *New England Journal of Medicine* 375(24):2349–58.

Khodyakov, Dmitry, and Deborah Carr. 2009. "The Impact of Late-Life Parental Death on Sibling Relationships: Do Advance Directives Help or Hurt?" *Research on Aging* 31:495–519.

Klinenberg, Eric. 2002. *Heat Wave: A Social Autopsy of Disaster in Chicago*. Chicago: University of Chicago Press.

Kochanek, Kenneth D., Sherry L. Murphy, Jiaquan Xu, and Elizabeth Arias. 2019. "Deaths: Final Data for 2017." *National Vital Statistics Reports*, 68(9).

Kontis, Vasilis, James E. Bennett, Colin D. Mathers, Guangquan Li, Kyle Foreman, and Majid Ezzati. 2017. "Future Life Expectancy in 35 Industrialised Countries: Projections with a Bayesian Model Ensemble." *The Lancet* 389(10076):1323–35.

Kramarow, Ellen. 2019. "Dental Care among Adults Aged 65 and Over, 2017." Washington, DC: *National Center for Health Statistics Data Brief, No. 337* (May). https://stacks.cdc.gov/view/cdc/78735, accessed July 7, 2021.

Kramarow, Ellen A., and Betzaida Tejada-Vera. 2019. "Dementia Mortality in the United States, 2000–2017." *National Vital Statistics Reports* 68(2):1–29.

Krause, Eleanor, and Richard V. Reeves. 2017. "Hurricanes Hit the Poor the Hardest." Brookings Institution (September 18). https://www.brookings.edu/blog/social-mobility-memos/2017/09/18/hurricanes-hit-the-poor-the-hardest/, accessed August 19, 2021.

Kripke, Pamela Gwyn. 2017. "Here's Another Way Baby Boomers Are Screwing the Rest of Us." *New York Post* (November 18). https://nypost.com/2017/11/18/you-can-count-on-getting-squat-when-your-parents-die/, accessed July 19, 2020.

Krogstad, Jens Manuel. 2015. "5 Facts about American Grandparents." Pew Research Center (September 13). https://www.pewresearch.org/fact-tank/2015/09/13/5-facts-about-american-grandparents/, accessed July 3, 2021.

Krueger, Alan B. 2015. "The Great Utility of the Great Gatsby Curve." Brookings Institution (May 19). https://www.brookings.edu/blog/social-mobility-memos/2015/05/19/the-great-utility-of-the-great-gatsby-curve/, accessed July 27, 2021.

Ku, Inhoe, and Chang-O. Kim. 2020. "Decomposition Analyses of the Trend in Poverty among Older Adults: The Case of South Korea." *Journals of Gerontology: Series B* 75(3):684–93.

Kunitz, Stephan J. 1984. "Mortality Change in America, 1620–1920." *Human Biology* 56(3):559–82.

Kurz, Christopher, Geng Li, and Daniel J. Vine 2018. "Are Millennials Different?" Finance and Economics Discussion Series 2018-080. Washington, DC: Board of Governors of the Federal Reserve System, https://doi.org/10.17016/FEDS.2018.080, accessed July 5, 2022.

Kutner, Mark, Elizabeth Greenberg, Ying Jin, and Christine Paulsen. 2006. *The Health Literacy of America's Adults: Results from the 2003 National Assessment of Adult Literacy (NCES 2006-483)*. Washington, DC: U.S. Department of Education, National Center for Education Statistics.

Kyff, Rob. 2012. "From Coots to Q-Tips, the Origins of Nicknames from Old-Timers." *Hartford Courant* (June 7, 2012). https://www.courant.com/hc-xpm-2012-06-07-hc-word-watch-kyff-0610-20120606-story.html, accessed July 5, 2022.

Laditka, James N., and Sarah B. Laditka. 2001. "Adult Children Helping Older Parents': Variations in Likelihood and Hours by Gender, Race, and Family Role." *Research on Aging* 23(4):429–56.

LaRoche, Julie. 2015. "Warren Buffett: 'Retirement Is Not My Idea of Living.'" *Business Insider* (October 14). http://www.businessinsider.com/why-buffett-says-he-wont-retire-2015-10, accessed August 2. 2020.

Lee, Yunhwan, Joung Hwan Back, Jinhee Kim, Si-Heon Kim, Duk L. Na, Hae-Kwan Cheong, Chang Hyung Hong, and Youn Gu Kim. 2010. "Systematic Review of Health Behavioral Risks and Cognitive Health in Older Adults." *International Psychogeriatrics* 22(2):174–87.

Leland, John. 2008. "In 'Sweetie' and 'Dear,' a Hurt for the Elderly." *New York Times* (October 6). http://www.nytimes.com/2008/10/07/us/07aging .html?_r=0, accessed September 20, 20120.

Levy, Becca R. 2003. "Mind Matters: Cognitive and Physical Effects of Aging Self-Stereotypes." *Journals of Gerontology Series B: Psychological Sciences and Social Sciences* 58(4):P203–P211.

Levy, Becca R., and Mahzarin R. Banaji. 2004. "Implicit Ageism." Pp. 37–76 in *Ageism: Stereotyping and Prejudice against Older Persons*, edited by T. D. Nelson. Cambridge, MA: MIT Press.

Levy, Daniel, Satish Kenchaiah, Martin G. Larson, Emelia J. Benjamin, Michelle J. Kupka, Kalon K. L. Ho, Joanne M. Murabito, and Ramachandran S. Vasan. 2002. "Long-Term Trends in the Incidence of and Survival with Heart Failure." *New England Journal of Medicine* 347(18): 1397–402.

Lichtenstein, Bronwen. 2020. "From 'Coffin Dodger' to 'Boomer Remover': Outbreaks of Ageism in Three Countries with Divergent Approaches to Coronavirus Control." *Journals of Gerontology: Series B* 76(4):e206–e12 (doi: 10.1093/geronb/gbaa102).

Lin, I-Fen, Susan L. Brown, and Cassandra Jean Cupka. 2018. "A National Portrait of Stepfamilies in Later Life." *Journals of Gerontology: Series B* 73(6):1043–54.

Lin, I-Fen, and Douglas A. Wolf. 2020. "Division of Parent Care among Adult Children." *Journals of Gerontology: Series B* 75(10):2230–39.

Link, Bruce G., and Jo Phelan. 1995. "Social Conditions as Fundamental Causes of Disease." *Journal of Health and Social Behavior* 35:80–94.

Lipka, Michael. 2015. "Mormons More Likely to Marry, Have More Children Than Other U.S. Religious Groups." Pew Research Center (May 22). https:// www.pewresearch.org/fact-tank/2015/05/22/mormons-more-likely-to -marry-have-more-children-than-other-u-s-religious-groups/, accessed July 15, 2020.

Lipnic, Victoria A. 2018. *The State of Age Discrimination and Older Workers in the U.S. 50 Years after the Age Discrimination in Employment Act (ADEA)*. Washington, DC: US Equal Employment Opportunity Commission. https://www.eeoc.gov/reports/state-age-discrimination-and-older -workers-us-50-years-after-age-discrimination-employment, accessed August 8, 2020.

Liu, Hui, Shannon Shen, and Ning Hsieh. 2019. "A National Dyadic Study of Oral Sex, Relationship Quality, and Well-Being among Older Couples." *Journals of Gerontology: Series B*, 74 (2):298–308.

Liu, Sze Yan, and Ichiro Kawachi. 2017. "Discrimination and Telomere Length among Older Adults in the United States: Does the Association Vary by Race and Type of Discrimination?" *Public Health Reports* 132(2):220–30.

Livingston, Gill, Andrew Sommerlad, Vasiliki Orgeta, Sergi G. Costafreda, Jonathan Huntley, David Ames, Clive Ballard et al. 2017. "Dementia Prevention, Intervention, and Care." *The Lancet* 390:2673–734.

Livingston, Gretchen. 2014. "Four-in-Ten Couples Are Saying 'I Do,' Again." Pew Research Center (November 14). (https://www.pewresearch.org/social-trends/2014/11/14/four-in-ten-couples-are-saying-i-do-again/), accessed March 12, 2021.

Lohr, Steve. 2021. "Seeking Not Just a Raise, but a Career." *New York Times* (August 19). https://www.nytimes.com/2021/08/18/business/workers-in-demand-have-a-new-demand-of-their-own-a-career-path.html, accessed August 19, 2021.

Lopez, Eric, Tricia Neuman, Gretchen Jacobson, and Larry Levitt. 2020. "How Much More Than Medicare Do Private Insurers Pay? A Review of the Literature." Kaiser Family Foundation (April 15). https://www.kff.org/medicare/issue-brief/how-much-more-than-medicare-do-private-insurers-pay-a-review-of-the-literature/, accessed July 7, 2021.

Lufkin, Bryan. 2020. "What the World Can Learn from Japan's Robots." *Japan 2020*, BBC (February 6). https://www.bbc.com/worklife/article/20200205-what-the-world-can-learn-from-japans-robots, accessed August 25, 2021.

Luhmann, Maike, and Louise C. Hawkley. 2016. "Age Differences in Loneliness: From Late Adolescence to Oldest Old Age." *Development Psychology* 52(6): 943–59.

Mahase, Elisabeth. 2021. "FDA Approves Controversial Alzheimer's Drug Despite Uncertainty over Effectiveness." *British Medical Journal* 373(1462). doi.org/10.1136/bmj.n1462, accessed July 7, 2021.

Mair, Christine A. 2019. "Alternatives to Aging Alone? 'Kinlessness' and the Importance of Friends across European Contexts." *Journals of Gerontology: Series B* 74(8):1416–28.

Makaroun, Lena K., Rachel L. Bachrach, and Ann-Marie Rosland. 2020. "Elder Abuse in the Time of COVID-19—Increased Risks for Older Adults and Their Caregivers." *American Journal of Geriatric Psychiatry* 28(8):876–80.

Malani, Preeti, Jeffrey Kullgren, Erica Solway, John Piette, Dianne Singer, and Matthias Kirch. 2020. *National Poll on Healthy Aging: Loneliness among Older Adults before and during the COVID-19 Pandemic.* Ann Arbor: University of Michigan. https://www.healthyagingpoll.org/report/loneliness-among-older-adults-and-during-covid-19-pandemic, accessed February 21.

Manheim, Karl. [1927] 1952. "The Problem of Generations." In *Essays in the Sociology of Knowledge*, edited by P. Kecskemeti. Boston: Routledge and Kegan Paul.

Manning, Wendy D., and Susan L. Brown. 2011. "The Demography of Unions among Older Americans, 1980–Present: A Family Change Approach." Pp. 193–210 in *Handbook of Sociology of Aging*, edited by R. A. Settersten Jr. and J. L. Angel. New York: Springer.

Manton, Kenneth G., XiLiang Gu, and Gene R. Lowrimore. 2008. "Cohort Changes in Active Life Expectancy in the US Elderly Population: Experience from the 1982–2004 National Long-Term Care Survey." *Journals of Gerontology Series B: Psychological Sciences and Social Sciences* 63(5):S269–S281.

Marans, David. 2017. "Senate Democrats Introduce Bill Allowing Medicare Buy-In At 55." *Huffington Post* (August 4). http://www.huffingtonpost.com /entry/democrats-medicare-expansion_us_598491c6e4b041356ebf7569, accessed August 29, 2021.

Margolis, Rachel, and Laura Wright. 2017. "Older Adults with Three Generations of Kin: Prevalence, Correlates, and Transfers." *Journals of Gerontology Series B: Psychological Sciences and Social Sciences* 72(6):1067–72.

Markides, Kyriakos S., and Karl Eschbach. 2005. "Aging, Migration, and Mortality: Current Status of Research on the Hispanic Paradox." *Journals of Gerontology Series B: Psychological Sciences and Social Sciences* 60:S68–S75.

Markides, Kyriakos S., and Richard Machalek. 2020. "Selective Survival, Aging, and Society." *Growing Old in America* (2020):187–205.

Marshall, Helen. 2004. "Midlife Loss of Parents: The Transition from Adult Child to Orphan." *Ageing International* 29(4):351–67.

Martikainen, Pekka T., and Tapani Valkonen. 1996. "Mortality after the Death of a Spouse: Rates and Causes of Death in a Large Finnish Cohort." *American Journal of Public Health* 86(8):1087–93.

Martin, Patricia P., and David A. Weaver. 2005. "Social Security: A Program and Policy History." *Social Security Bulletin* 66. https://www.ssa.gov/policy /docs/ssb/v66n1/v66n1p1.html, accessed August 1, 2020.

Mather, Mara. 2012. "The Emotion Paradox in the Aging Brain." *Annals of the New York Academy of Sciences* 1251:33–49.

Mather, Mark, and Lillian Kilduff. 2020. "The U.S. Population Is Growing Older, and the Gender Gap in Life Expectancy Is Narrowing." Population Reference Bureau (February 19). https://www.prb.org/the-u-s-population-is -growing-older-and-the-gender-gap-in-life-expectancy-is-narrowing/, accessed October 15, 2020.

Mathews, T. J., and Brady E. Hamilton. 2018. "Total Fertility Rates by State and Race and Hispanic Origin: United States, 2017." *National Vital Statistics Reports* 68(1):1–11.

Mathews, T. J., and Marian F. MacDorman. 2013. "Infant Mortality Statistics from the 2010 Period Linked Birth/Infant Death Data Set." *National Vital Statistics Reports* 62(8):1–26.

McDonald, John. 2021. "The Secret to a Long Life? Just Keep Living, Says 100-Year-Old Artist." *Sydney Morning Herald* (April 8). https://www.smh .com.au/culture/art-and-design/australia-s-ol5dest-artist-remains-at-the -canvas-reaching-a-century-20210401-p57fsu.html, accessed July 7, 2021.

McDonough, Ian M., Gérard N. Bischof, Kristen M. Kennedy, Karen M. Rodrigue, Michelle E. Farrell, and Denise C. Park. 2016. "Discrepancies between Fluid and Crystallized Ability in Healthy Adults: A Behavioral Marker of Preclinical Alzheimer's Disease." *Neurobiology of Aging* 46:68–75.

McPherson, Christine J., Keith G. Wilson, Michelle M. Lobchuk, and Susan Brajtman. 2007. "Self-Perceived Burden to Others: Patient and Family Caregiver Correlates." *Journal of Palliative Care* 23(3):135–42.

Meara, Ellen R., Seth Richards, and David M. Cutler. 2008. "The Gap Gets Bigger: Changes in Mortality and Life Expectancy, by Education, 1981–2000." *Health Affairs* 27(2):350–60.

Mechanic, David, and Donna D. McAlpine. 2011. "Mental Health and Aging: A Life-Course Perspective." Pp. 477–94 in *Handbook of Sociology of Aging*, edited by Richard A. Settersten Jr. and Jacqueline L. Angel. New York: Springer.

Medina, Lauren D., Shannon Sabo, and Jonathan Vespa, 2020. "Living Longer: Historical and Projected Life Expectancy in the United States, 1960 to 2060," Current Population Reports, P25-1145. Washington, DC: US Census Bureau.

Meisner, Brad A. 2020. "Are You OK, Boomer? Intensification of Ageism and Intergenerational Tensions on Social Media amid COVID-19." *Leisure Sciences* 43(1–2):56–61. doi.org/10.1080/01490400.2020.1773983.

MetLife Mature Market Institute. 2011. *The MetLife Study of Elder Financial Abuse: Crimes of Occasion, Desperation, and Predation against America's Elders.* New York: MetLife. https://www.metlife.com/assets/cao/mmi /publications/studies/2011/mmi-elder-financial-abuse.pdf, accessed March 25, 2017.

Meyer, Ilan H. 2003. "Prejudice, Social Stress, and Mental Health in Lesbian, Gay, and Bisexual Populations: Conceptual Issues and Research Evidence." *Psychological Bulletin* 129(5):674–97.

Meyer, Madonna Harrington, and Amra Kandic. 2017. "Grandparenting in the United States." *Innovation in Aging* 1(2):1–10.

Mills, C. Wright. 1959. *The Sociological Imagination.* New York: Oxford University Press.

Minkler, Meredith, and Carroll L. Estes. 2019. *Readings in the Political Economy of Aging.* New York: Routledge.

Mocatta, Gabi, and Rebecca Harris. 2021. "More Reasons for Optimism on Climate Change Than We've Seen for Decades." *The Conversation* (April 25). https://theconversation.com/more-reasons-for-optimism-on-climate-change -than-weve-seen-for-decades-2-climate-experts-explain-159233, accessed August 19, 2021.

Monahan, Caitlin, Jamie Macdonald, Ashley Lytle, MaryBeth Apriceno, and Sheri R. Levy. 2020. "COVID-19 and Ageism: How Positive and Negative Responses Impact Older Adults and Society." *American Psychologist* 75(7):887–96. http://dx.doi.org/10.1037/amp0000699.

Moore, Deborah, and Ross Keat. 2020. "Does Dental Appearance Impact on Employability in Adults? A Scoping Review of Quantitative and Qualitative Evidence." *British Dental Journal.* doi: 10.1038/s41415-020-2025-5.

Moran, Gwen. 2022. "Why Older Workers Are Switching Jobs Now." AARP (January 3). https://www.aarp.org/work/job-search/info-2022/older-workers -switching-jobs.html, accessed January 19, 2022.

Morrow-Howell, Nancy, Natalie Galucia, and Emma Swinford. 2020. "Recovering from the COVID-19 Pandemic: A Focus on Older Adults." *Journal of Aging & Social Policy* 32(4–5):526–35.

Moss, Sidney Z., and Miriam S. Moss. 1989. "The Impact of the Death of an Elderly Sibling: Some Considerations of a Normative Loss." *American Behavioral Scientist* 33(1): 94–106.

Mouzon, Dawne M. 2013. "Can Family Relationships Explain the Race Paradox in Mental Health?" *Journal of Marriage and Family* 75(2):470–85.

Musi, Nicolas, and Peter Hornsby, eds. 2021. *Handbook of the Biology of Aging.* New York: Academic Press.

National Academies of Sciences, Engineering, and Medicine. 2016. *Families Caring for an Aging America.* Washington, DC: The National Academies Press.

National Alliance for Caregiving, American Association of Retired Persons, and Public Policy Institute. 2015. *Caregiving in the U.S. 2015.* Washington, DC: National Alliance for Caregiving in collaboration with American Association of Retired Persons. http://www.caregiving.org/wp-content/uploads/2015/05 /2015_CaregivingintheUS_Final-Report-June-4_WEB.pdf, accessed October 22, 2016.

National Cancer Institute. 2021. "Age and Cancer Risk." . https://www.cancer .gov/about-cancer/causes-prevention/risk/age, accessed July 9, 2021.

National Center for Health Statistics. 2020. "Mortality Statistics." National Vital Statistics System. https://www.cdc.gov/nchs/nvss/deaths.htm.

National Centers for Environmental Information (NCEI). 2021. "U.S. Billion-Dollar Weather and Climate Disasters." accessed August 18, 2021. https:// www.ncei.noaa.gov/access/billions/, DOI: 10.25921/stkw-7w73.

National Council on Aging. 2017. "2015 Results: The United States of Aging Survey." Washington, DC: National Council on Aging. https://www.ncoa.org /news/resources-for-reporters/usoa-survey/2015-results/, accessed September 27, 2020.

———. 2021. "Elder Abuse Facts." . https://www.ncoa.org/public-policy-action /elder-justice/elder-abuse-facts/, accessed February 5, 2021.

National Institute of Mental Health. 2021. "Suicide." https://www.nimh.nih.gov /health/statistics/suicide, accessed July 6, 2021.

Neumark, David, Ian Burn, and Patrick Button. 2017. "Age Discrimination and Hiring of Older Workers." *Age* 6(1):1–5.

*New York Times* Editorial Board. 2020. "Nursing Home Patients Are Dying of Loneliness." *New York Times* (December 29). https://www.nytimes.com/2020 /12/29/opinion/coronavirus-nursing-homes.html, accessed January 1, 2021.

Newport, Frank. 2018. "In U.S., Estimate of LGBT Population Rises to 4.5%." Gallup (May 22). https://news.gallup.com/poll/234863/estimate-lgbt -population-rises.aspx.

Noël-Miller, Claire M. 2011. "Partner Caregiving in Older Cohabiting Couples." *Journals of Gerontology Series B: Psychological Sciences and Social Sciences* 66(3):341–53.

Noppert, Grace A., Rebecca C. Stebbins, Jennifer B. Dowd, Robert A. Hummer, and Allison E. Aiello. 2020. "Life Course Socioeconomic Disadvantage and the Aging Immune System: Findings from the Health and Retirement Study." *Journal of Gerontology: Series B* 76(6):1195–205. doi.org/10.1093 /geronb/gbaa144.

Nyce, Steven A., and Sylvester J. Schieber. 2005. *The Economic Implications of Aging Societies: The Costs of Living Happily Ever After*. Cambridge: Cambridge University Press.

Odlum, M., N. Moise, I. M. Kronish, et al. 2020. "Trends in Poor Health Indicators among Black and Hispanic Middle-Aged and Older Adults in the United States, 1999–2018." *JAMA Netw Open*. doi:10.1001/jamanetwork open.2020.25134.

Oliva, Jessica Lee, and Kim Louise Johnston. 2020. "Puppy Love in the Time of Corona: Dog Ownership Protects against Loneliness for Those Living Alone during the COVID-19 Lockdown." *International Journal of Social Psychiatry* 67(3):232–42.

Oliver, Melvin, and Thomas Shapiro. 2013. *Black Wealth/White Wealth: A New Perspective on Racial Inequality*. New York: Routledge.

Oliynyk, Roman Teo. 2019. "Age-Related Late-Onset Disease Heritability Patterns and Implications for Genome-Wide Association Studies." *PeerJ* 7. doi: 10.7717/peerj.7168.

Olshansky, S. Jay, and A. Brian Ault. 1986. "The Fourth Stage of the Epidemio-logic Transition: the Age of Delayed Degenerative Diseases." *Milbank Quarterly* 64(3):355–91.

Omran, Abdel. 1971. "The Epidemiologic Transition: A Theory of the Epidemiol-ogy of Population Change." *Milbank Memorial Fund Quarterly* 49(4):509–38.

O'Rand, Angela M. 1996. "The Precious and the Precocious: Understanding Cumulative Disadvantage and Cumulative Advantage over the Life Course." *The Gerontologist* 36(2):230–38.

Organisation for Economic Co-operation and Development (OECD). 2017. *Pensions at a Glance 2017: OECD and G20 Indicators.* Paris: OECD Publishing. http://dx.doi.org/10.1787/pension_glance-2017-en, accessed July 15, 2021.

———. 2021a. "Elderly Population." OECD Data. doi: 10.1787/8d805ea1-en, accessed July 11, 2021.

———. 2021b. "Life Expectancy at Age 65." Paris: OECD Data. doi: 10.1787/0e9a3f00-en, accessed July 11, 2021.

———. 2021c. "Poverty Rate." OECD Data. https://data.oecd.org/inequality/poverty-rate.htm, accessed July 11, 2021.

Ornstein, Charles, and Jessica Huseman. 2016. "Federal Officials Seek to Stop Social Media Abuse of Nursing Home Residents." *Shots: Health News from NPR* (August 8). http://www.npr.org/sections/health-shots/2016/08/08/489195484/federal-officials-seek-to-stop-social-media-abuse-of-nursing-home-residents, accessed February 10, 2021.

Osborn, Robin, Michelle M. Doty, Donald Moulds, Dana O. Sarnak, and Arnav Shah. 2017. "Older Americans Were Sicker and Faced More Financial Barriers to Health Care Than Counterparts in Other Countries." *Health Affairs* 36(12):2123–32.

Osterman, Michelle J. K., Brady E. Hamilton, Joyce A. Martin, Anne K. Driscoll, and Claudia P. Valenzuela. 2022. "Births: Final Data for 2020." *National Vital Statistics Report* 70(17). https://stacks.cdc.gov/view/cdc/112078, accessed July 6, 2022.

Osterman, Paul. 2017. *Who Will Care for Us? Long-Term Care and the Long-Term Workforce: Long-Term Care and the Long-Term Workforce.* New York: Russell Sage Foundation.

Paine, Thomas. [1775–1776] 1986. *Common Sense.* New York: Penguin.

———. 1795. *Agrarian Justice.* Philadelphia, PA: R. Folwell.

Palmore, Erdman. 2001. "The Ageism Survey: First Findings." *The Gerontologist* 41(5):572–75. https://doi.org/10.1093/geront/41.5.572.

Pampel, Fred C., Patrick M. Krueger, and Justin T. Denney. 2010. "Socioeconomic Disparities in Health Behaviors." *Annual Review of Sociology* 36:349–70.

Paraprofessoinal Healthcare Institute. 2021. *Caring for the Future: The Power and Potential of America's Direct Care Workforce.* Bronx, NY: PHI. https://phinational.org/resource/caring-for-the-future-the-power-and-potential-of-americas-direct-care-workforce/, accessed August 29, 2021.

Parkes, Colin Murray, and Holly G. Prigerson. 2013. *Bereavement: Studies of Grief in Adult Life.* New York: Routledge.

Pasupathi, Monisha, and Corinna E. Löckenhoff. 2002. "Ageist Behavior." Pp. 201–46 in *Ageism: Stereotyping and Prejudice against Older Persons,* edited by T. D. Nelson. Cambridge, MA: MIT Press.

Pew Research Center. 2015. "Women and Leadership: Public Says Women Are Equally Qualified, but Barriers Persist." https://www.pewsocialtrends.org /2015/01/14/women-and-leadership/, accessed July 11, 2020.

———. 2019. "Religion and Living Arrangements Around the World." https:// www.pewforum.org/2019/12/12/religion-and-living-arrangements-around -the-world/, accessed July 23, 2021.

Phelan, Jo C., and Bruce G. Link. 2015. "Is Racism a Fundamental Cause of Inequalities in Health?" *Annual Review of Sociology* 41:311–30.

Piketty, Thomas. 2014. *Capital in the 21st Century.* Cambridge, MA: Harvard University Press.

Pillemer, Karl, and J. Jill Suitor. 20124. "Who Provides Care? A Prospective Study of Caregiving among Adult Siblings." *The Gerontologist* 54(4):589–98.

Pinquart, Martin, and Silvia Sörensen. 2005. "Ethnic Differences in Stressors, Resources, and Psychological Outcomes of Family Caregiving: A Meta-Analysis." *The Gerontologist* 45(1):90–106.

Pitman, Alexandra L., Fiona Stevenson, David P. J. Osborn, and Michael B. King. 2018. "The Stigma Associated with Bereavement by Suicide and other Sudden Deaths: A Qualitative Interview Study." *Social Science & Medicine* 198:121–29.

Ploeg, Jenny, Lynne Lohfeld, Christine A. Walsh. 2013. "What Is 'Elder Abuse'? Voices from the Margin: The Views of Underrepresented Canadian Older Adults." *Journal of Elder Abuse & Neglect* 25(5):396–424. doi: 10.1080/ 08946566.2013.780956.

Poon, Leonard W., Gloria M. Clayton, Peter Martin, Mary Ann Johnson, Bradley C. Courtenay, Anne L. Sweaney, Sharan B. Merriam, Betsy S. Pless, and Samuel B. Thielman. 1992. "The Georgia Centenarian Study." *International Journal of Aging and Human Development* 34:1–17.

Poon, Linda, and Sarah Holder. 2020. "The 'New Normal' for Many Older Adults Is on the Internet." *CityLab* (May 6). https://www.bloomberg.com /news/features/2020-05-06/in-lockdown-seniors-are-becoming-more-tech -savvy, accessed February 19, 2021.

Posner, Richard A. 1995. *Aging and Old Age.* Chicago: University of Chicago Press.

Preston, Samuel H. 1984. "Children and the Elderly: Divergent Paths for America's Dependents." *Demography* 21(4):435–57.

Preston, Samuel H., and Michael R. Haines. 1991. *Fatal Years: Child Mortality in Late Nineteenth-Century America.* Princeton, NJ: Princeton University Press.

Pruchno, Rachel. 2019. "Technology and Aging: An Evolving Partnership." *The Gerontologist* 59(1):1–5.

Qualls, Sara Honn. 2021. "Family Caregiving." Pp. 221–38 in *Handbook of Aging and the Social Sciences*, 9th ed., edited by K. F. Ferraro and D. Carr. New York: Academic Press.

*QC Metro.* 2019. "Hester Ford of Charlotte Now Listed as Oldest American." *QC Metro* (December 1). https://qcitymetro.com/2019/12/01/hester-ford-of -charlotte-now-listed-as-oldest-american/, accessed July 1, 2022.

Raifman, Matthew A., and Julia R. Raifman. 2020. "Disparities in the Population at Risk of Severe Illness from COVID-19 by Race/Ethnicity and Income." *American Journal of Preventive Medicine* 59(1):137–39.

Raley, R. Kelly, Megan M. Sweeney, and Danielle Wondra. 2015. "The Growing Racial and Ethnic Divide in U.S. Marriage Patterns." *Future Child* 25(2): 89–109. doi: 10.1353/foc.2015.0014.

Raymond, Amanda. 2020. "Live Long and Prosper: Hester Ford Celebrates Her 115th Birthday." *Charlotte Post* (August 19). http://www.thecharlottepost.com /news/2020/08/19/life-and-religion/live-long-and-prosper-hester-ford -celebrates-her-116th-birthday/, accessed December 6, 2020.

Read, Jen'nan Ghazal, and Bridget K. Gorman. 2010. "Gender and Health Inequality." *Annual Review of Sociology* 36:371–86.

Reinhardt, Uwe E. 2019. *Priced Out.* Princeton, NJ: Princeton University Press.

Rexbye, Helle, Inge Petersen, Mette Johansens, Louise Klitkou, Bernard Jeune, and Kaare Christensen. 2006. "Influence of Environmental Factors on Facial Ageing." *Age and Ageing* 35:110–15.

Richardson, Robin A., Katherine M. Keyes, José T. Medina, and Esteban Calvo. 2020. "Sociodemographic Inequalities in Depression among Older Adults: Cross-Sectional Evidence from 18 Countries." *The Lancet Psychiatry* 7(8): 673–81.

Rindfuss, Ronald R., and James A. Sweet. 2013. *Postwar Fertility Trends and Differentials in the United States.* New York: Elsevier.

Roberto, Karen A. 2016. "Abusive Relationships in Late Life." Pp. 335–56 in *Handbook of Aging and the Social Sciences*, edited by L. K. George and K. F. Ferraro. New York: Academic Press.

Roberto, Karen A., and Emily Hoyt. 2021. "Abuse of Older Women in the United States: A Review of Empirical Research, 2017–2019." *Aggression and Violent Behavior* 57:101487.

Roberto, Karen A., and Pat Ianni Stanis. 1994. "Reactions of Older Women to the Death of Their Close Friends." *OMEGA: Journal of Death and Dying* 29(1):17–27.

Roberts, Andrew W., Stella U. Ogunwole, Laura Blakeslee, and Megan A. Rabe. 2018. *The Population 65 Years and Older in the United States: 2016.* Suitland, MD, USA: US Department of Commerce, Economics and Statistics Administration, US Census Bureau.

Robinson, Linda, and Margaret M. Mahon. 1997. "Sibling Bereavement: A Concept Analysis." *Death Studies* 21(5):477–99.

Roepke-Buehler, Susan K., Melissa Simon, and XinQi Dong. 2015. "Association between Depressive Symptoms, Multiple Dimensions of Depression, and

Elder Abuse: a Cross-Sectional, Population-Based Analysis of Older Adults in Urban Chicago." *Journal of Aging and Health* 27: 1003–25.

Rogers, Catherine H., Frank J. Floyd, Marsha Mailick Seltzer, Jan Greenberg, and Jinkuk Hong. 2008. "Long-Term Effects of the Death of a Child on Parents' Adjustment in Midlife." *Journal of Family Psychology* 22(2):203–11.

Romig, Kathleen, and Arloc Sherman. 2016. "Social Security Keeps 22 Million Americans Out of Poverty: A State-by-State Analysis." Center for Budget and Policy Priorities (October 25). http://www.cbpp.org/research/social-security -keeps-22-million-americans-out-of-poverty-a-state-by-state-analysis, accessed October 5, 2020.

Roscigno, Vincent J., Sherry Mong, Reginald Byron, and Griff Tester. 2007. "Age Discrimination, Social Closure and Employment." *Social Forces* 86(1):313–34.

Rossen, Lauren M., Amy M. Branum, Farida B. Ahmad, Paul Sutton, and Robert N. Anderson. 2020. "Excess Deaths Associated with COVID-19, by Age and Race and Ethnicity—United States, January 26–October 3, 2020." *Morbidity and Mortality Weekly Report* 69 (42):1522–27. https://www.ncbi .nlm.nih.gov/pmc/articles/PMC7583499.

Rossi, Alice S., and Peter Henry Rossi. 1990. *Of Human Bonding: Parent-Child Relations across the Life Course.* Piscataway, NJ: Transaction Publishers.

Rothstein, Richard. 2017. *The Color of Law: A Forgotten History of How Our Government Segregated America.* New York: W. W. Norton.

Rowe, John W., and Robert L. Kahn. 2015. "Successful Aging 2.0: Conceptual Expansions for the 21st Century." *Journals of Gerontology: Series B* 70(4): 593–96.

Rowe, Timothy. 2006. "Fertility and a Woman's Age." *Journal of Reproductive Medicine* 51(3):157–63.

Ruggles, Steven. 2007. "The Decline of Intergenerational Coresidence in the United States, 1850 to 2000." *American Sociological Review* 72(6):964–89.

Rurka, Marissa, J. Jill Suitor, and Megan Gilligan. 2020. "The Caregiver Identity in Context: Consequences of Identity Threat from Siblings." *Journals of Gerontology: Series B*:1–12.

Saltzman, Leia Y., Tonya Cross Hansel, and Patrick S. Bordnick. 2020. "Loneliness, Isolation, and Social Support Factors in Post-COVID-19 Mental Health." *Psychological Trauma: Theory, Research, Practice, and Policy* 12(S1):S55–S57.

Samuel, Sigal. 2020. "You Can Buy a Robot to Keep Your Lonely Grandparents Company. Should You?" *Vox* (December 8). https://www.vox.com/future -perfect/2020/9/9/21418390/robots-pandemic-loneliness-, accessed August 25, 2021.

Samuelson, Robert. 2019. "Don't Expand Social Security. Our Elderly Are Mostly Fine." *Washington Post* (February 10, 2019). https://www.washington post.com/opinions/dont-expand-social-security-our-elderly-are-mostly-fine

/2019/02/10/a65ae6ce-2bc9-11e9-b011-d8500644dc98_story.html, accessed July 30, 2020.

Sanders, Jason L., and Anne B. Newman. 2013. "Telomere Length in Epidemiology: A Biomarker of Aging, Age-Related Disease, Both, or Neither?" *Epidemiologic Reviews* 35(1):112–31.

Sanger-Katz, Margot. 2021. "Five Decades Later, Medicare Might Cover Dental Care." *New York Times* (August 29). https://www.nytimes.com/2021/08/29/upshot/medicare-dental-care.html, accessed August 29, 2021.

Santos-Lozano, Alejandro, Ana Santamarina, Helios Pareja-Galeano, Fabian Sanchis-Gomar, Carmen Fiuza-Luces, Carlos Cristi-Montero, Aranzazu Bernal-Pino, Alejandro Lucia, and Nuria Garatachea. 2016. "The Genetics of Exceptional Longevity: Insights from Centenarians." *Maturitas* 90:49–57.

Saraceno, Benedetto, Itzhak Levav, and Robert Kohn. 2005. "The Public Mental Health Significance of Research on Socio-economic Factors in Schizophrenia and Major Depression." *World Psychiatry* 4(3):181–85.

Sarkisian, Natalia, Mariana Gerena, and Naomi Gerstel. 2007. "Extended Family Integration among Euro and Mexican Americans: Ethnicity, Gender, and Class." *Journal of Marriage and Family* 69(1):40–54.

Sarkisian, Natalia, and Naomi Gerstel. 2008. "Till Marriage Do Us Part: Adult Children's Relationships with Their Parents." *Journal of Marriage and Family* 70(2):360–76.

Schaeffer, Katherine. 2019. "The Most Common Age among Whites in U.S. Is 58—More Than Double That of Racial and Ethnic Minorities." Pew Research Center (July 30). https://www.pewresearch.org/fact-tank/2019/07/30/most-common-age-among-us-racial-ethnic-groups/, accessed October 8, 2020.

Schafer, Markus H., and Jonathan Koltai. 2014. "Does Embeddedness Protect? Personal Network Density and Vulnerability to Mistreatment among Older American Adults." *Journals of Gerontology Series B: Psychological Sciences and Social Sciences* 70(4):597–606.

Scherer, Zachary, and Rose M. Kreider. 2019. "Exploring the Link between Socioeconomic Factors and Parental Mortality." Washington, DC: US Census Bureau. https://www.census.gov/content/dam/Census/library/working-papers/2019/demo/sehsd-wp2019-12.pdf, accessed July 6, 2022.

Schieber, Sylvester J., and John B. Shoven. 1999. *The Real Deal: The History and Future of Social Security.* New Haven, CT: Yale University Press.

Schroeder, Steven A. 2007. "We Can Do Better—Improving the Health of the American People." *New England Journal of Medicine* 357(12):1221–28.

Scully, Eileen P., Jenna Haverfield, Rebecca L. Ursin, Cara Tannenbaum, and Sabra L. Klein. 2020. "Considering How Biological Sex Impacts Immune Responses and COVID-19 Outcomes." *Nature Reviews Immunology* 20:442–47. https://doi.org/10.1038/s41577-020-0348-8.

Shadel, Doug, and Karla Pak. 2017. *AARP Investment Fraud Vulnerability Study*. Washington, DC: AARP Research. https://www.aarp.org/content /dam/aarp/research/surveys_statistics/econ/2017/investment-fraud -vulnerability.doi.10.26419%252Fres.00150.001.pdf.

Shanahan, Michael J., and Scott M. Hofer. 2005. "Social Context in Gene–Environment Interactions: Retrospect and Prospect." *Journals of Gerontology Series B: Psychological Sciences and Social Sciences* 60(Special Issue 1): 65–76.

Shankar, Aparna, Anne McMunn, James Banks, and Andrew Steptoe. 2011. "Loneliness, Social Isolation, and Behavioral and Biological Health Indicators in Older Adults." *Health Psychology* 30(4): 377.

Shear, M. Katherine, Naomi Simon, Melanie Wall, Sidney Zisook, Robert Neimeyer, Naihua Duan, and Charles Reynolds et al. 2011. "Complicated Grief and Related Bereavement Issues for DSM-5." *Depression and Anxiety* 28(2):103–17.

Shellman, Juliette, Camella Granara, and Gabrielle Rosengarten. 2011. "Barriers to Depression Care for Black Older Adults: Practice and Policy Implications." *Journal of Gerontological Nursing* 37:13–17.

Sherman, Carey Wexler, Noah J. Webster, and Toni C. Antonucci. 2013. "Dementia Caregiving in the Context of Late-Life Remarriage: Support Networks, Relationship Quality, and Well-Being." *Journal of Marriage and Family* 75:1149–63.

Silver, Laura, Patrick Van Kessel, Christine Huang, Laura Clancy, and Sneha Gubbala. 2021. *What Makes Life Meaningful? Views from 17 Advanced Economies*. Washington, DC: Pew Research Center. https://www.pew research.org/global/wp-content/uploads/sites/2/2021/11/PG_11.18.21 _meaning-in-life_fullreport.pdf, accessed July 5, 2022.

Singh, Gopal K., and Hyunjung Lee. 2021. "Marked Disparities in Life Expectancy by Education, Poverty Level, Occupation, and Housing Tenure in the United States, 1997–2014." *International Journal of MCH and AIDS* 10(1): 7–18. doi:10.21106/ijma.402.

Sleep Foundation. 2020. *Insomnia and Seniors* (September 18). https://www .sleepfoudation.org/insomnia/older-adults, accessed April 10, 2021.

Smith, Adam. 2021. "2020 U.S. Billion-Dollar Weather and Climate Disasters in Historical Context." National Oceanic and Atmospheric Administration (January 8). https://www.climate.gov/news-features/blogs/beyond-data /2020-us-billion-dollar-weather-and-climate-disasters-historical, accessed July 27, 2021.

Smock, Pamela J., and Christine R. Schwartz. 2020. "The Demography of Families: A Review of Patterns and Change." *Journal of Marriage and Family* 82(1):9–34.

Social Security Administration. 2022. *Retirement Benefits*. Washington, DC: Social Security Administration. https://www.ssa.gov/pubs/EN-05-10035.pdf, accessed July 5, 2022.

Solomon, Barbara Miller. 1985. *In the Company of Educated Women: A History of Women and Higher Education in America*. New Haven, CT: Yale University Press.

Span, Paula. 2020. "When Romance Is a Scam." *New York Times* (March 27). https://www.nytimes.com/2020/03/27/well/elderly-romance-scam.html, accessed February 20, 2021.

Springer, Kristen W., and Dawne M. Mouzon. 2011. "'Macho Men' and Preventive Health Care: Implications for Older Men in Different Social Classes." *Journal of Health and Social Behavior* 52(2):212–27.

Steptoe, Andrew, Aparna Shankar, Panayotes Demakakos, and Jane Wardle. 2013. "Social Isolation, Loneliness, and All-Cause Mortality in Older Men and Women." *Proceedings of the National Academy of Sciences* 110(15): 5797–801.

Sterrett, David, Jennifer A. Titus, Jennifer K. Benz, and Liz Kantor, L. 2017. "Perceptions of Aging during Each Decade of Life after 30." Issue Brief. West Health Institute; NORC. https://www.norc.org/PDFs/WHI-NORC-Aging-Survey/Brief_WestHealth_A_2017-03_DTPv2.pdf, accessed April 10, 2021.

Stokes, Andrew C., Jordan Weiss, Dielle J. Lundberg, Wubin Xie, Jung Ki Kim, Samuel H. Preston, and Eileen M. Crimmins. 2020. "Estimates of the Association of Dementia with US Mortality Levels Using Linked Survey and Mortality Records." *JAMA Neurology* 77(12):1543–50.

Stone, Robyn L., and Natasha Bryant. 2021. "Feeling Valued Because They Are Valued: A Vision for Professionalizing the Caregiving Workforce in the Field of Long-Term Services and Supports." LeadingAge LTSS Center @UMass Boston. https://leadingage.org/sites/default/files/Workforce%20Vision%20Paper_FINAL.pdf, accessed January 17, 2022.

Stroebe, Margaret, and Henk Schut. 2010. "The Dual Process Model of Coping with Bereavement: A Decade On." *OMEGA—Journal of Death and Dying* 61(4):273–89.

Stuber, Jennifer, Kathleen Maloy, Sara Rosenbaum, and Karen C. Jones. 2000. "Beyond Stigma: What Barriers Actually Affect the Decisions of Low-Income Families to Enroll in Medicaid?" Health Policy and Management Issue Briefs paper 53. The George Washington University.

Sugarman, Samantha. 2018. "Maine's New Recruitment Tool Targeting Out-of-State College Graduates." *News Center Maine* (October 28, 2018). https://www.newscentermaine.com/article/news/local/maines-new-recruitment-tool-targeting-out-of-state-college-graduates/97-609313582, accessed July 15, 2020.

Taylor, Shelley E., and Teresa E. Seeman. 1999. "Psychosocial Resources and the SES-Health Relationship." *Annals of the New York Academy of Sciences* 896:210–25.

Thomas, John, D. Johniene Thomas, Thomas Pearson, Michael Klag, and Lucy Mead. 1997. "Cardiovascular Disease in African American and White

Physicians: The Meharry Cohort and Meharry-Hopkins Cohort Studies." *Journal of Health Care for the Poor and Underserved* 8(3): 270–83.

Thomas, Patricia A., and Seoyoun Kim. 2020. "Lost Touch? Implications of Physical Touch for Physical Health." *Journals of Gerontology: Series B* 76(3):e111–e115.

Thompson, Andrea. 2020. "How the Environment Has Changed since the First Earth Day 50 Years Ago." *Scientific American* (April 22). https://www .scientificamerican.com/article/how-the-environment-has-changed-since -the-first-earth-day-50-years-ago/, accessed July 25, 2021.

Tolbert, Jennifer, Kendal Orgera, and Anthony Damico. 2020. "Key Facts about the Uninsured Population," Kaiser Family Foundation (November 6). https:// www.kff.org/uninsured/issue-brief/key-facts-about-the-uninsured -population/, accessed July 7, 2021.

Traub, Amy, Laura Sullivan, Tatjana Meschede, and Tom Shapiro. 2017. "The Asset Value of Whiteness: Understanding the Racial Wealth Gap." *Demos* (February 6). https://www.demos.org/publication/asset-value-whiteness -understanding-racial-wealth-gap, accessed October 3, 2020.

Turner, R. Jay, and William R. Avison. 2003. "Status Variations in Stress Exposure: Implications for the Interpretation of Research on Race, Socio-economic Status, and Gender." *Journal of Health and Social Behavior* 44(4):488–505.

Umberson, Debra, and Meichu D. Chen. 1994. "Effects of a Parent's Death on Adult Children: Relationship Salience and Reaction to Loss." *American Sociological Review* 59:152–68.

Umberson, Debra, Julie Skalamera Olson, Robert Crosnoe, Hui Liu, Tetyana Pudrovska, and Rachel Donnelly. 2017. "Death of Family Members as an Overlooked Source of Racial Disadvantage in the United States." *Proceedings of the National Academy of Sciences of the United States of America* 114(5):915–20.

Umberson, Debra, Mieke Beth Thomeer, Rhiannon A. Kroeger, Corinne Reczek, and Rachel Donnelly. 2016. "Instrumental- and Emotion-Focused Care Work during Physical Health Events: Comparing Gay, Lesbian, and Heterosexual Marriages." *Journals of Gerontology Series B: Psychological and Social Sciences* 72(3):498–509.

United Nations Department of Economic and Social Affairs, Population Division. 2016. *Income Poverty in Old Age: An Emerging Development Priority.* New York: United Nations. https://www.un.org/esa/socdev/ageing /documents/PovertyIssuePaperAgeing.pdf, accessed July 20, 2021.

———. 2019. *World Population Ageing 2019: Highlights* (ST/ESA/SER.A/430). New York: United Nations.

———. 2020. *World Population Ageing 2020 Highlights: Living Arrangements of Older Persons.* New York: United Nations. https://www.un.org/development

/desa/pd/sites/www.un.org.development.desa.pd/files/undesa_pd-2020
_world_population_ageing_highlights.pdf, accessed August 30, 2021.

US Census Bureau. 2016. *Measuring America: Our Changing Landscape.*
Washington, DC: Census Bureau (December 8). https://www.census.gov
/library/visualizations/2016/comm/acs-rural-urban.html, accessed July 12,
2020.

———. 2019a. "Historical Living Arrangements of Adults." Census Bureau
(November). https://www.census.gov/data/tables/time-series/demo/families
/adults.html, accessed August 2, 2020.

———. 2019b. "Historical Poverty Tables: People and Families—1959 to 2018."
Census Bureau. https://www.census.gov/data/tables/time-series/demo
/income-poverty/historical-poverty-people.html, accessed August 3, 2020.

———. 2020a. "America's Families and Living Arrangements: 2019." Census
Bureau. https://www.census.gov/data/tables/2019/demo/families/cps-2019
.html.

———. 2020b. "Annual Estimates of the Resident Population for Selected Age
Groups by Sex: April 1, 2010, to July 1, 2019." Census Bureau, Population
Division (June). https://www.census.gov/data/tables/time-series/demo
/popest/2010s-state-detail.html, accessed July 12, 2020.

———. 2020c. "65 and Older Population Grows Rapidly as Baby Boomers Age."
Census Bureau (June 25). Release Number CB20-99. https://www.census.gov
/newsroom/press-releases/2020/65-older-population-grows.html, accessed
July 30, 2020.

———. 2021. "State Population by Characteristics: 2010–2020." Washington, DC:
U.S. Census Bureau. https://www.census.gov/programs-surveys/popest
/technical-documentation/research/evaluation-estimates/2020-evaluation
-estimates/2010s-state-detail.html, accessed July 8, 2022.

US Department of Agriculture, National Agricultural Statistics Service. *Census
of Agriculture: 2007, 2012, 2017.* February 2020. https://www.nass.usda.gov
/AgCensus/index.php, accessed July 5, 2022.

US General Accountability Office. 2016. *Retirement Security: Low Defined
Contribution Savings May Pose Challenges.* Washington, DC: US GAO.
https://www.gao.gov/assets/gao-16-408.pdf, accessed August 30, 2021.

Vadnal, Julie. 2020. "'I Don't Want to Be a Nurse, a Purse, or Worse': 5 Seniors
on Dating Online." *Vox* (September 24). https://www.vox.com/first-person
/21453215/online-dating-seniors-older-singles-covid-19, accessed February 14,
2021.

Venkataramani, Atheendar S., Rourke O'Brien, and Alexander C. Tsai. 2021.
"Declining Life Expectancy in the United States: The Need for Social Policy
as Health Policy." *JAMA* 325(7):621–22.

Verbrugge, Lois M. 2020. "Revisiting the Disablement Process." Pp. 275–85
in *International Handbook of Health Expectancies.* New York: Springer.

Villarroel, Maria A., and Emily P. Terlizzi. 2019. "Symptoms of Depression among Adults: United States, 2019." *NCHS Data Brief, no 379.* Hyattsville, MD: National Center for Health Statistics. 2020. https://www.cdc.gov/nchs /data/databriefs/db379-H.pdf, accessed July 7, 2021.

Vogels, Emily A., Andrew Perrin, Lee Rainie, and Monica Anderson. 2020. "53% of Americans Say the Internet Has Been Essential during the COVID-19 Outbreak" Pew Research Center, April 30. https://www.pewresearch.org /internet/2020/04/30/53-of-americans-say-the-internet-has-been-essential -during-the-covid-19-outbreak/, accessed February 15, 2021.

Wagner, David. 2005. *The Poorhouse: America's Forgotten Institution.* Lanham, MD: Rowman & Littlefield.

Waite, Linda J., Louise Hawkley, Ashwin A. Kotwal, Colm O'Muircheartaigh, L. Philip Schumm, and Kristen Wroblewski. 2021. "Analyzing Birth Cohorts with the National Social Life, Health, and Aging Project." *Journals of Gerontology: Series B* 76, Supplement 3:S226–S237.

Waite, Linda J., Edward O. Laumann, Aniruddha Das, and L. Philip Schumm. 2009. "Sexuality: Measures of Partnerships, Practices, Attitudes, and Problems in the National Social Life, Health, and Aging Study." *Journals of Gerontology Series B: Psychological Sciences and Social Sciences* 64(suppl 1): i56–i66.

Waite, Linda J., and Janet Xu. 2015. "Aging Policies for Traditional and Blended Families." *Public Policy & Aging Report* 25(3):88–93.

Wallevand, Kevin. 2020. "North Dakota's Oldest Living Resident Celebrates 115th Birthday." *InForum* (August 28). https://www.inforum.com/lifestyle /family/6638852-North-Dakotas-oldest-living-resident-celebrates-115th -birthday, accessed December 6, 2020.

Wang, XiaoRong, Karen M. Robinson, and Heather K. Hardin. 2015. "The Impact of Caregiving on Caregivers' Medication Adherence and Appointment Keeping." *Western Journal of Nursing Research* 37(12):1548–62.

Ward, Brian W., James M. Dahlhamer, Adena M.,Galinsky, and Sarah S. Joestl. 2014. "Sexual Orientation and Health among U.S. Adults: National Health Interview Survey, 2013." *National Health Statistics Reports,* no. 77:1–10.

Ware, Erin B., and Jessica D. Faul. 2021. "Genomic Data Measures and Methods: A Primer for Social Scientists." Pp. 49–62 in *Handbook of Aging and the Social Sciences,* 9th ed., edited by Kenneth Ferraro and Deborah Carr. New York: Academic Press.

Warner, Bernhard. 2020. "Warren Buffett Lays Out a Succession Plan—for His Berkshire." *Fortune* (February 22). https://fortune.com/2020/02/22/warren -buffett-succession-plan-shares/, accessed August 1, 2020.

Warren, John Robert. 2009. "Socioeconomic Status and Health across the Life Course: A Test of the Social Causation and Health Selection Hypotheses." *Social Forces* 87(4):2125–53.

Warren, Molly, Stacy Beck, and Daphne Delgado. 2020. *The State of Obesity 2020: Better Policies for a Healthier America* Washington, DC: Trust for America's Health. https://www.tfah.org/wp-content/uploads/2020/09 /TFAHObesityReport_20.pdf, accessed August 10, 2021.

Weekman, Kelsey. 2020. "This Fitness-Obsessed 80-Year-Old Will Inspire You to Move Your Body." *Yahoo Sports* (May 11). https://sports.yahoo.com/2020 -05-11-this-fitness-obsessed-80-year-old-will-inspire-you-to-move-your -body-24272936.html, accessed August 5, 2020.

Weiss, Robert S. 1973. *Loneliness: The Experience of Emotional and Social Isolation.* Cambridge, MA: MIT Press.

Wheeler, Inese. 2001. "Parental Bereavement: The Crisis of Meaning." *Death Studies* 25, 1: 51–66.

White, Lynn. 2001. "Sibling Relationships Over the Life Course: A Panel Analysis." *Journal of Marriage and Family* 63(2):555–68.

Wiemers, Emily E., and Sung S. Park. 2021. "Intergenerational Transfers of Time and Money over the Life Course." Pp. 201–20 in *Handbook of Aging and the Social Sciences,* 9th ed., edited by K. F. Ferraro and D. Carr. New York: Academic Press.

Wiglesworth, Aileen, Laura Mosqueda, Ruth Mulnard, Solomon Liao, Lisa Gibbs, and William Fitzgerald. 2010. "Screening for Abuse and Neglect of People with Dementia." *Journal of the American Geriatrics Society* 58(3):493–500.

Wilkinson, Richard G., and Kate Pickett. 2009. *The Spirit Level: Why More Equal Societies Almost Always Do Better.* London: Allen Lane.

Williams, David R., and Pamela Braboy Jackson. 2005. "Social Sources of Racial Disparities in Health." *Health Affairs* 24(2):325–34.

Williams, David R., Jourdyn A. Lawrence, and Brigette A. Davis. 2019. "Racism and Health: Evidence and Needed Research. *Annual Review of Public Health* 40:105–25.

Williams, Grant R., Amy Mackenzie, Allison Magnuson, Rebecca Olin, Andrew Chapman, Supriya Mohile, Heather Allore et al. 2016. "Comorbidity in Older Adults with Cancer." *Journal of Geriatric Oncology* 7(4):249–57.

Williams, Joah L., Melba Hernandez-Tejada, Emily S. Fanguy, and Ron Acierno. 2016. "Elder Abuse." In *Gerontology: Changes, Challenges, and Solutions: Changes, Challenges, and Solutions,* Vol. 2, *Health and Wellbeing,* edited by M. Harrington Meyer and E. A. Daniele, 205–22. Santa Barbara, CA: Praeger Publishers.

Wilmoth, Janet M. 2012. "A Demographic Profile of Older Immigrants in the United States." *Public Policy and Aging Report* 22(2):8–11.

Wilson, Bianca D. M., and Ilan H. Meyer. 2021. *Nonbinary LGBTQ Adults in the United States.* Los Angeles: The Williams Institute. https://williams institute.law.ucla.edu/publications/nonbinary-lgbtq-adults-us/, accessed January 17, 2022.

Wilson, Robert S., Lei Yu, Melissa Lamar, Julie A. Schneider, Patricia A. Boyle, and David A. Bennett. 2019. "Education and Cognitive Reserve in Old Age." *Neurology* 92(10):e1041–e1050.

Wolf, Douglas. 2016. "Late-Life Disability Trends and Trajectories." Pp. 77–99 in *Handbook of Aging and the Social Sciences*, edited by Linda K. George and Kenneth Ferraro. New York: Academic Press.

Wolff, Jennifer L., and Judith D. Kasper. 2006. "Caregivers of Frail Elders: Updating a National Profile." *The Gerontologist* 46(3):344–56.

Wolff, Jennifer L., John Mulcahy, Jin Huang, David L. Roth, Kenneth Covinsky, and Judith D. Kasper. 2018. "Family Caregivers of Older Adults, 1999–2015: Trends in Characteristics, Circumstances, and Role-Related Appraisal." *The Gerontologist* 58(6): 1021–32.

Wolff, Margaret, Brooke Wells, Christina Ventura-DiPersia, Audrey Renson, and Christian Grov. 2017. "Measuring Sexual Orientation: A Review and Critique of U.S. Data Collection Efforts and Implications for Health Policy." *Journal of Sex Research* 54(4–5):507–31.

Wood, Lisa, Karen Martin, Hayley Christian, Andrea Nathan, Claire Lauritsen, Steve Houghton, Ichiro Kawachi, and Sandra McCune. 2015. "The Pet Factor—Companion Animals as a Conduit for Getting to Know People, Friendship Formation and Social Support." *PloS One* 10(4): e0122085.

Woolf, Steven H., Derek A. Chapman, and Jong Hyung Lee. 2020. "COVID-19 as the Leading Cause of Death in the United States." *JAMA* 325(2):123–24.

Woolf, Steven H., Ryan K. Masters, and Laudan Y. Aron. 2021. "Effect of the COVID-19 Pandemic in 2020 on Life Expectancy across Populations in the USA and Other High Income Countries: Simulations of Provisional Mortality Data." *British Medical Journal* 373 doi.org/10.1136/bmj.n1343.

World Bank. 2021. World Bank Open Data. https://data.worldbank.org/, accessed August 30, 2021.

World Health Organization. 2020. *Ageing Data Portal*. https://www.who.int/data/maternal-newborn-child-adolescent-ageing/ageing-data, accessed July 7, 2021.

Wright, Patricia Moyle. 2016. "Adult Sibling Bereavement: Influences, Consequences, and Interventions." *Illness, Crisis & Loss* 24(1):34–45.

Wu, Huijing. 2018. *Grandchildren Living in a Grandparent-Headed Household*. Family Profile No. 01, 2018. Bowling Green, OH: National Center for Family & Marriage Research (NCFMR). https://www.bgsu.edu/ncfmr/resources/data/family-profiles/wu-grandchildren-living-with-grandparent-hhh-fp-18-01.html, accessed February 1, 2021.

Yahirun, Jenjira J., Sung S. Park, and Judith A. Seltzer. 2018. "Step-Grandparenthood in the United States." *Journals of Gerontology: Series B* 73(6):1055–65.

Yedjou, Clement G., Jennifer N. Sims, Lucio Miele, Felicite Noubissi, Leroy Lowe, Duber D. Fonseca, Richard A. Alo, Marinelle Payton, and Paul B.

Tchounwou. 2019. "Health and Racial Disparity in Breast Cancer." *Advances in Experimental Medicine and Biology* 1152:31–49. doi.org/10.1007/978-3-030-20301-6_3.

Yuan, Anastasia S. Vogt. 2007. "Perceived Age Discrimination and Mental Health." *Social Forces* 86(1):291–311.

Yuccas, Jamie. 2020. "98-Year-Old Swimmer 'Mighty Mo' Refuses to Slow Down." *CBS Evening News* (January 2). https://www.cbsnews.com/news/maurine-kornfeld-97-year-old-swimmer-mighty-mo-refuses-to-slow-down-2020-01-02/, accessed July 30, 2020.

Zarit, Steven H., and Judy M. Zarit. 2011. *Mental Disorders in Older Adults: Fundamentals of Assessment and Treatment*. New York: Guilford Press.

Zhang, Bing, Sai Ma, Inbal Rachmin, Megan He, Pankaj Baral, Sekyu Choi, William A. Gonçalves et al. 2020. "Hyperactivation of Sympathetic Nerves Drives Depletion of Melanocyte Stem Cells." *Nature* 577:676–81.

# Index

401K plans, 144

abuse. *See* elder abuse.
Activities of Daily Living (ADLs), 99, 118; and
activity limitation, 128
activity theory, 36
Affordable Care Act (ACA), 134
African Americans/Blacks, 44, 47, 63, 64, 65,
77, 95, 116, 129, 130, 156; assistance given
by adult children to their older parents,
81; Black military veterans, 56–57; and
COVID deaths compared to whites, 106;
as especially vulnerable to loss and
bereavement, 84; COVID-19 vaccine hesi-
tancy, 135; higher death rates of than
white Americans, 46; history of mistrust
among regarding the health care system,
135; as less likely to report depressive
symptoms, 126; and life expectancy, 110;
and mobility issues, 117; risk of for
dementia, 122. *See also* Black women
Age Discrimination in Employment Act
(ADEA), 59
"age-as-leveler" effect, 169n8
ageism, 26, 27, 71, 100–102; negative effects
of, 101; in the workplace, 101–3. *See also*
elder-speak

aging, demography of, 5–6; population aging,
8–11; projections of birth rates for whites,
Blacks, Latinx, and Asian women, 46–47;
truths concerning, 1–2. *See also* global
population aging, statistics concerning
aging, health and well-being issues, 103–5;
among elite athletes, 104, 104*fig.*; poor
health and memory loss as the greatest
concerns of older adults, 103; role of biological, genetic, and social issues regarding health decline, 104–5; sleep issues,
103; weakening immune systems, 105
aging, health and well-being issues, biological
and genetic perspectives on, 105–8;
cellular aging approaches to, 106;
immunosenescence, 106–7; oxidative
stress models, 106. *See also* late-life
health, statistics concerning
aging, health and well-being issues, mental
health and functioning issues, 170n10; and
cognitive reserve, 123; and crystallized
intelligence, 121; and educational levels,
122–23; and fluid intelligence, 121; mental
health issues, 124–28; mental health issues
and symptom management, 127; and mild
cognitive impairment (MCI), 121–22;
neurocognitive health, 120–21

old age, history of (*continued*)
    Depression, 30; waning status and honor
    bestowed on older adults through the late
    nineteenth and early twentieth centuries,
    25–26
old age, predicting the future of, 157–58; and
    climate change, 160–63; and health crises
    (from COVID to opioids), 163–65; and
    rising economic inequality, 158–60
"old-age dependency ratio," 171n1
older adults, 167n1; assistance provided to by
    their adult children, 80–81; better health
    of in wealthy nations, 149; common chal-
    lenges faced by, 71; as a global resource,
    153–55; in nations with a "collectivist"
    orientation, 148
older adults, demographic characteristics, 41;
    current dating patterns of, 73–74; family
    status, 49–50 (*see also* marriage); as the
    "majority minority," 44; nativity status,
    47–49; race and ethnicity, 44–47, 45*fig.*;
    sex, 41–43; sexual orientation, 43–44, 44*fig.*
older adults, socioeconomic characteristics,
    54; amount of older adults living beneath
    the poverty line, 64–65; educational
    attainment, 54–57, 55*fig.*, 56*fig.*; employ-
    ment rates of, 57–61, 59*fig.*; income and
    poverty, 61–65, 62*fig.*; medium income for
    older adults, 64, 65*fig.*
"old miserly man," 25
opioid crises, 163, 164–65
oral health, 118–19. *See also* dental health.
Organization for Economic Co-Operation
    and Development (OECD), 139, 140,
    139*fig.*, 140*fig.*; life expectancy at age
    sixty-five by sex for OECD nations,
    146*fig.*; poverty rates for OECD nations,
    141, 142*fig.*
"Over the Hill to the Poor House," 21, 28, 29;
    poster for the 1920 film of, 22*fig.*
oxidative stress, 106

paid caregivers, 151–52
Paine, Thomas, 28
Panel Study of Income Dynamics (PSID),
    80, 81
"parent" green cards, 48–49
pensions, 29–30, 168n4; access to, 171n3;
    employer-provided pensions, 63'
    government-supported pensions, 148–49
personal savings, 63–64
pets/animal companions,78–79
Philippines, the, 47

poor houses, 21
population growth: of age over sixty-five and
    over, 5*fig.*, 5. *See also* population pyramid
population pyramids, 10–11, 167n2; popula-
    tion pyramids of Florida, Utah, Japan,
    and Niger, 12–13*fig.*
populations, how do they age, 14–17. *See also*
    fertility
Portugal, 139
poverty: income and poverty, 61–65; poverty
    rates of older adults, 30–32
public policies: community-based programs
    for health care, 151; economic and eco-
    nomic security, 19, 141–44; family and
    caregiver policies, 19, 148–53; health care,
    19, 144–48

Rahe, Richard H., 83
Readjustment Benefits Act (1966), 56
re-partnering, 70
retirement, 25; mandatory retirement ages,
    59; three-legged stool of, 61, 64
Robinson, Mary, 154
robots, 153
romantic relationships, 72–74

Santana, Carlos, 40
Seinfeld Jerry, 79–80
selective survival, 111
sex, 74; sex ratio, 11; sexual relationships, 74;
    sexual satisfaction, 74
Silent Generation, the, 160
singlehood, 50
Sinopoli, Angie, 89–90
Sinopoli, Steven, 89–90
smoking, 34, 42, 132
social causation, 129
social isolation, 44, 70, 89–92, 96
social relationships, 71, 102. *See also* late-life
    family and social relationships; social
    relationships, the bleak side of, loss and
    bereavement
social relationships, the bleak side of, loss and
    bereavement, 83–84; among the LGBTQ
    community, 86–87; bereavement as espe-
    cially common in later life, 84; other types
    of losses (death of a child, parent, friend,
    or sibling), 87–89; spousal and partner
    loss, 84–87. *See also* elder abuse
Social Security, 17, 18, 22, 26–27, 28, 49, 58,
    59; history of, 30–31; importance of to
    lower-income households, 62–63; as the
    most important source of income for older

adults, 61–62; reliance of women on, 63; structure of Social Security benefits, 143

Social Security Act Amendments, 32

social selection, 129

socioeconomic status (SES), 101, 125, 133, 156; SES gaps, 128–29

*Sociological Imagination, The* (Mills), 156

"solo agers," 70, 91–92

*Sopranos, The*, 66

South Asia, 47

Southeast Asia, 47

South Korea, 141, 171n2

Springsteen, Bruce, 40

stepchildren, 76

stepfamilies, 75–76

Sternberg, Joseph, 27

stress, and heightened cortisol ("stress hormone"), 131–32

stroke, 84

sub-Saharan Africa, 10, 47–48, 141, 142, 149

suicide, 42, 87, 89, 109–10, 112, 125, 129, 170n11

*Suicide* (Durkheim), 83

Taiwan, single-payer insurance system of, 146–47

Takei, George, 40

testosterone, 42

*Theft of a Decade, the: How the Baby Boomers Stole the Millennials' Economic Future* (Sternberg), 27

Thunberg, Greta, 160–61

Total Fertility Rate (TFR), 46

transgender persons, 169n1

Trump, Donald, 76, 120

United States, 41, 138, 142, 172n2; aging population of, 14, 23–24 (*see also* old age, history of); economic downturn in (2020), 60; gross domestic product (GDP) of (2021), 171n4; labor force participation in, 57–58; as lagging behind more than a dozen high-income nations in respect to older adults' health and longevity, 145–46; population of as older than ever before, 4; racial and ethnic composition of, 47; racial oppression in, 126. *See also* feminization, of the US population

US Department of Health and Human Services, 164

US Supreme Court, 43

US Veterans Association, 56

Utah, 14

Vermont, 9

Village movement, the, 151

Villages, The, 16

Warren, Elizabeth, 40, 61

Warren, Guy, 107

Westman, Iris, 3, 69, 70

West Virginia, 9, 16–17

White, Betty, 137

widowhood, 84–86; as more likely to die of accidents and alcohol-related deaths, 86

Winfrey, Oprah, 40

"within-family difference," 81

women, 63, 101, 142–43; close relationships with their children, 54; "female" jobs, 60; mobility limitations in older age, 116–17; living arrangements of, 149; protection of by the biological benefits of estrogen, 42; reliance on Social Security benefits, 63; strains on women caregivers, 98–99; women caregivers as "kin keepers," 86; women's living arrangements by race/ethnicity, 53*fig*.

youth culture, 25

Zhang, Bing, 169n1

Zoom, 82; Zoom funerals, 84

Founded in 1893,
UNIVERSITY OF CALIFORNIA PRESS
publishes bold, progressive books and journals
on topics in the arts, humanities, social sciences,
and natural sciences—with a focus on social
justice issues—that inspire thought and action
among readers worldwide.

The UC PRESS FOUNDATION
raises funds to uphold the press's vital role
as an independent, nonprofit publisher, and
receives philanthropic support from a wide
range of individuals and institutions—and from
committed readers like you. To learn more, visit
ucpress.edu/supportus.